Local Government and
Politics in Britain

CONTEMPORARY POLITICAL STUDIES

Series Editor: John Benyon, *Director, Centre for the Study of Public Order, University of Leicester*

A series which provides authoritative, yet concise introductory accounts of key topics in contemporary political studies.

Other titles in the series include:

Elections and Voting Behaviour in Britain
DAVID DENVER, *University of Lancaster*

Pressure Groups, Politics and Democracy in Britain
WYN GRANT, *University of Warwick*

UK Political Parties since 1945
Edited by ANTHONY SELDON, *Institute of Contemporary British History*

Politics and Policy Making in Northern Ireland
MICHAEL CONNOLLY, *University of Ulster*

British Political Ideologies
ROBERT LEACH, *Leeds Polytechnic*

CONTEMPORARY POLITICAL STUDIES

Local Government and Politics in Britain

JOHN KINGDOM

Sheffield Business School, Sheffield City Polytechnic

Philip Allan

NEW YORK LONDON TORONTO SYDNEY TOKYO SINGAPORE

First published 1991 by
Philip Allan
66 Wood Lane End, Hemel Hempstead
Hertfordshire HP2 4RG
A division of
Simon & Schuster International Group

Typeset in 10 on 12 pt Times Roman
by Inforum Typesetting, Portsmouth

Printed and bound in Great Britain by
Billing and Sons Ltd., Worcester

British Library Cataloguing in Publication Data

Kingdom, John
  Local government and politics in Britain.
  1. Great Britain. Local government
  I. Title
  352.041

  ISBN 0–86003–831–9
  ISBN 0–86003–832–7 (pbk)

---

3 4 5   95 94 93 92

Contents

Preface

The 1980s was a traumatic decade for British politics, marked by a shattering of the consensus of the earlier post-war decades. During the consensus years local government, although having a key role in the welfare state, occupied the political backwaters. All changed from the mid-1970s, when the end of the long boom of western capitalism meant that the cost of social democracy led to fiscal crisis. The New Right Thatcher government came to power with a mission to draw in the state frontiers and local government was seen to inhabit the vulnerable marginal territory. At the same time, the New Urban Left, disillusioned with Labour's earlier performances in office, and despairing of further parliamentary power in the face of the rise of the centre parties and greater electoral volatility, began to see in the urban a theatre for battle. Thus local government became a major site for politics and few corners of the municipal landscape were to be untouched. When the Chinese place a curse they say: 'May you live in interesting times.' From the point of view of the student, local government became exceedingly interesting.

I would like to thank series editor John Benyon for the opportunity to write this book and for his help and encouragement throughout. I am also grateful to Clare Grist of Simon & Schuster for her enthusiasm and guidance. My colleague Roger Ottewill, combining the skills of an ex-district auditor with those of a political scientist, has given generously of his time to read the whole manuscript and make many helpful suggestions. As always I owe an enormous debt to my wife, Ann, who has made many stylistic improvements and compiled a superb index. Needless to say, the particular interpretation, and any errors, are mine alone.

I would like to dedicate this book to the memory of my uncle, Alderman E.W. Kingdom. His long conversations with my father, heard by me literally from the cradle, made me think that talking about politics was the very epitome of adult behaviour. It was gratifying to discover in due course that Aristotle agreed with me.

1

Discovering Local Government

From being rather a constitutional fringe-show, local government has emerged as one of the most important theatres of British politics. Local government is big government; indeed, it is big business. Its expenditure accounts for around one-tenth of the entire gross domestic product and it employs some three million people. The populations under some British local authorities and the expenditure levels incurred actually exceed those of the smaller nations of the world.

The neglect of local government is in no small measure a product of the media construction of events which tends to see in Westminster, Whitehall and the Cabinet the holy trinity of all political life. This is a centrist orientation which places the thermometer rather too near the radiator of London when taking the temperature of the body politic. When ordinary people feel the presence of the state, it is not usually through the great institutions of Westminster and Whitehall but through the town hall. Indeed, while 650 MPs inhabit the House of Commons, the nation elects some 26,000 representatives to its council chambers.

Popular lack of interest in local government is itself a factor in politics; it serves the interests of the political right. The great cities which grew up during the process of industrialisation were necessary for the new factory-owning bourgeoisie, yet at the same time they posed a threat which was appalling to contemplate. The vast work-force represented an urban leviathan with the potential to sweep away the pattern of privilege and social domination upon which it was predicated. To this day, the city remains a social formation deeply disturbing to the right, who prefer to keep local politics well off the political agenda.

However, academic interest quickened from the 1970s through the contemplation of a body of European neo-Marxist thinking which stressed the potential of the urban level of the state as a site for political struggle (Castells, 1977). At the same time, interest developed on the right in a body of work termed public choice theory, which applied the logico-deductive reasoning characteristic of classical economics to the study of politics. Here the individual, and his/her personal self-interest, was made the fundamental building block of all analysis with some bizarrely anti-communitarian results (Tiebout, 1956; Niskanen, 1973). This approach was bound to generate an unsympathetic view of local government, with its basis in concepts such as community and welfare and a concern with collectivist issues such as roads, clean air, safe streets and so on.

However, in 1979 nature began to resemble art. A Conservative government came to power at Westminster espousing an ideology termed the New Right, which incorporated the ideas of the public choice theorists along with a set of free-market doctrines disinterred from the nineteenth century when the role of the municipality was serving industry not people. This provoked a strong resistance movement, the New Urban Left, committed to preserving the role of local government in providing collectivist services and even reviving the idea of municipal, as opposed to Westminster-based, socialism. The result was an unprecedented degree of political tension in the world of local government, with consequences penetrating to the very foundations of the modern British state. By the beginning of the 1990s no one could think that local government was outside mainstream politics. Equally, no one could be sure where the developments were leading.

This chapter sets the scene for study by introducing some key terms and concepts and takes an overview of the local government system, indicating briefly the focal points of subsequent chapters. It concludes with a discussion on the values of local government.

What is local government?

Today, local government means the self-government of Britain's counties, cities and towns. Generally the term denotes the separate government of a sub-national territorial unit of the state. It may be undemocratic, as in the days of feudal barons, or democratic, when members of the community are able to play a part in decision making. Most importantly, the idea of local government implies some degree of autonomy from the central government at Westminster.

Modern local government has lain at the very heart of the country's greatest modern political achievement, the welfare state. Its study is no dry exercise in public administration; it can be a site for fierce political controversy. Front-page issues such as the Dewsbury case of racism in education, the Cleveland child abuse affair, repeated scandals of child suffering, wife battering, racist attacks, poverty, homelessness, drug dependency, low literacy rates, high crime rates, violence in the playground, racism in our police force, sexism in society, the profound problem of the decay of our inner cities, pollution and traffic congestion all centre upon local government.

This section introduces three closely related concepts central to the study of local government: local administration, local democracy and local politics. It begins by describing the basic unit of local government: the municipality or local authority.

Anatomy of a municipality

The institutional manifestation of local government is the local authority. More precisely it is the *elected* local authority, to distinguish it from a variety of other public authorities which mark the local political landscape. Its anatomy is a Lilliputian version of central government, with two fundamental elements: a body of elected politicians and a large permanent work-force comprising a bureaucracy of administrators and a great army of employees ranging from park-keepers to teachers.

Local authorities do not merely administer one single service (like, for instance, a health authority); they have multifunctional portfolios. Throughout the post-war era much of our housing, education, parks, buses and so on have been provided by local government. It is also responsible for the maintenance of countless miles of highway, protection from fire, environmental protection, help with a myriad social problems, and even regulates the specific gravity of the comforting liquid consumed in public houses. With advice on family planning and well-kept municipal graveyards it can safely be said that local government has tended our welfare needs from womb to tomb, from sperm to worm.

The politicians form the *council*, a kind of local parliament, and the bureaucrats resemble civil servants, though they are known as local government officers. These central actors are examined in Chapters 8 and 9, respectively. Councillors are, in principle, ordinary citizens who have put themselves forward in local elections (see Chapter 6). Their formal role is to make public policy on behalf of the rest of the community, while that of the bureaucrats is to implement their decisions. Of course, matters are not quite as simple as this in practice and the relationship between the two is a key issue in the study of local politics (Chapter 10).

Local public administration

This is the running of public services for the community and is the job of the local government officers. However, local administration is not necessarily wedded to local government as it is defined here. In fact the majority of all civil servants are actually located outside London in *field agencies* and, in addition, there is an exotic menagerie of quasi-autonomous local administrative bodies existing within the territory of each local authority. This exerts complex pressures on the elected authorities, an issue examined in Chapter 4.

The presence of these bodies leads some writers to speak of 'non-elected local government', but there is a profound difference between local *government* and local *administration*. The former involves the right of a community to decide things for itself, while the latter amounts to rule by bureaucrats. This leads to a second key concept: local democracy.

Local democracy

Above all else local government embodies local democracy (rule by the people; from the Greek *demos*); it is this which makes the municipalities unique in the state. There is nothing new in the idea of local democracy. The earliest accounts of democracy as such are of the city-states of ancient Greece existing around 300 BC. Although not units of local government, they were very small and there are grounds for arguing that a true spirit of democracy can only be engendered in intimate communities. Local democracy in Britain predates the great nineteenth-century democratisation of the central state. In medieval times there were ancient forms of parish government where members of small communities would come together to make decisions in the church or its vestry. Modern local democracy, in which decision makers are chosen by the community, is known as *representative democracy*. In such a system elections play a central part (see Chapter 6).

Local politics

Generally speaking, politics arises from the fact that, because people tend naturally to live in communities, there will be various sources of disagreement over such things as moral standards and the way resources are to be distributed. Such disputes can be settled in various ways. The most elemental is by using force; many of our great wealthy families gained their positions in this way, the problems of Northern Ireland continue to invoke physical violence, and the state maintains a major capability to use such methods with its police force.

Alternatively, there is the operation of the economic market. In a capitalist society such as Britain this is accorded a prime place, determining what we eat, what we wear, whom we make friends with, where we work and so on. Finally, decisions may be entrusted to experts. In modern society they abound as doctors, architects, judges and so on. While these modes of decision making are greatly in evidence in the modern state, their complete domination would be very dangerous, leading respectively to rule by the mighty (tyranny), rule by the wealthy (class rule) or rule by an elite (technocracy).

Not only are such forms of rule unpopular (and hence unstable); they do not work. Thus, for example, the use of force patently fails to solve the problem of Northern Ireland for either side. Economic solutions operate on the principle of 'to him that hath shall be given', and are harsh in a different way; the wallet and cheque book replace the sword and shield. Technical solutions appeal to many well-meaning people, but chase the elusive butterfly of rationality. Again, the idea that there is a single 'right' solution to society's problems is a myth; in a kind of perverse law of human knowledge we find that 'for every expert there is an equal and opposite expert', and who is to choose between them? Hence people call for a 'political solution'. What exactly is this?

A classic definition of politics is that given by Bernard Crick, which sees it as the settling of disagreements by a harmonious process of reconciling the different interests within society through peaceful, reasoned means. This may be seen as morally superior to methods which permit the rich, or otherwise powerful, to get what they want at the expense of the rest (Crick, 1964: 141). However, this process cannot take place without some powerful, legitimately accepted body at the centre to enforce the collective decisions. David Easton, in another famous definition, calls politics 'the authoritative allocation of values' (Easton, 1953: 129). In local government this centre of authority is the council, its legitimacy derived from popular election.

Yet the processes which may be termed political do not end with the election of councillors, or even with discussions in council chambers. Political activity (the attempt to influence the authoritative allocation of values) permeates all aspects of local government. It involves a jockeying between various affected interests. This introduces another key factor in politics: power – the ability to influence who gets what, when, how (Lasswell, 1936). The question of where power lies in a local community is of central concern to our study. It directs attention to a complex of activity including the formation of political parties (Chapter 7) and pressure groups, and entails a search into more shadowy political territory for the less overt forms of power, such as that held by the wealthy owners of capital (Chapter 12). Politics also surrounds the processes of local government finance (Chapter 11), the relationship of local government with central government (a recurring theme) and its place in the wider system of national politics (Chapter 15).

Moreover, although centring largely on the municipal institutions, local politics also takes place around the other local centres of administration: health authorities, urban development corporations and so on (Chapter 4). It can even embrace the institutions of national government (Chapter 13), as in the case of, for instance, a

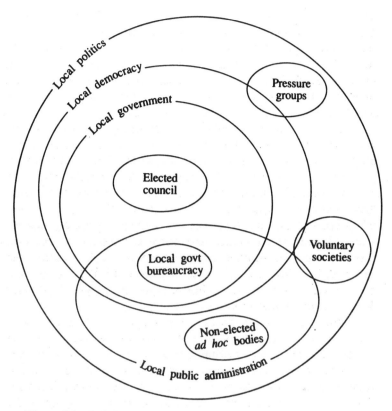

Figure 1.1 Relationship between local government, local public administration, local politics and local democracy.

decision to site a power station or a nuclear waste disposal plant. Indeed, local politics is inextricably linked with national politics; few issues are entirely local in their origins and implications (Chapter 14). Figure 1.1 shows the complicated overlap between local government, local democracy, local public administration and local politics.

Urban spacemen

Much writing on local government speaks of the 'urban'. In normal usage the term denotes life in towns and cities, to be contrasted with the rural. However, its meaning today goes further. It is urbanisation which has created modern local government.

Early studies of urbanisation were made by an influential group of scholars writing between 1920 and 1940, known collectively as the Chicago School. One of their themes was the idea of 'urban ecology', which sees the process as analogous to the adaptation of plant and animal life to the environment. Hence towns grow up in accordance with geographical features: by rivers to provide transport and water power, near sources of raw materials and food, on high ground to afford fortification and so on. Later development follows various processes of natural selection; people best suited to city life thrive, others decline, perhaps leaving for rural areas (Park, 1952: 79). Generally, cities tend to grow as firms set up near the work-forces, more people arrive in search of employment, and so on. Spatially the pattern looks rather like the growth rings in a tree trunk: concentric circles extending outwards. Different types of neighbourhoods develop, from the central business districts and the threatening inner city areas to the more salubrious outer fringes. In later stages a process of suburbanisation sees colonisation of further areas, as villages are engulfed by the outflowing city. Figure 1.2 shows the growth of Sheffield between 1843 and 1972.

The ecological view of urbanisation may be criticised in that it tends to underestimate the importance of conscious human design and the political forces of power and domination. For Harvey (1973; 1985) the urban is created, and constantly restructured, by the movements of industrial capitalism. Spatial patterns result from the decisions of private firms to set up in one place and close down in another. People do not choose where to live; they must follow the economic giants which provide them with jobs. Castells (1983) sees the urban as the spatial manifestation of social forces; towering glass office blocks replace cathedrals as the defining physical features of the city, proclaiming the might of the wealthy. At the same time, the slums speak of the powerlessness of others, though their numbers suggest a latent form of political power which gives the right sleepless nights.

When Britain is said to be urbanised, it means that not only are there towns and cities, but that the whole country is dominated by urban forces. Rural areas are themselves locked into the urban process, producing food, not for local communities, but for national markets. Moreover, the methods are largely those of mass

Figure 1.2 Growth of the city of Sheffield.

production, the natural landscape being ravaged to produce a terrain suitable for the iron feet of the gigantic machines.

Part of this process is the growth of local government. What local government is, and what it does, cannot be understood other than through an appreciation of the urban context. The urban area is not merely a place, but a key part in a process of collective (or socialised) consumption which is an inherent feature of capitalism (see Chapter 3). Local government is driven by complex and contradictory forces. While it must necessarily serve capitalist interests, it also offers a power base for ordinary people though local democracy. The contradictory implications of this conundrum will manifest themselves throughout this book.

A local government constitution? – unwritten and silent

What is the formal position of local government in the state? All civilised government is bound by a constitution: a set of rules laying down the powers of the state and the rights of citizens and associations. In many countries of the developed world we find that the constitution specifies the position of local government within the totality of the state. There are two ways in which this may be done. In the first place the constitution may give to local authorities a *general competence* which means that they may perform any function in their area providing that it is legal. This is usually qualified by making certain crucial functions obligatory. Examples of this kind are found in Scandinavian countries such as Denmark, Sweden and Norway. Alternatively, the constitution may *entrench* the right of local authorities to perform certain defined functions. Examples of this kind of provision are found in European countries such as France, West Germany and Italy with their complexly tiered systems. The states of the USA vary, but generally have adopted one or other of these models. The important thing about both forms of constitutional status is that local government autonomy is afforded constitutional protection; central government cannot ride roughshod over its rights and responsibilities. However, Britain's constitution is notoriously vague to the extent of being unwritten, existing only in the form of a dense legal undergrowth of statute, common law and mere convention (Kingdom, 1991: ch. 2). Although these are not silent on the legal position of local government, they do not speak loudly.

Constitutionally each local authority is a corporation (or body corporate) with a legal *persona* or identity in law. It can do many of the things which real persons do (own property, enter into contracts, employ people, lend and borrow money and so on). However, in other ways this strange legal entity is different from a real person. It belongs to that category of monsters which, even if stakes be driven through their hearts, cannnot die, enjoying immortality through the principle of *perpetual succession*. It will live to honour its obligations quite independently of the health or longevity of any of those (councillors or employees) who labour in its name.

Moreover, this persona is restricted in a way that a real person is not. Indeed, rather than guarantee the rights of local authorities against the state, the constitution stresses their curtailment. This it does through the doctrines of the supremacy of Parliament and *ultra vires*.

The supremacy of Parliament

Constitutional theorists regard the concentration of power within the state as a fatal sign of totalitarianism. This is why the US constitution enshrines a separation of government powers. In the first place there is separation between the executive, legislature and judiciary (sometimes termed *capital* division) and secondly, there is a spatial separation of power between the central government and the states (federal division). The state governments are sovereign in their own territories: constitutionally they are said to have relinquished certain of their 'original' powers to the federal (central) government but those they retain may be exercised freely. Thus, the laws of individual states may vary; if one state wishes to allow easy divorce, or impose the death penalty for certain crimes, it may do so legally.

However, Britain does not have either a capital or a federal separation of powers. Indeed, it has quite the opposite. The one fundamental principle of the British constitution as enunciated in the nineteenth century by the great constitutional lawyer Albert Venn Dicey (1835–1922) is the doctrine of the supremacy of Parliament. This means that all constitutional authority is concentrated in one single place. It means that any powers which local government may have are not guaranteed by the constitution; they can be removed by Parliament at any time. Thus, for example, the GLC was wiped off the constitutional map in 1983. How then can the local authorities be self-governing?

The short legal answer to this is that Parliament voluntarily relinquishes, or delegates, certain powers to the local authorities. However, there is more than one way to do this. It may set up field agencies (such as local offices of the Department of Social Security) and *ad hoc* bodies (such as district health authorities). This is termed 'administrative devolution' and it is much in evidence in the British state. Alternatively, Parliament can actually delegate some of its power to make political decisions. This may be termed 'political devolution' and is justified on the grounds that the bodies receiving the power are themselves popularly elected. This is where local government in Britain fits in. Figure 1.3 shows the various ways in which the sovereign power of the state may be shared out.

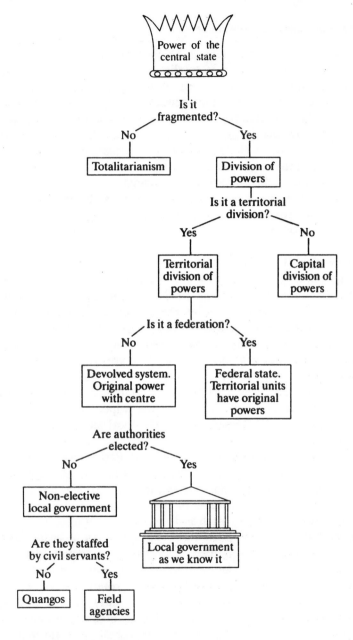

Figure 1.3   Dividing state power.

Ultra vires

Local authorities, although controlled by elected representatives, still lack the authority of federal states. Individuals can do anything they like providing it is not forbidden by the law. If they wish to stand on the steps of the town hall distributing £10 notes to passers-by, they cannot be arrested. (The only impediments will be their alarmed families and the two physicians required to certify them.) However, if a local authority were to do the same, the councillors responsible would be in serious trouble. This is because the vitally important doctrine of *ultra vires* (beyond the powers) decrees that the local authority can provide only those services which Parliament has specifically empowered it to. Thus, the distribution of largesse in the above manner would be illegal, and the councillors would be *surcharged* (that is, required by the courts to pay back the money misused) and perhaps banned from holding office.

This restrictive system was necessary to soothe the minds of the Victorian nineteenth-century capitalists who could not sleep easy with the thought that councillors might use their rates in a profligate manner for purposes such as poor relief. While not even the most extreme left councils have yet resorted to the wanton distribution of £10 notes, their political opponents feel that they have not fallen far short of this, and the anti-socialist forces raised by Thatcherism from their nineteenth-century mausoleums have scrutinised the local account books with the zeal of Dickens's Ebenezer Scrooge (see Chapter 11). This restriction leads us to appraise another term sometimes used in discussion of local government: the local state.

A local state?

Some writers on local government speak of the idea of the 'local state'. However, while it is helpful to view the processes of a local authority as a kind of 'political system in miniature' (Stanyer, 1976: ch. 3), with parties, pressure groups, elections and so on, detailed like the figures, cars and pillar boxes on a model railway layout, the idea that this constitutes a local state fails to take account of the constitutional and political context of local government.

In simple terms a state is a community formed for the purpose of government. The ancient Greeks talked of the *city-state* (sometimes termed the *polity*) and today we speak of the nation-state. In much general usage the local authority has many of the characteristics of a fully fledged state, including a clearly defined territory, a legitimate government, an existence recognised by other states, a legal persona, perpetual succession and universality of jurisdiction over its territory (Lasswell and Kaplan, 1950: 181). Moreover, in the existence of police forces local authorities have an ability to use legitimate force and coercion against members, a feature which the sociologist Max Weber saw as the most singular characteristic of the state, distinguishing it from all other organisations.

However, there are various important respects in which a local authority falls short of being a true local state, including the following:

(1)   The presence within the territory of various other public agencies means that the local authority cannot have the jurisdictional sovereignty associated with a fully fledged state. (Furthermore, the idea that a local authority controls its police force is wildly fanciful – see pp. 62–4.)

(2)   Patterns of settlement (for instance, dormitory towns around cities) and economic communications create spatial networks of urban political behaviour transcending the formal municipal boundaries. Hence, it may have jurisdiction over only a part of the organic urban space.

(3)   Most importantly, the central government dominates the House of Commons through party discipline, effectively hijacking the sovereignty of Parliament, so that it is able to exert overwhelming levels of influence over all local authorities.

Clearly local authorities have only a very low level of autonomy (Castells, 1977: 247). Moreover, it will become evident throughout this book that they are subject to the iron will of the wider economic system, which is largely beyond their influence.

Local government values

Why do we have local government? In what ways does it improve the quality of life in the state? These are fundamental questions and were seriously addressed in the nineteenth century, the formative years of the liberal democratic state, when local government was in the melting pot (see Chapter 2). A dominant influence was the thought of Jeremy Bentham (1748–1832) and the Philosophical Radical movement he inspired. Bentham argued that the rational pursuit of maximum happiness (or utility, hence *utilitarianism*) should be the guiding principle behind all law and government. The utilitarian most associated with the liberal case for democratic local government was J. S. Mill (1806–73). Values the utilitarians particularly associated with local government in liberal democracy were freedom, participation and efficiency.

Freedom

The liberal view of freedom is the right to do as one pleases providing it does not restrict the freedom of others. This view entails a minimal state, one which interferes in people's lives as little as possible. Local government can make a major contribution to freedom by limiting the power of the central state. It represents a fragmentation of power, a pluralist check against autocracy. In addition, each authority can act as a territorial pressure group, protecting the interests of its citizens.

Participation

Aristotle's view that political participation is a necessary part of the good life is one of the premises of western political thought; it is a necessary condition of democracy. In modern local government participation is facilitated at three levels: through elections, council membership and lobbying. Participation in local government can not only ensure that policy reflects local wishes; it can enrich social life by engendering a spirit of community. For Mill one of the most important features of local participation was its educative function; it helped create a harmonious political culture. People learn about democracy by experiencing it at close quarters. Indeed, local government can be a training ground for national politicians. It can be argued that without local democracy the country would be less (would certainly *feel* less) democratic at national level.

Efficiency

This was the value of local government most venerated by the Philosophical Radicals. They saw a duality in the state with the centre setting the overarching goals and the localities trimming them to fit local circumstances. In this way local government enables the state to accommodate territorial diversity. Further efficiency can accrue from the multi-purpose nature of local authorities, which are able to coordinate related sets of services such as housing, social services and education. Again, local government offers ordinary people an opportunity to control the professional experts who, left to their own devices, would tend towards inefficiency by promoting a decision-making regime based on their own self-interests rather than those of citizens (Sharp, 1970: 174).

Liberal values and class interest

However valid these values might seem, the motives of the nineteenth-century liberals and their successors are open to question. The values can be seen to serve the interests of a capital-owning bourgeoisie, the class supported by the Philosophical Radicals against the land-owning conservatives. In practice the freedoms most valued by liberal thinkers were the rights to own property and pursue economic profit. The exercise of these, far from leaving intact other people's freedom, resulted in an epic period of poverty and suffering. Moreover, the value of efficiency meant, to the Philosophical Radicals, a high degree of central government domination over the municipalities (mainly to ensure that they would not spend too much in poor relief), with a consequent erosion of the participatory values. Indeed, it will be seen in Chapter 2 that full democratic participation was by no means what the nineteenth-century bourgeoisie understood as the goal of municipal reform.

Social democratic values

This is not to say that the liberal values could not, under other circumstances, serve the general interest, and they continue to be reaffirmed in modern debate. Even so, they do not all fit comfortably with the goals of social democracy, where equality and rights to welfare take precedence over freedom and participation. The diversity promised by the liberals is but another word for inequality. Under social democracy local government can become an instrument for the redistribution of wealth (central government can use national progressive taxation to take from the richer areas and give to the poorer by means of a grant), but this begins to erode the participatory rights as areas become dependent upon the centre. It will be seen in later chapters that this was a major problem for local government in the period of post-war social democracy.

Does it then logically follow that the political right, with its preference for freedom of choice over equality, will be more sanguine in its attitude towards the values of local government? It has indeed been argued by the New Right that local government should be a vehicle for maximising local choice, with variations in standards determining where people will choose to live. This, it is said, will lead ultimately to an optimum allocation of municipal resources (Tiebout, 1956). Yet, paradoxically, the New Right Conservatism of Mrs Thatcher, while loudly declaiming the rhetoric of choice in theory, was deeply incensed by choice when made by left-wing councils in practice. It will be seen throughout this book that the result was a regime of centralism more draconion than that under social democracy.

Does this mean that the values of local government must, in practice, receive a hostile reception from both right and left? If so, how does it manage to survive? A start to answering this can be made by looking deeper and recognising the limitation of the traditional liberal-inspired view. It is impossible to appreciate the value of local government *in vacuo*; it is part of the larger state system and must be evaluated in terms of its function within this.

Local government in the state

Britain is a state with a capitalist economy, which means that the all-important means of producing the things society needs in order to survive are owned, not by the people, but by certain individuals who are, as a result, extremely powerful.

Although a capitalist system purports to favour the doctrine of *laissez-faire* (let act) in which the state keeps meddling fingers out of the economy, in reality it asks much of the state. It requires an extensive range of (non-profitable) public services, including an infrastructure for the economy (roads, telecommunications and so on) and social services to maintain the work-force (to facilitate lower wages than are really necessary), environmental protection against pollution and laws which protect private property (the key to an economy based on ownership). In addition, the economic inequalities which arise from the massive accumulation of profit by certain people promise potentially disruptive social tension. The state must contain this in two ways: first, by running a strong police force to maintain law and order and secondly (and more effective than the use of force), by nourishing a culture in which people are generally content with the system. This is accomplished by *legitimation*, a diffuse process whereby people come to accept, as a matter of 'common sense', that inequality (in wealth, education, health, opportunity, and so on) is necessary for the success of the economy and that they are not, as Marx suggested, helpless exploited victims of economic forces.

An Achilles heel?

It will be seen (Chapter 15) that local government can serve capitalism very well with both infrastructure and social services. The city is a 'residential unit of labour power' (Castells, 1976: 148). In addition, by allowing ordinary people to participate in politics as councillors, it plays a major role in legitimation by reducing feelings of powerlessness. However, in so doing, local government at the same time threatens the capitalist state. It can be described as its Achilles heel, because it allows ordinary people to be involved in decision making and affords them a moral right to dissent from, and oppose, central government. This right is derived from various sources, including the pattern of its history (where self-government by communities can be portrayed as a constitutional convention), the fact that it alone among public bodies outside Parliament has enjoyed a right to tax and, most important of all, the fact that councillors are, like MPs, Cabinet and Prime Minister, democratic representatives of the people.

This means that local government in the modern state is placed in a position of constitutional and political contradiction. The central state both needs local government and fears it. Orthodox textbooks usually consign discussion on 'central–local relations' to a single chapter, making it a generally apolitical matter of management (often evaluating the relative merits of 'agency' or 'partnership' management models). The effect of this is to depoliticise the issue and emasculate debate. Throughout this book it will be apparent that central government places tension upon local government in almost all its aspects. This was to reach new levels of intensity from the beginning of the 1980s, when an entirely new political dimension entered municipal life. For various reasons central government decided it could dispense with the legitimating power of local self-government. Yet events revealed that there was more to the constitution than met the eye of the lawyer. Local government demonstrated a tenacious power to resist the heavy centralism in the system.

2

Genesis

This chapter examines the birth of modern local government in Britain, identifying two contradictory traditions: localist and centralist. A dominant theme of the chapter is the process of industrialisation and the social revolution it produced. In these forces lay the genesis of modern local government.

The localist and centralist traditions

Like much of the machinery of the British state, modern local government is largely a creation of the nineteenth century, a product of the same kind of innovating energy which drove industry and commerce in this period of social revolution. The form and functions of modern local government were largely set out in Acts passed by a newly sovereign Parliament under the control of the newly dominant class, the industrial bourgeoisie. Their very title meant 'town dweller', distinguishing them from both rural peasantry and landowning gentry. The emergence of modern local government can be seen as symptomatic of the great social revolution which altered the balance of power within the state. It was largely determined by the imperatives of the capitalist mode of production.

Yet excessive concentration upon the nineteenth century and its reforming legislation can imply that central government created local government. This is misleading, in that it predisposes all further analysis to a centralist interpretation, with the implication that local government must always be subservient. Central government is not God nor local government Adam; before the industrial revolution there had been an organic evolutionary tradition of local government predating not merely the Victorians, but the central state itself (Redlich and Hirst 1958). The thick trunk of this ancient constitutional oak was not to be felled by the statutory axe of the Philosophical Radicals, and traditions of old remain deeply ingrained in the modern system.

Hence, the full evolution of local government must be conceived as a twin-track development embracing two traditions: the *localist* and the *centralist.*

The localist tradition

To ignore this tradition is to make the mistake of those school textbooks which chronicle the past exclusively through the tales of 'great men', whose machinations have focused exclusively on the central institutions of state. However, when the monarchs of old pursued their intrigues and fought their epic battles, ordinary people remained largely untouched; their politics were more of the parish pump than the court. It is here that the heart of real local government began to beat and where its spiritual history is written.

The development arose from the natural impulse of small communities to meet their collective needs, such as the upkeep of roads and bridges, care of the poor and the maintenance of order. It is seen in the tradition of parish government, which to ordinary people was far more real than that of the nation-state (Webb, S. and B. 1963: 5). Other sources of localism came from the boroughs and the craftsmen's guilds.

Parish government
There were numerous parishes throughout the country (well over 15,000 by the seventeenth century), but little uniformity in size, population and function. Each reflected a local character; the populations of the smallest could be numbered in tens, while others grew to be veritable cities. Over time parishes tended to amalgamate, forming larger areas, subdivided into smaller units known variously as tythings, hundreds, townships, vills, hamlets and so on.

Anglo-Saxon parish government has been represented as an idyllic form of democracy. The process of decision making was undertaken by all in a truly populist manner, with parishioners assembled as a *vestry* within the precincts of the church, summoned by the tolling bell. Similarly, implementation of decisions was shared, parishioners taking turns to do the work required. The importance of the parishes was increased through the statutory Elizabethan Poor Law of 1601 which formally gave them responsibility for caring for paupers.

However, the idyll is tarnished by the fact that, in practice, parish government was prey to domination by local elites, representing the church and local landed gentry. They would rule and collect dues in their own interests, transforming the 'open vestry' into its corrupt form, the 'closed vestry'. Yet, despite the failings, two fundamental rights of local government emerged naturally and spontaneously; they were not *bestowed* by the centre.

(1)   The right of all citizens to *participate* in local decision making.

(2)   The right of a community to provide itself with such services as it desired.

The boroughs

The localist dynamic was not confined to small ecclesiastical communities. Although Anglo-Saxon England was by no means an urban society, from the tenth century larger settlements grew up as market centres and to provide fortification against enemies. These evolved communal services of a more advanced nature and some promoted the localist tradition further by seeking freedom from royal interference. They would apply for a Royal Charter of incorporation, which bestowed the right to regulate town life, raise money by taxation (though paying a fixed amount to the Crown), administer their own system of justice and return members to Parliament. (Tudor and Stuart monarchs used the device to increase their support in Parliament, creating 'rotten boroughs'.)

The guilds

From the twelfth century municipal development in the boroughs was augmented by another localist dynamic in the emergence in the towns of associations, or guilds, of craftsmen and merchants. These were formed to regulate trade and for other forms of economic self-protection. Guild members benefited from well-conducted town life and became involved in civic administration to the extent that the *Guild Hall* often became in effect the *Town Hall* (many retaining the name today). Guild practices usually included some form of internal democracy, with the election of Grand Masters for limited terms of office, and these became part of municipal life, producing various forms of representative and accountable government, financial probity and efficient administration. Here was a mould for modern local government.

The centralist tradition

The essence of this alternative tradition was central domination rather than local self-determination. It too shows an ancient lineage. Before England became a unitary state, fused under one monarchy, it consisted of separate kingdoms. When the conquering Danes advanced across the country they preserved these boundaries as the shires, units for the imposition of central rule. Each was placed under a royal agent, a shire reeve (sheriff). The system was retained in principle by the Normans after the conquest of 1066. The king aimed to gain the following four things from the shires:

(1)   *Finance*. The reeve would be the tax collector.

(2)   *Military support*. Officers of array would recruit men. Today, army regiments still carry the names of the shires.

(3)   *Maintenance of law and order*. Each shire would have a court. This did more than dispense royal justice, it was an assembly of citizens to appoint officials and receive orders from the king.

(4)   *Advice*. The shires would send knights to Parliament, the forerunners of our MPs.

The confluence of the traditions

The centralised model of local rule contained an intrinsic tension. Local courts began to threaten royal authority, and in response the king established a rival system by sending his own justices around the country on circuits. In time these *Justices of the Peace* (JPs) became key figures in local administration. Their powers were extended by the Tudor monarchs through a succession of statutes giving them a direct supervisory role over important parish functions such as roads, bridges and the relief of poverty. Thus, through the Justices, the localist and centralist traditions were amalgamated, although a centralist–localist tension remained.

By the eighteenth century the local government map contained a basic duality. There was a system of counties covering the whole of the country, encompassing parishes of various sizes and status operating under the eyes of the JPs, and a set of incorporated boroughs standing largely free of the county administration. Although this system had been able to survive the constitutional upheavals of the seventeenth century it was too fragile to withstand the traumas of the industrial revolution.

The industrial revolution

The industrial revolution saw the emergence of a new mode of production with far-reaching consequences. It produced a new class of people (capitalists or bourgeoisie) made incredibly powerful by the fact that they personally owned the materials (factories and machines) which the rest of the community needed for its very survival. This new class was to redraw the architecture of the entire state. Local government was directly affected through the process of urbanisation, which was central to the power of the bourgeoisie. As the new factories grew up to produce goods, so great new cities emerged to house and reproduce the labour force demanded by their gargantuan appetites.

Industrialisation lured people from the rural towns and villages to form populous urban communities the like of which had never existed before. At the beginning of the nineteenth century only one-fifth of the population dwelt in towns, but by the end of the century this had increased to around four-fifths. Moreover, the population grew in absolute terms. Estimated at some 5.5 million in 1695, it had reached 11 million by the time of the first census in 1801. Thirty years later it stood at 16.5 million (Flinn, 1963: 30). Urbanisation had cataclysmic social effects, including the following:

(1) *The slum.* Urban population growth generated an unprecedented demand for housing, resulting in the hasty construction by capitalists of poorly built, small dwellings, densely packed around the factories. Before long these were labelled irredeemable slums of which nineteenth-century chronicler Engels wrote:

True poverty often dwells in hidden alleys close to the palaces of the rich; but, in general a separate territory has been assigned to it, where, removed from the sight of the happier classes, it may struggle along as it can. (Engels, 1969: 60)

(2) *Disease.* The cities were constructed without an infrastructure of drainage and sanitation. Privy middens provided foul rudimentary lavatories. Epidemics of cholera, tuberculosis and scarlet fever ravaged the working population. Indeed the germs, unaware of any divinely ordained class system, even invaded the nostrils of the bourgeoisie and gentry, and as a salutary lesson, Prince Albert himself died of typhoid fever in 1861.

(3) *Inadequate transportation.* In the early stages of the industrial revolution roads, so vital for the transport of raw materials and products, were hopelessly inadequate in both quality and quantity.

(4) *Vice and corruption.* Large, impersonal, dimly lit cities provided opportunities for vice undreamed of in the pre-urban age. Cities like London and Manchester contained thousands of prostitutes, many of whom were children. In an underworld chronicled by Dickens, footpads and pickpockets roamed freely. The bourgeoisie feared for their lives as well as their rapidly accumulating property.

(5) *Exploitation.* Although academic disputants argue about factory conditions, there is little doubt that they were harsh and dangerous. A ruling establishment which had enjoyed the advantages of cheap, plentiful, human labour through slavery in the colonies had clear ideas on what to expect from workers on the home front. Men and women sweated from morning to night in dull, physically fatiguing, life-shortening tasks. Children, with fingers more nimble than their parents, and cheaper to hire, were in great demand. Their stunted growth produced the additional advantage that they could work in cramped places around clattering machines and up in sooty chimneys.

(6) *Pollution.* Here was another of capitalism's new products. Factories were erected in the most economically advantageous locations with no concern for atmosphere, rivers or landscape. The bourgeoisie built their grand houses west of the cities, so that the prevailing winds would waft the noxious factory fumes away from them. In the old agrarian order nature's great biological cycles had ensured the elimination of waste material, including human and

animal excrement, but in the new cities it remained where it fell, dank and polluting. Engels observed:

> The streets are generally unpaved, rough, dirty, filled with vegetable and animal refuse, without sewers or gutters, but supplied with foul stagnant pools instead. (Engels, 1969: 60)

(7) *Poverty*. Despite the burgeoning production, making Britain the proud workshop of the world and producing wealth beyond the dreams of avarice, workers received pitiful wages and the spectre of unemployment moved among the community as ubiquitously as that of disease. Around one-third of the population lived below the poverty line. Charles Booth graphically detailed the dire conditions of the people of London (Fried and Elman 1971) and, as late as 1901, Seebohm Rowntree (1980) exposed horrors in the city of York.

(8) *Fear*. In spite of (or because of) the vast wealth generated, this was a society living on a knife-edge. The social harmony, based on a sense of acceptable hierarchy and community which had existed under the *ancien régime* of the agrarian order was replaced with hard-edged individualism, competition and a new and provocative form of inequality. To the wealthy all was made more alarming by the haunting example of the French revolution and its bloody aftermath. The factories of the bourgeoisie had created another dangerous by-product, a Frankenstein's monster posing a constant sense of threat – the working class – and the city was its natural home. Radical movements and trade unions were feared and opposed, sometimes with savagery.

The municipal response

The new urban centres did not necessarily emerge in the boroughs where municipal institutions had become well established. Factory location was dictated by the logic of communications, power (mainly coal) and raw materials. Rural hamlets were transformed within a few decades into teeming anthills. The old system of aristocratic, county-based, local government was rendered entirely lost. The responses to the trauma were both localist and centralist.

The localist impetus came from the capitalists whose business success was contingent upon effective urbanisation. While proclaiming an ideology of *laissez-faire* they paradoxically required much from the municipality, including the guarantee of a strong and passive work-force, good roads, freedom from disease, public transport, street lighting and law and order to crush incipient radicalism. In the longer term this class was to fight successfully for control of the state at national level, but initially they took over the municipalities, bringing to them a pomp and splendour to match the importance they placed upon themselves and their enterprises. The ancient cities had been marked with great cathedrals but, in the new ones, the town halls built by the bourgeoisie often surpassed the ecclesiastical architecture in splendour and opulence. They were the new cathedrals and they honoured a puritan God who spoke more of hard work and competition than contemplation and love of one's neighbour.

Centralist impetus came in the form of legislation inspired by Bentham and the Philosophical Radicals (see pp. 15–16). The utilitarians had no patience with localist ideas of organic evolution or the veneration of the past, arguing that each age should fashion anew its institutions and laws. They were impatient to sweep away the old pattern. Bentham had little confidence in local endeavour and drew up elaborate plans for the central control and supervision of local bodies. His devoted disciple, the administrator Edwin Chadwick, was to become one of the most prominent reformers (Finer, 1952).

The reforms

The practical response came in two ways: the establishment of *ad hoc* bodies to provide new services directly, and the reform of the municipal institutions themselves. Although both were important, the latter was ultimately to create the modern local government system.

Ad hoc *bodies*
Ad hoc bodies were created to provide particular services and were controlled by boards of leading citizens gaining statutory authority by means of private Acts of Parliament. They arose because local capitalist interests were sceptical of the ability of the old institutions to cope with new demands. The movement gained great momentum and produced a complex mosaic of bodies responsible for a large range of functions, including gaols, asylums,

schools, civic improvement, slaughterhouses, roads, hospitals, burial of the dead and so on. The boards varied in composition and nature but were often elected, in receipt of grants from central government, and with power to levy a rate. They would employ both skilled and unskilled workers.

Reforming the municipal institutions

The early incursion of the new middle class into municipal affairs was facilitated by property-based extensions of the franchise (see pp. 90–3). In the early 1830s, following the 1832 Reform Bill, two Royal Commissions were established to conduct enquiries into the parish administration of the Poor Law and the state of municipal corporations, respectively. They were dominated by Philosophical Radicals and both reports were voluminous, running into many thousands of pages. In addition there was a public health movement, also dominated by utilitarians, which sought to make local government formally responsible for sanitation. All these added up to a comprehensive programme of municipal reform, which effectively created the modern system.

The Poor Law Reform Act 1834

The report on the Poor Law was determined to justify centralist reforms and alleged scandalous misuse of funds by the parishes. It appeared that the sufferings of the poor were matched only by the agonies inflicted by local guardians (those running the system) on their own livers, few appearing able to function without the lubrication of copious wining and dining at public expense. The report also dwelt upon the uneven and unsystematic nature of the boundaries and their discrepant sizes (Checkland and Checkland, 1973: 29–33).

However, it may be argued that the commissioners 'deliberately selected the facts so as to impeach the existing administration' (Blaug, 1963: 161). The real complaint of the bourgeoisie was against the over-generous aid to the poor through the 'Speenhamland system' (devised by the Justices of Berkshire, meeting on 6 May 1775, in the Pelican Inn in the village of Speenhamland) which used money from the poor rate to supplement the wages of farm labourers on the basis of their family commitments and the price of bread. Bentham saw this as 'a bounty to indolence and vice', insidiously undermining the capitalist system.

The result of the report was the Poor Law Reform Act 1834, a highly centralist measure. It rationalised the system of poor relief by amalgamating parishes into larger units (poor law unions) and subjecting them to strict central control. The new authorities were to effect a harsh system of poor relief to force people to work for the lowest possible wages. The hand of Chadwick was starkly visible and he assumed control of the central board, demonstrating with his uncompromising zeal a considerable capacity to irritate.

The Municipal Corporations Act 1835

The enquiry into the state of the boroughs was also scathing, alleging nepotism, jobbery and other forms of corruption. Many municipalities were judged to have outlived their time (Old Sarum being the most infamous 'rotten borough' for having an MP but no voters at all), and provided few services. Yet this was again a calculated hatchet-job by the forces of utilitarianism. Painstaking research by Sidney and Beatrice Webb was to present an alternative judgement, finding many efficient municipalities, often superior to the central government administration, which had not yet been subject to the attentions of Messrs Northcote and Trevelyan.

This report led to the Municipal Corporations Act which applied to 178 large towns (the City of London, with a long history of guild management and with powerful financial interests, managed to get itself exempted) and aimed to spread the best practices developed in the go-ahead corporations – including representative government, extensive ratepayer franchise, financial probity and administrative efficiency – to the rest of the country. Unlike the poor law reforms it was not centralising. It did not need to be; the large towns were already under the control of the bourgeoisie.

The public health movement

In administering the reformed poor law system Chadwick's attention was drawn to public health, which he recognised as being at the very root of social problems. He conducted a campaign for improvements in sewerage and water supply. Two large-scale reports aroused public feeling and Chadwick managed to win establishment support for reform by the pragmatic expedient of pointing out that, if the poor were healthier, they would be less likely to infect the wealthy. Eventually he secured the Public Health Act 1848, which followed the model of the new poor law administration with centrally controlled local boards of health responsible for sanitary districts. Where municipal corporations existed, they took on the public health functions themselves.

Administratively speaking, this measure was never as successful as the Poor Law reforms. Once the epidemics had been conquered the capitalists, like the burghers of Hamelin Town in Brunswick who declined to pay the Pied Piper once he had rid their town of rats, awakened to the fact that public health cost private money. A *laissez-faire* reaction swept the Central Board from the stage, though the sanitary districts remained. In 1871 a report from a Royal Commission on sanitation reaffirmed the importance of public health provision in a 'civilised life' and a new sperm was implanted in the Whitehall womb: the Local Government Board, to grow by stages into the Department of the Environment of today (see pp. 217–18).

The Local Government Act 1888

In 1884 the third major Reform Act granted the right to vote in parliamentary elections to the rural working class. This highlighted the anomaly that the counties had remained untouched by municipal reform. It also became apparent that certain parish services, particularly roads, would be better administered over wider areas. In Parliament the radical campaigner for municipal reform, Joseph Chamberlain, pressed the government. The result was the Local Government Act of 1888, which (together with a later one of 1894) established the modern model of local government.

The original intention had been to establish for almost all the country a two-tier system of new administrative counties, divided into districts. This was a centralist model and was resisted by the forces of localism in the form of the municipal corporations. They resented the idea of losing autonomy to the counties and lobbied strongly to amend the Act. As a result, all boroughs with populations of over 50,000 were permitted to remain independent of county jurisdiction. They were to combine the powers of county and borough; hence their name – county boroughs.

This duality in the system is often portrayed in textbooks as a most curious anomaly. However, in reality it was no more than a recognition of the organic fact of social and economic life; the densely populated urban boroughs presented problems entirely different from those of the rural counties. The dual pattern was irritating only to those with a passion for administrative neatness and uniform centralism. Redlich and Hirst (1903: 115), in a classic work, described the system as one 'condemned by logic . . . [but] approved by experience'. Far from being irrational, it represented the very essence of local government: the accommodation of diversity within the state. As the new system became established municipal institutions acquired more and more functions as the *ad hoc* bodies were swallowed up (see Chapter 4). Local government was to enter a period often termed its 'golden age'.

Conclusion – golden age to golden opportunity

It would be a mistake to conclude that this 'golden age' was a democratic and caring system protecting citizens from the cradle to the grave. It was essentially a machine to facilitate the working of capitalism. In so far as the new cities offered a vehicle for working-class organisation they were deeply feared. The economic leaders of society were also the political leaders and baroque towns halls and procedural splendour testify to their municipal dominance. Participation in this new arm of the state was, for the working class, limited to a choice between elites – Whigs or Tories, Liberals or Conservatives.

However, the model established by the bourgeoisie was to endure into the following century to become, with the extension of the franchise, an important instrument of democracy. As the structure of industry changed, with the fragmentation of ownership through joint stock companies and, more importantly, the emergence of giant monopolistic undertakings, links with their localities ceased to be so vital to the capitalist class. Yet when they deserted the town halls they left not only architectural splendour but a site for political struggle. The golden age gave way to a golden opportunity in the form of a portal of the state through which ordinary people could pass. It will be seen throughout this book that in so doing they would create tensions unanticipated when the bourgeoisie built their municipal palaces.

3

What Local Government Does

Local democracy is meaningless unless linked with a mechanism for providing important services to the community. Thus, for example, parish government today, with no major responsibilities, is considered little more than a quaint relic of a bygone age, to be ranked with well-dressings and the celebrations taking place around the maypoles on the village greens of Olde England. This chapter begins by stressing the flexibility of the local government functional portfolio, noting in broad outline its pattern of development. After considering the classification of functions and their allocation between tiers, the basic question of how the service-providing role of local government fits into the capitalist state is addressed. The implications of this lead into a final section, which considers the dramatic changes that began during the 1980s under an extreme right-wing impetus from central government.

Studying functions

It is conventional in discussing the things that state agencies provide (education, defence and so on) to refer to them as functions. This can be confusing, because in the social sciences the term has a different meaning. However, the convention is generally followed in this chapter although sometimes, when it seems more appropriate, the word services is used.

Textbooks have paid little attention to the political importance of the local government functional portfolio. For the most part it was treated rather like the rules of a game, to be accepted rather than discussed. This was a symptom of the post-war consensus which took for granted the role of the state in modern civilised life. Functions were seen merely as apolitical technical facts of public administration. However, in the 1980s this complacency was shattered, as the right of local government to provide some of its most cherished services was subjected to unrelenting political attack. This policy promised to do far greater harm to local democracy than any of the other acts of political aggression perpetrated during the period. It was a case of shooting the horse from under the rider.

A brief history of functions

The principles of parliamentary sovereignty and *ultra vires* mean that local authorities can only undertake those functions for which they have statutory approval. Acts of Parliament confer mandatory (compulsory) or permissive (optional) powers to do this or that activity. If an authority wishes to take on some new function it must promote a private bill in Parliament – a commonplace practice in the nineteenth century but infrequent today owing to the great expense involved. Local government's functional portfolio can be seen to have evolved through four eras.

A golden age

In the nineteenth century, the number of functions burgeoned. Although the new industrial order favoured a doctrine of *laissez-faire*, with the free market being allowed to allocate the resources within society, the reality was that capitalism needed a wide range of services from the state. Industrial cities mushroomed to serve the new smoking mechanical leviathans: the factories. A workforce was required which was healthy, sheltered, able to read and count, able to travel to work and so on. Thus the provision of many social services was motivated, not by altruism, but by the seemingly divine mission of the bourgeoisie to amass profits in honour of their Calvinistic God. In addition, an infrastructure of roads, street lighting, water supply, sewerage and law and order was needed to support the local economies.

All *laissez-faire* meant was that the state kept out of areas where profits could be made. Advocates of genuinely minimalist government were alarmed; by the time of the Great Exhibition of 1851, Herbert Spencer had written two books deploring the insinuation of state tentacles into economic life (Fraser, 1973: 102). Vital functions were provided locally and by the turn of the century the municipalities reached a high point as *multi-purpose* authorities by taking over the responsibilities of *ad hoc* bodies, voluntary societies and private enterprises (providing public utilities), often amid bitter political in-fighting.

The era of municipal socialism

By the first decade of the twentieth century the fledgling Labour Party was able to capitalise on this large portfolio. The emphasis changed from directly serving industry to improving social conditions. Stealthy social reform could be pursued through the 'gas and water socialism' advocated by the Fabian Society. Here the intention was to municipalise basic utilities (gas, electricity and water supply, street lighting, public transport) so that local working people could, through council membership, gain a greater say in the life of the community without seeming to threaten the capitalist order in a fundamental way. In addition, the Education Act of 1902 drew the vitally important function of secondary education into the municipal net. Municipal socialism was further advanced in 1929 when local government took over the responsibilities of the Poor Law guardians, inheriting the extensive range of rudimentary social services which had been developed since 1834.

Local government in the social democratic state

A new era opened after the Second World War as social democracy replaced liberal democracy. The Beveridge Report of 1942, published during the grim days of battle, promised people that, if they continued to fight, those remaining alive would witness the dawn of a new age of citizenship where new social rights would confer positive freedoms from the 'five giants' of want, disease, squalor, ignorance and idleness. In addition, governments generally accepted that the state should enter the hallowed precincts of the free market to regulate the economy in the general interest of all. This marked the beginning of a great consensus era in British politics in which local government assumed a key role as the provider of a comprehensive range of social services.

The New Right era

The social democractic era seemed set to go on for ever. However, it had depended upon an unprecedented 'long boom' of western capitalism based on a world economy with exchange rates fixed to the US dollar. All collapsed in the mid-1970s, producing a fiscal crisis in which the capitalist economy became unable to sustain the state services it required. When the Thatcher government came to power in 1979 it embarked upon a process of painful functional depilation as a large range of services were plucked, or partially plucked, from the local government breast. There was a general desire to reduce the role of local government and change it to one of 'coordinating' or 'enabling' the provision of services by a charity-funded voluntary sector and the profit-hungry private sector. We return to these developments later in this chapter.

Classifying functions

Local authorities administer two main categories of functions: those delivered to the community and those needed to sustain itself. The latter may be termed 'housekeeping' functions, or the management of resources (land, personnel and finance), and are not relevant here (although, as will be seen in later chapters, they are vitally important). Conventional textbook accounts have placed the community functions into categories such as the following:

Protective: fire, police, consumer protection, etc.
Environmental: roads, pollution control, planning, etc.
Personal: education, careers, housing, social services, etc.

Recreational: parks, leisure centres, dry ski-slopes, theatres, art
galleries, etc.

Commercial: markets, restaurants, transport, etc.

In addition, some authorities run unusual services which are *sui
generis*. For example, there is Doncaster Racecourse, Manchester
Airport, various seaports controlled by local authorities, and the
city of Hull has successfully operated its own telephone service.

Such lists are of only limited use. They do nothing to distil the
essence of the functional specificity of local government (that is, to
explain why local government does what it does). This is one of the
big questions of local government analysis and, from the 1980s, its
importance was heightened. This is considered below.

Allocating functions within the state

Why have some functions been performed by local government
and others by central government? This question is important because it helps in the discovery of the essential nature and role of
local government, and its location in the context of the totality of
the state.

The division between state agencies has not remained fixed;
functions have moved between local government, central government and a variety of centrally created quangos. Why do these
movements occur? Is there any inherent logic determining that
which should be rendered to the Caesars of local government, and
that belonging to the God of Westminster? It is intuitively obvious
that certain services are best controlled locally; it would be absurd
to organise the emptying of the nation's dustbins from Whitehall.
This operation, like a great many others, requires intimate local
knowledge. Yet by no means all such operations lie in the hands of
the municipalities (see Chapter 4). We may identify three sources
of explanation: the rational, the political and the holistic.

Rational explanation

A rational explanation would suggest that there is some allocation
of functions within the state which optimises some desirable goal,
such as efficiency, effectiveness or democracy. This was the

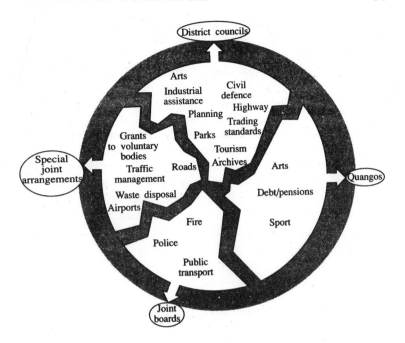

Figure 3.1   Abolishing the Mets: where the function went.

approach of Bentham when he sought to redesign the state to maximise the sum of total utility (see pp. 15–16). In a later era, health minister Aneurin Bevan argued in rational vein that a system of special-purpose health authorities would be more efficient than local government for the administration of the NHS. Again, when the GLC and the metropolitan counties were relieved of all functions (by abolition) by the Thatcher government, the official explanation was that they were being 'streamlined' in the interests of efficiency (see Figure 3.1).

However, the problem with 'rational' explanations is that they can be mutually contradictory. While sensitivity to the popular will offers a better prospect that a service such as education will reflect the desires of a particular community, other goals, such as territorial justice (equality), are sacrificed. Indeed, it is unlikely that the distribution of state functions could ever be entirely rational. In the first place, no government starts with a *tabula rasa*; there are always historical factors and the inertia of the status quo to be taken into account. Moreover, decision-makers always have interests of their own which they will tend to place first. Hence, putative rational argument is often no more than a rationalisation of a political decision. This introduces the next form of explanation.

Political explanations

Political factors lead us to the view that the distribution of functions may be expected to serve the advantage of the powerful. Thus, nineteenth-century councillors in the thriving industrial centres were in a strong bargaining position; the municipalities had resources, expertise and organisation at a time when the apparatus of central government was small, weakly organised, poorly staffed, corrupt, and bound in a philosophical straitjacket of minimal government.

During the twentieth century the balance of power has changed in favour of the centre. Thus, in spite of Bevan's protestations, local government's loss of the hospital service reflected the power of the medical profession. Income maintenance was removed from local government as a result of central fears of 'Poplarism': that is, excessive generosity from working-class councillors to the poor and their own staff (see p. 230). We shall see shortly that an attempt by the Thatcher government to completely reconstitute local government's functional portfolio in the 1980s was almost entirely political. Hence, the services which local government has lost during the century have not been mislaid out of carelessness; they have been removed by the purposive hand of the central state.

Or have they? Do politicians have the power to shape the state according to their whims? This question leads to the third possible source of explanation, and takes us into deeper levels of social causation.

A holistic explanation

A holistic explanation is one which looks to the politico-economic system in its totality as a determinant of much in social life. From early times the state has fulfilled certain basic functions, including guaranteeing property rights, maintaining law and order, conducting foreign relations and defence and accepting some responsibility for the poor.

As Britain became an advanced capitalist economy state functions were not reduced, but increased. James O'Connor (1973) identifies three categories of public expenditure: social investment, social consumption and social expenses. Social investment expenditure provides the infrastructure for the economy (roads, telecommunications and so on); social consumption expenditure provides things people consume (housing, health care, welfare and so on) in order to remain alive, healthy and even happy. This vitally assists capitalism by maintaining the work-force and socialising production costs (so that wages can be kept low). Finally, social expenses are incurred in maintaining social stability through various forms of legitimation, defence and law and order. Some of these things could in principle be provided by the market but they would not be profitable. Others, such as defence, would not be legitimate if provided by private endeavour.

Is any one of these categories particularly characteristic of local government? It can be argued that, as the factory was the place where production took place, so the city has been the place where labour power is sustained and reproduced. The urban organisation provides the things people need to consume in order to live and bring up their families: O'Connor's 'consumption expenditures'. Indeed, for Castells the 'city' is something very special in capitalism:

> a residential unity of labour power . . . a unity of collective consumption corresponding . . . to the daily organization of labour power (Castells, 1976: 148).

Of course, it is clear that not all local government functions in the real world would be classed as collective consumption services. However, they constitute the essential character of the urban, in much the same way that production of goods is the essential characteristic of the factory. Thus, private firms can run social and sports clubs, brass bands, provide various forms of employee insurance and so on, but this is not their *raison d'être*. It was shown in Chapter 2 how the emergence of the modern cities coincided with the unparalleled need for labour by the new industries.

Local government serving the state

Why is it beneficial for capitalism if social consumption services are provided by local government? There are a number of possible reasons, including the following:

(1) *Cost saving.* The existence of local taxes produces ever-present local pressures for thrift and low levels of social provision. In the nineteenth century such pressure came from the 'economisers' and in the post-war era from the Conservative middle-class ratepayers. The Thatcher community charge ('poll tax') was designed to increase this pressure.

(2) *Deflecting criticism.* While dominating a service from the centre, the capitalist state can allow local government to suffer the odium for unpopular policies (such as rent rises in the early 1970s).

(3) *Containing opposition.* Free-market capitalism stands in constant threat of retaliation from those who must of necessity lose out, and one of its best sources of defence is fragmentation of opponents. Councils in working-class areas are obliged to compete with each other for a share of central government funds and in enticing firms to their territories. The latter may even involve attempts to suppress radical elements in local trade unions (Massey, 1985: 86) and on councils.

(4) *Limiting democracy.* The central–local division of functions means that participation by ordinary people is confined to the sphere of social consumption. Important investment decisions can be made in closed secretive forums of capitalist interests and central politicians (see Chapter 12).

(5) *Legitimation.* Although 'Keep Out' signs are erected around the central decision-making forums, the real degree of popular participation permitted at local level allays fear that the state is an instrument of the capitalist class.

Of course, it does not follow that capitalist interests will recognise these advantages. Indeed, the 1980s saw dramatic events which promised to entirely redraw the functional contours of local government. This was nothing less than a challenge to the basic idea of local authorities as service providers at all.

Privatising democracy – the Thatcher assault

For a number of reasons the Thatcher government proved particularly hostile to the state. When coming to power in Orwell's

Animal Farm the pigs had worked on a simple premise of 'four legs good, two legs bad'; the New Right rewrote this to read with equal decisiveness: 'private sector good, public sector bad'. The idea of local government was felt to be particularly bad.

Attacks were to come on several fronts (to be detailed throughout this book) but the removal of functions was perhaps the most deadly of all. With nothing to do local government becomes like a miner in one of Britain's abandoned collieries: redundant and discarded. The overall thrust was in the direction of privatisation; the idea was not to dispense with functions, they were merely to be shipped into the private sector. Indeed, by slicing functions away like servings of salami it became possible, not merely to leave local government with less to do, but to undermine its very core role of providing collective consumption services. This was attempted in various ways.

Selling the local silver

Some assets could be sold outright. Council housing proved an easy target; supplementing Britain's historic constitutional rights came a 'right to buy' (at tempting knock-down prices). By 1987 more than a million had been disposed of. Although most went to owner-occupiers, unoccupied dwellings and sometimes whole estates were bought by private property developers. The government played a very active part in encouraging tenants to purchase. In addition, local authorities were obliged to sell unused land for private development.

Competitive tendering

This policy enshrined the key New Right all-purpose nostrum – competition. Although not a new practice, it was to be extended to a much wider range of functions. Rather than use its own workforce to do a job, the authority was to seek tenders (estimates of the cost) from the private sector. The 'in-house' work-force could also tender, but would have to take its chances with the rest. In addition, one part of an authority could even award a contract to another part, establishing an 'internal market' in place of cooperation. The first legislation came in the Local Government Planning and Land Act 1980, which required competitive tendering in the areas of highways, building construction and maintenance. The Local Government Act 1988 extended the requirement to refuse collection, street cleaning,

catering, cleaning buildings and vehicle maintenance, while the Edu
cation Reform Act 1988 allowed schools to shop around for service
such as ground maintenance and cleaning.

New Right apologists argued that there was no local governmen
service which could not be put out to tender, even the collection o
taxes (Ridley, 1988). Indeed, the Conservative policy of care in th
community, which involved transferring responsibility for the ol
and handicapped from the hospitals to local authorities, saw th
role of local government as contracting for 'packages of care' fron
the private and voluntary sectors (Griffiths, 1988: 1).

Deregulation
This policy entailed the ending of public-sector monopolies
Public-sector operators (mainly local authorities) had long bee.
the monopolistic providers of public transport services. Statutor
regulation had limited competition for environmental and safet
reasons. However, legislation from 1980 made it progressivel
easier for private operators to compete. The Transport Act of 198
forced the public-sector operators to break away from the loca
authorities altogether and form themselves into private companie
operating according to market criteria (see Chapter 4).

Opting out
Here the idea is that certain local authority clients opt to com
under some other body. Thus the Housing Act 1988 enabled coun
cil tenants to choose some other landlord approved by centrall
created bodies or manage their own estates as tenant cooperative
In addition, housing action trusts could be set up by central gov
ernment in areas of its own choice to take over council estates an
subsequently sell them to the private sector. The Education Re
form Act 1988 made provision for schools to opt out of loca
government ownership and control, to be financed by means of
direct grant from Whitehall (see DES, 1987). Polytechnics an
colleges of higher education were also removed from local govern
ment to become 'independent', largely controlled by loca
businessmen.

Quango culture
From being the party of quangocide the Conservatives began t
cultivate a whole range of new administrative predators to tak

over local government functions (see Chapter 4). These stood as evidence that, to the government, local democracy was not really necessary at all. The most significant were the urban development corporations. By the end of the 1980s local authorities were but one species in a densely crowded and hostile environment (see Chapter 4). There were even rivals in education; government training schemes proliferated and city technical colleges were schools established by central government and sponsored by local industry, their emphasis on serving business rather than education in its wider sense.

Encouraging rivals

The government played an active part in fostering the emergence of private sector rivals to local government. Private education and health care were praised (and enjoyed a boom period). Firms were urged to tender for contracted-out work and legislation was repeatedly passed whenever it was felt their chances might be impaired. The 'care in the community' policy urged the development of private homes for the mentally and physically handicapped and the old and chronically ill. There was even encouragement for the private sector to engage in urban renewal through the use of enterprise zones and grants (see Brindley and Stoker, 1987).

Family matters

Privatisation could even enter the home. Much government rhetoric spoke of the importance of the family, a coded message reminding women of their duties to care for their children, their elderly and their chronically sick. This would help reduce local government's social services responsibility. 'Granny grants' were offered to families willing to take the elderly off the hands of the state. Here was a strategy for those unable to afford the caring services of the private sector.

Not serving but enabling

The vast amount of piecemeal legislation necessary to promote the changes did not look like a coordinated programme to restructure local government. However, by a process of trial, a great deal of error, considerable audacity and no little surprise at what could be accomplished, something resembling a programme did emerge. Broadly this claimed to be replacing the idea that local government provided services with the idea that it merely coordinated their provision by others. The buzz term became 'the enabling authority', put forward as an alternative to the rather outmoded 'serving authority'. Central to the approach is the concept of the *contract*. The authority ensures that the community receives services by awarding contracts to private firms, voluntary societies (operating on the basis of charity in areas where capitalists cannot see profit) and perhaps non-elected public agencies.

This meant replacing democratic decision making and control with the free market; it also meant replacing the concept of need with that of demand (that is, ability to pay) as the basis for determining who gets what. What kind of local government would this be? The centre may have rid itself of some left-wing municipal bathwater, but was democracy also to gurgle down the plughole?

Why privatise local government?

It was seen earlier that local government actually serves capitalism by socialising labour costs and providing a means of legitimation. Why then should a far right government wish to go to such lengths to bite a hand (indeed remove an arm) which was helping to feed it?

Overriding all is the question of cost. Profitability can fall to the point that capitalists are unwilling to pay for the state services they require and a fiscal crisis is threatened (O'Connor, 1973). This point was reached in the mid-1970s with the collapse of the long post-war boom period of western capitalism. The economic environment was such that a government of any persuasion was going to face hard choices over collective consumption. Indeed, it was a Labour Secretary of State who first proclaimed 'the party's over' (see Chapter 11). However, the Conservative government of the 1980s went far beyond economy. The reducing of functions showed a fundamentalist zeal reflecting various motives.

Ideological commitment

The Thatcher government was more overtly ideological than any in the post-war era. 'Thatcherism', an amalgam of economic liberalism, monetarism, individualism, anti-corporatism, authoritarianism and populism (Benyon, 1989: 170–1), became a standard term in the ideological lexicon. Its implications were not confined to local government; the rolling back of the state frontiers meant just about all frontiers apart from defence and police. The earlier belief that the private sector could not be trusted to place the common good before profit was banished in free-market euphoria. In an age that had forgotten the horrors of cholera, even water was to be privately owned.

Monetarism

The Thatcherite version of monetarism, which informed early economic strategy, placed great stress on reducing public expenditure. Local government, with its services responsible for around a third of this, was bound to be in the firing line. While cost-cutting could help, removing functions altogether was by far the simplest solution. Indeed, the actual sale of assets did more than reduce public spending, it brought revenue into the state coffers.

Dispensing with legitimation

Those representing capital may not recognise the value of local government to their interests. The legitimating role may seem particularly invisible through *petit bourgeois* spectacles. Indeed, a failure to recognise the value of various forms of legitimation was a general characteristic of Thatcherism throughout the 1980s, when media freedom, the House of Lords, the trade unions, the opposition party, progressive taxation, the Church of England, established patterns of consultation and so on were all threatened. The result was civil unrest and ugly scenes of violence in the streets. Although this was contained by massively increased expenditure on the police, wet (non-Thatcherite) Conservatives were nervous. By the end of the 1980s the party's popularity had hit an all-time low, to culminate dramatically in the resignation of the Prime Minister herself.

Fear of democracy

Under democracy the who gets what, when, how decisions are determined by votes rather than wallets. The power of the market to legitimate inequality (which it does by saying 'if you can't afford it, you can't have it') is lost and poor people have an opportunity to call for an equal share of the cake. Hence, full democracy is essentially antithetical to the interest of the right. This is why urban politics can be an important site for political struggle. In the 1970s, when Labour seemed able to win office regularly, there was grave talk in establishment circles of 'elective dictatorship'. Clearly a privatisation policy reduces the sphere of democratic decision-making.

Attacking the dependency culture

Broadly it can be said that the New Right philosophy, with its emphasis on individualism, resented the welfare state as feather-bedding for the weak and lazy. Much rhetoric lamented the 'dependency culture'. Social democracy was characterised by leading Conservative Norman Tebbit as 'post-war-funk'. The extensive social service functions of local government could hardly have been more provocative.

Party politics

In addition there was a straight party political fight. Despite the technical and economic jargon this was an intensely political programme. Urban councils sometimes appeared to be hotbeds of socialism; reducing their sphere of responsibility lessened their power. Moreover, competitive tendering undermined the public-sector unions; win or lose the contract, things were bound to be tougher. With council house sales, enforced *embourgeoisement* created new tranches of owner-occupier Conservatives. Not content with disposing of living accommodation, Westminster City Council sold accommodation for death - in 1987 three large cemeteries passed into the private sector, though in this case the cold tenants could not be expected to make their way to the polling stations, at least not during the hours of daylight. Overall, the policy offered a huge boost to the private sector, where the government desperately needed growth to legitimate its economic policies.

Conclusion – enabling or disabling?

New Right apologists believed the functional reforms to be profound. At the most extreme it could mean no less than the complete demise of local government (Mather, 1989). Yet the extent of real change remained questionable, and, in so far as legitimation of the policy would come in terms of outcome, there were few grounds for optimism. Deregulation did not improve public transport (Hoyle, 1987), and competitive tendering could be adjudged to have largely failed (Ascher, 1987: 227–8). Schools proved loath to opt out and the devolved management was not welcomed by teachers. Although council house sales were hailed as a major success, the pattern of purchase was variable, reflecting the north–south divide. Many tenants steadfastly resisted the tempting offer and the government fell short of its target of 80 per cent owner-occupation (Forrest, 1987). The result of private-sector-led urban renewal has been consumerist hypermarket theme parks and office blocks with little to offer inner city residents. Reduced social services will mean more unpaid work for women in the home, inner city decline will mean social tension.

Although the extreme enactment of the policy of functional depilation would represent a fundamental change, and perhaps the end of local democracy, reform was consistently impeded by local government resistance. Yet the challenge to the traditional service-providing role of local government was to send shocks and currents throughout the system, with implications for councillors, employees, management practices, finance, and of course for the operation of local democracy itself. This chapter has made it clear that the issue of what local government does is no apolitical matter of administrative theory; it lies at the heart of politics and the tensions generated will be apparent throughout the following chapters.

4

The Administrative Environment

Not all state services organised territorially lie within the remit of elected local government. This chapter explores a world of non-democratic life-forms, which constitutes the administrative environment of local government, beginning with a broad overview of the range of bodies to be sighted. Following this some particular specimens are selected for more detailed examination, including those responsible for water (before privatisation), passenger transport, health, police and the local economy. These are crucially important services. Why do they lie beyond the eyes and ears of local democracy? What are the implications for local government in the arrangements? In seeking answers to these questions it will become apparent that the examination of the local adminstrative environment is no dry study of red-taped public administration. The issue is highly political and the implications run deep.

Non-elective local government

An understanding of the system of non-elected local state agencies is profoundly important because of the systemic nature of urban politics. The agencies do not stand *in vacuo*, like marble statues in a garden staring sightlessly at each other and powerless to complete the promised embrace; they are parts of an urban whole, locked in a network of interdependence. This has implications for local democracy. Where rival authorities exist there is potential for friction and for a limitation of the right of the community to decide things for itself.

Justifying *ad hocery*

Of course, few official utterances will ever say that the reason for non-elective local bodies is the evasion of local democracy. Various pious arguments are advanced to suggest that they are in some way better for particular jobs than the elected authorities. Hence the reasons for creating *ad hoc* bodies are said variously to be commercial, technical (medicine), artistic, socially sensitive (race relations) or unsuitable for political control (policing).

Yet all these reasons are open to debate. As the previous chapter demonstrated, one of the major effects of reducing the functions of local government is to restrict the area in which ordinary people have control over their lives. This is replaced with the paternalistic judgement of experts, central government decisions or, where the private sector becomes involved, the hand of the market. The theme of this chapter is that local government exists in a hostile environment.

Populating the environment

The idea of *ad hoc* bodies providing single services outside the framework of the municipal institutions is by no means new. Indeed, as a response to nineteenth-century urbanisation, it predates the modern system of all-purpose authorities (see Chapter 2). However, a significant difference between nineteenth-century *ad hoc* bodies and their modern counterparts is the fact that they were intimately wedded to their communities, often popularly elected, and formed because municipalities were often undeveloped.

The early decades of the post-war era saw the creation, in 1948, of a complex system of hospital authorities (see below). In addition there were various joint boards drawing together groups of local authorities to administer services needing wider areas, such as public transport, police and land-use planning. Around the large urban areas (particularly London) new town development

corporations were established, creating satellite towns to accommodate the swelling urban work-force. During the 1970s the economic recession bit deeply into the northern industrial cities
creating large-scale unemployment. The Labour government created economic development agencies in Wales and Scotland and in
the cities themselves authorities, sometimes in partnership with
central government, established various quasi-autonomous enterprise boards and cooperative development agencies in efforts to
arrest decline.

However, the most dramatic growth occurred from 1979. This
was ironic since the Conservative government professed itself
committed to roll back the state rather than advance it. However
all fitted into an anti-socialist political strategy; for the most part
the new bodies were designed to relieve local government of
powers and enhance the opportunities for private business to influence economic development. In addition there was the abolition of
the GLC and metropolitan counties in 1986, which led to the creation of a host of new agencies to take over their functions.

It is not easy to categorise the bewildering collection of non-
elected public bodies jostling for position in the local environment.
The following catalogue can help in the quest to understand, but it
is neither exclusive nor exhaustive.

Caging the animals

The species found in the local administrative environment exhibit
a bewildering variety of forms. What they share is some degree of
insulation from the communities they serve – none are directly
elected. Dunleavy and Rhodes (1986: 115–16) provide the useful
acronym QUELGO (quasi-elected local government organisation)
to encompass many of them. However, the categories below go
further, to include bodies which are entirely non-elected, ranging
from those wedded to the central state to those with feet planted
largely in the private sector.

'Colonial' administrations

When Britain ruled the waves, bowler-hatted Whitehall-style civil
servants could be found in all outposts of the empire. Today the

United Kingdom comprises four provinces, three of them remnants of nations conquered and subjugated by the fourth. As compensation there are separate 'colonial' civil services (the Welsh, Scottish and Northern Ireland Offices) to betoken some degree of nationhood. In their respective territories these civil services deal with local government and become part of a complex network of central–local relationships. However, they weaken local democracy because, in any case of conflict, they will defer to Whitehall.

Non-central civil service departments

Not all the so-called Whitehall departments are located in the capital. The Driver and Vehicle Licensing Centre is at Swansea, the Training Agency is located in Sheffield and the Department of Social Security is centralised upon Newcastle. Like big private firms, these leviathans cannot be ignored by the host local authorities.

Whitehall's field agencies

It would surprise the casual observer to discover the extent to which the tentacles of Whitehall penetrate into the heart of Britain's towns and cities: some 75 per cent of all civil servants work outside London (see Figure 4.1). The revenue departments, the Department of Social Security and the Department of the Environment are dispersed down to regional and/or local offices. Other departments also have extensive field agency networks and the host local authorities will be very conscious of their cuckoo-like presence in the administrative nest. They can be important agents in getting local authorities to toe a centrally prescribed line.

Quangos

This term is one of the least exact in the political science lexicon, referring as it does to an astonishingly wide range of government-created bodies. The basis of the acronym is itself debatable; some writers take it to stand for quasi-autonomous national government organisation, which makes sense, though most take it to mean quasi-autonomous non-government organisation, which does not. A better term is quasi-government agency, but QGA lacks the

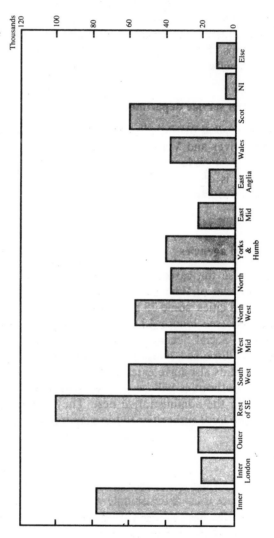

Figure 4.1 The national distribution of civil servants.

resonance of 'quango'. The essential feature of the quango is some degree of freedom from control by, and accountability to, the democratic institutions, which is why they are sometimes called 'arm's-length' agencies. Although most belong in the arena of central government some, like the regional arts associations, have a clear territorial structure and manifest a visible local presence, particularly where the service must be tailored to the characteristics of the locality. The health authorities and (until privatised) water authorities provide good examples (see below). Although in some cases local councillors are represented on the controlling boards, relations are often acrimonious.

Promotional bodies

A particular type of quango is concerned not with administering anything but with encouraging particular activities such as sport, leisure, tourism, the arts and so on. Centrally based agencies such as the Arts Council work through regional arts associations. In similar fashion the Sports Council operates regionally, aiming to develop facilities on the basis of local requirements. Tourist boards promote the holiday delights of the regions, from the sewers of the great Victorian cities to improbable and chilly naturist resorts along the east coast. Local authorities can be closely involved in the activities of these bodies, often providing part of their grant income and with representation on their boards.

Locally based quangos

These are set up by central government to operate specifically in certain areas. Early examples of such arrangements were the new town development corporations which were to provide a model for the very significant growth of urban development corporations (UDCs) (see below). These are controlled by government-appointed boards comprising civil servants and local business interests and are largely funded by central government. Clearly they will follow policies desired by the centre. Although not elected, as centres of power they are subject to the formal and informal attentions of pressure groups and have proved most amenable to the demands of industry and commerce.

The Housing Act of 1988 made provision for the establishment of housing action trusts (HATs), set up by central government to take over run-down estates and improve them with public and private subsidy. Once the renovation was complete the HAT would dispose of the stock to private ownership. However, the idea of being taken over in this way aroused considerable opposition from tenants fearful of falling into private sector hands. By 1989 the scheme appeared to have run out of steam (Spencer, 1989: 89).

Local government quangos

Local authorities may themselves establish and fund bodies to operate at arm's length from the town hall. These may be constituted in the form of companies run by directors appointed by the council. The development became particularly prevalent in Labour metropolitan counties during the early 1980s (thus, for example, Manchester appointed a Greater Manchester Economic Development Corporation) as they sought ways to deal with economic problems, particularly the large-scale unemployment brought about by the great Thatcherite 'shake-out' of the economy.

Local authorities maintained a degree of control through funding and appointments, receiving regular reports and monitoring performance. However, the essential point of establishing such bodies was to free them to act commercially, and often the best source of recruitment was the private sector, resulting in a narrow community vision. Hence the relationship is paradoxical in that, if they are working well they may displease a left-wing council, yet if they are pleasing their council they may not be achieving their economic goals. Generally, they were not very successful (they were operating in a very inclement climate) and were not welcomed by central government (see below).

Authorities have experimented with other forms of arm's-length agencies including workers' cooperatives and community business associations. The contracting-out and deregulation policies could result in more local authority services being delivered in this way; the 1985 Transport Act forced the hiving off of bus operations as separate companies. In such cases the ability of local authorities to exert control is considerably reduced, since the centre imposes conditions largely designed to protect the private sector (see below).

Joint boards

Joint boards are formed from a number of adjacent local authorities and have a similar constitutional status, being corporate bodies with legal personas. They obtain funds from the member authorities through a precept (a demand that the authority collect a certain amount of tax on their behalf) or by borrowing. However, funds are not unlimited: central government can impose 'precept capping' (see Chapter 11). The abolition of the GLC and metropolitan counties in 1986 produced a new brood of some twenty joint boards to take over functions like police, fire, waste disposal and passenger transport services.

The boards are nominally under the control of councillor representatives of the constituent authorities, but they cannot generate the political dynamic of a council or committee of a single authority. Local democracy is deliberately neutered by dampening down party politics. Although a party may dominate the council at district level, it is not permitted to send a party phalanx to the board; representatives must be in proportion to party strengths (to reduce Labour domination). Because they come from different district councils members do not have strong interpersonal links and this inhibits the development of political networks. The effect is to depoliticise the service, placing the chief officers on top (Gyford *et al.* 1989: 302–3). Moreover, in the case of the police, the fact that non-elected magistrates must comprise one-third of the membership (see below) reduces the democratic voice to little more than a murmur.

Decentralised units

The local authority can itself add to the administrative complexity. Large urban authorities have moved to decentralised forms of administration, with area-based management teams and committees to provide housing and social services closer to the community. Further complication arises where the areas for different services are not coterminous. Thus, for example, the Family and Community Services Department of Sheffield City Council was reorganised into seven area divisions, while the Housing Department had fifteen (Seyd, 1990: 342).

User organisations

These consist of representatives from certain clientele groups and perhaps the local authority. They may be advisory only, or may actually administer a service. The increased emphasis on the market and the concept of consumer choice in the 1980s led authorities to establish such organisations to permit users a greater say in the nature of services. They include neighbourhood forums, tenant associations (Clapham and English, 1987), and parent–teacher associations. The opting-out legislation gives tenants the right to form a cooperative. Similarly, opted-out schools are managed by school councils composed of parents and business interests. There have also been experiments in the user management of leisure facilities.

Yet user organisations pose a major ethical problem since, for many services, it is by no means easy to identify the true users. For example, drivers benefit from cheap public transport if roads are less congested and safer. Schools do not only serve parents and children; they also serve the community at large by producing doctors, builders and so on, and generally civilise society. User organisations will, by definition, tend to run services in their own narrowly defined interests. The city of Sheffield encountered this problem in 1982. Labour's manifesto had pledged the abolition of corporal punishment in schools, but school boards (representing parents), when asked for their views, overwhelmingly opposed the change. There was cynicism when the council went ahead with abolition but, as the representative of the whole community, it had a responsibility to consider what was conducive to a humane society. What happens if a school council wants to restrict admission on the grounds of ability, colour or religion? The essential point about local government services is that they are collectively provided for the benefit of all.

Voluntary organisations

The very nature of local government services makes them of central concern to a wide range of voluntary bodies formed to protect the interests of the vulnerable (children, the poor, the aged and the physically and mentally handicapped). With considerable expertise and knowledge, these often play a key role, working in partnership with the authority in delivering services. Conservative policy in the late 1980s promised a dramatic increase in this role (see Chapter 3).

Yet such organisations present local government with various difficulties. In the first place, despite the volunteers' commitment, they are essentially amateurs, lacking training and skill. This has the additional problem of alienating professional social workers and others who may feel threatened. Their much applauded fund-raising skills are also dangerous in that, because some charities are more popular than others, there can be a maldistribution of resources. Generally the effect of an enlarged voluntary sector is a return to the idea that care is an act of charity. People cannot claim rights by virtue of being citizens and are robbed of dignity, appearing as humble supplicants before middle-class benefactors, as in Victorian times. Moreover, they are denied a democratic voice in the nature of the services they receive.

Public–private partnership organisations

These combine industry and commerce with central or local government (or both). Funding comes from both partners. Organisations of this kind became very important in the 1980s as central government sought to increase the voice of the private sector in municipal affairs, particularly in economic development (Moore *et al.*, 1985). The relationships were resisted by left-wing councils in the early 1980s as they tried to revive their economies alone but, by the close of the decade, they were increasingly drawn in as part of a movement of 'new realism' which accepted the power of private capital.

City councils and chambers of commerce began to bury hatchets and embrace. Thus, for example, a Sheffield Economic Regeneration Committee was established in 1986, uniting representatives from the business community, the trade unions, the university and polytechnic, regionally based civil servants and the local authority. Bodies of this kind have been involved in projects such as the development of science parks, workers' cooperatives, housing and urban renewal. In Sheffield, a special public–private partnership board was established to manage the World Student Games.

For local government such partnerships are *liaisons dangereuses*. The private sector is primarily interested in making profit. While it may, in the short term, sacrifice this for good community relations, it will only do so as part of a longer-term profit-maximisation strategy.

The private state?

Finally, during the 1980s, the private sector had to be seen almost as a branch of the state. The 'care in the community' policy envisaged local government even relinquishing much of its social services role to the private sector. The increased emphasis on contracting-out meant that services previously provided by the authority would come from private firms. This did not merely mean local firms. The lucrative contracts attracted the attentions of multinationals, able to submit crushing loss-leader tenders to gain a foothold in Britain. The prospect of further European integration after 1992 promised to place local authorities in a world market.

Figures on the local landscape

In the following section a few particular local administrative bodies are selected for closer examination. Although each poses its own unique problems, it is possible to generalise in terms of their propensity to press the mute button on local democracy.

Liquid assets – the water market

In 1989 the ten water authorities of England and Wales were privatised. Although no longer part of the public sector, their story is instructive. In the nineteenth century it became generally apparent, partly through the great public health movement, that leaving sewerage, drainage and the supply of water to private enterprise could seriously damage health. Drinking water was often polluted and drainage rudimentary or non-existent. Engineering was also hazardous. For example, on one dark night in 1864 large areas of Sheffield were fatally submerged beneath a deluge of water and slime when the ill-constructed Dale Dyke Dam fractured. Hence the services were almost entirely entrusted to local government. The 1974 reorganisation saw the function removed from local government and placed in the hands of new quangos, the Regional Water Authorities, with boundaries reflecting the major watersheds. Although this represented a serious loss of democratic control, it could be justified on technical and economic grounds.

Members of the authorities were appointed by the minister and nominated by the constituent local authorities. It was considered important that links between the water authorities and councils be retained to coordinate activities such as the siting of houses and factories and to make recreational use of reservoirs. Although relations were not always harmonious, the democratic voice could still be heard.

However, democratic influence was entirely killed in 1989 when the quangos became Britain's 'water businesses', their prime concern being to make profits for shareholders rather than to serve and protect the community. No other privatisation measure aroused so much opposition as the Bill made its tortuous journey through Parliament, probably costing environment minister Nicholas Ridley his job. Nevertheless, government resolution ensured that public opinion played no part in the decision and the nation's water was channelled from the many to the few. There was no compensation for the ratepayers whose forebears had purchased the old water companies. In place of community control came state regulatory apparatus, though the government's avowed preference for a 'light touch' in all matters of regulation did not augur well in the eyes of those who thought water, falling equally upon rich and poor alike, too precious a resource to be claimed as the property of a wealthy few. Yet the fact that this resource could be privatised sent out a clear message that literally nothing in the public domain could be regarded as sacred.

Transport of delight

Passenger transport was an area where local authorities did much pioneering work. If the essential function of the cities was to provide workers for the factories, getting them to the gates was crucial to the urban enterprise.

After 1974 public transport became one of the most important functions of the new metropolitan counties and some impressive advances were made. In Tyne and Wear a streamlined coordinated Metro system was developed, while in South Yorkshire fares were held down in an impressive social policy with widespread environmental, personal stress, shopping and road safety benefits. However, this triumph for local government was to be but brief; the abolition of the GLC and metropolitan counties saw the service transferred to joint boards.

More dramatic changes came when the deregulation of road service licensing opened up public transport provision to private competition, weakening further the management role of elected representatives. They were restricted to some influence on fare levels, concessionary fares, selecting routes for fare subsidies and planning new schemes. In 1985, the Transport Act obliged local authorities running bus services (and airports) to hive them off as separate companies. Although the authorities continue to own the capital and can appoint up to seven non-executive directors, the companies must compete with private companies on equal terms and are forced to place market considerations before those of service to the community. The result is higher fares, traffic congestion, more danger and more pollution.

Arm's-length health

Of all the public services provided locally while remaining outside the remit of elected local government, the NHS is the most curious. It is essentially local in character; hospitals and general practitioners (GPs) must be within easy reach of all sections of the community, particularly the old and infirm. Health is vital to the quality of life, more important than wealth, education, property, friends, or even good looks. It would seem fundamental that a community should influence its health service; to say whether it wants hi-tech medicine, more stress on community services, more preventative techniques and so on.

This case is strengthened by the fact that many hospital and domiciliary nursing services were pioneered by local authorities. Yet, when the NHS was created in 1948, great care was taken to exclude local democracy from both hospital and general practitioner services. This anomaly was accomplished by breeding some curious new constitutional animals, forming a kind of quasi-local government system, but divested of any provision for popular election. Why was this? The answer lies in the political forces at play during the creation of the service (Klein, 1989: ch. 1). Local democracy was a victim of one of the most powerful pressure groups in British politics – the medical establishment.

Today some 200 district health authorities (DHAs) constitute the operational tier of the NHS. They are responsible for hospitals, community care and certain other health services in their areas.

The resemblance to local government is quite marked; there is a substantial permanent bureaucracy and, at the policy making level, a board with members drawn from the NHS professions, voluntary societies and other community interests. Initially, councillors from the local authorities were also included. The members of the DHAs assemble about once a month. Although open to the public, the level of interest in the meetings is generally low: a predictable and intentional result of non-elected activity.

Of particular importance is the chairperson, the only member commanding a salary and an important patronage position of the Secretary of State. During the 1980s appointments became more nakedly political than ever before; by the end of the decade there was really no authority not under the control of a 'Thatcherite', often with experience gained in the world of local business rather than the welfare state. They came increasingly into conflict with council representatives, resulting in a typical Thatcher strategy – annihilation. A 1989 White Paper announced that local councils would no longer be represented on health authorities. This marked the disappearance of the only vestige of democracy in the NHS.

In 1974 the DHAs had been provided with democratic fig leaves in the form of Community Health Councils (CHCs) – in effect consumer councils to compensate for the unelected nature of the health authorities. Ironically, they too are unelected; indeed, their composition bears a striking resemblance to that of the DHA, with a predominantly middle-class odour, unlikely to empathise with the problems of ethnic minorities, one-parent families, the unemployed, aged and poor. Despite publicity campaigns, they remained unknown to over 98 per cent of the population. However, the 1980s saw the CHCs drawn more deeply into the political fray, though they enter at their peril, and there have been right-wing calls for abolition.

NHS–local government relations
The principal recipients of local authority social services – the old, children, the handicapped, post-natal and ante-natal cases – are also prime clients of the NHS. It is clearly unsatisfactory if the right hand of the welfare state does not know what the left is doing. Various official reports, including Merrison on the NHS and Redcliffe-Maud on local government, have argued the desirability of uniting the services under local government but their pleas have fallen upon studiously deaf ears. Attempts to conceal the cracks

with constitutional wallpaper have included coterminous boundaries, local authority health centres, joint consultative councils to bring together officers and members of both types of authority and joint funding arrangements.

However, there have been many problems in collaboration, mainly arising from the different cultures of the two kinds of authority (Ottewill and Wall, 1990: 390–1). They are essentially different constitutional animals, one driven by the idea of democracy and the other by technocratic elitism and the shifting sands of central government whim. The ultimate victims are the patients, who stand obediently in the waiting lists with no effective way of voicing their needs and feelings.

The democratic blues

The police service displays particularly problematic features. While formally classed as a local government function, it is quite different from any other, with many of the features of an independent agency. Hence we must classify the service with those lying in the dangerous marshland beyond the firm terrain of true local democracy. Here we find all the problems of non-elected local government: professional domination, strong central control from Whitehall and precious little opportunity for ordinary members of the community to influence policy.

There are 42 forces in England and Wales and eight in Scotland, while Northern Ireland is policed by the Royal Ulster Constabulary (RUC). It is a county function (joint boards in the metropolitan areas and the regions in Scotland), though in some cases the counties are combined. *Prima facie* the administration of the police is not dissimilar to that of any other major local government service (see p. 140). In each authority there is a police committee, a chairperson, a chief officer (the chief constable), a permanent bureaucracy and a work-force (the bobbies on the beat and elsewhere). However, the resemblance is entirely superficial.

The police committee
Unlike any other local authority committee, councillors constitute only two-thirds of the membership, the rest being non-elected Justices of the Peace. In 1986 the Widdicombe Report questioned this, but the government side-stepped the issue (Leach, 1989: 108–9).

The chief constable

This is the most significant figure in the force, quite unlike any other chief officer in local government, having sole control in matters relating to all operations, discipline and logistics. The chief constable receives no orders from any elected representatives and is not obliged to answer questions, attend meetings or give reports. The constitutional reason for this regal autonomy is the fact that the police are Officers of the Crown, not employees of the local authority. Originally the Bains Report on local government management spoke of the chief constable as a member of the chief officers' team. However, this so alarmed the Assistant to the Chief Inspector of Constabulary, James Anderton, that he complained to the Home Office and the report was hastily redrafted to read unequivocally: 'The Chief Constable is not an officer of the local authority but an independent officer of the crown' (Oliver, 1987: 51–2).

The local authority is left with one source of influence, the threat of cutting off the supply of funds, although this can be countered by the Home Secretary, effectively the minister for the police. Home Secretaries, both Labour and Conservative, have proved exceedingly timid (Rollo, 1980: 183), tending to side with the chief constable against the police authority at times of conflict. In 1984 South Yorkshire County Council, dismayed at what it considered to be brutal police tactics in the miners' strike, tried various means of influence, including threatening to withhold funds and to sell off police dogs and horses to prevent their use against miners. The Chief Constable called upon Home Secretary Leon Brittan for support, and did not call in vain (Oliver, 1987: 215–21).

It is argued in defence of the position that democratic involvement is unnecessary because policing is merely the application of professional techniques involving no political judgement. This is fallacious; there is considerable leeway for the exercise of politically significant discretion in the two principal aspects of policing – fighting crime and maintaining public order. Because resources are limited, conscious decisions must be made every day as to which types of crime to pursue – muggers or curb-crawlers, flashers or fraudsters, and so on. On the public order front, the police must decide whether to allow a particular march or demonstration to take place, how to police strikes, whether to protect left-wing groups from right-wing ones and so on. Modern policing has seen problems of racism, sexism, class bias, false confessions and brutality (Smith and Gray, 1985). The problems of control become greater as the modern police force becomes more centralised, militaristic and political.

Centralisation is promoted by the Association of Chief Police Officers. In addition, central government influence became more visible during the 1980s, particularly in the policing of the miners' strike; heading the operations was a special Cabinet committee chaired by Mrs Thatcher herself (Boateng, 1985: 239). In July 1989 Peter Imbert, Metropolitan Police Commissioner, promised further centralisation by calling for the creation in Britain of a centrally funded US-style FBI. Centralisation is also advanced through hi-tech policing methods and the collection of vast amounts of data through the National Computer Unit at Hendon, North London.

The voice of the community

The fact that local authorities have no real control over policing generates perpetual tensions. Some police committees, such as those of Greater Manchester and Merseyside, have operated under considerable stress as a result of their willingness to challenge the chief constable. There is even a feeling that such authorities are transgressing the proper tradition of British policing. Yet such a 'tradition' is a recent invention; nineteenth-century watch committees exercised considerable control and were even prepared to dismiss officers not following policy (Baldwin and Kinsey, 1982: 106). In 1962 a Royal Commission on the police expressed concern over the balance of power between elected local authorities and their forces. In 1981 the Scarman Report on the Brixton riots argued that much crime and social disorder was the result of economic and environmental conditions and saw the main solution in greater community involvement in policing (Scarman, 1981: para. 2.38).

The local economy

One of the most important areas in which local government has experienced the presence of rival agencies has been the local economy.

Rediscovering poverty

The post-war decades had been years of plenty, where social democracy appeared to have solved the serious problems besetting capitalism. However, in the 1960s, academic sociologists led by Peter Townsend (1979) 'rediscovered' poverty in the hearts of the cities, which were declining as a natural part of the process of advancing capitalism (Pahl *et al.*, 1983: 90).

Various schemes followed, including an Urban Programme (Higgins *et al.* 1983: 73), Community Development Projects and Inner Area Studies (Department of the Environment, 1977b: 297), whereby central government encouraged local authorities to assume responsibilities for economic revival. 'Partnership' schemes were established with committees of central and local politicians supported by civil servants and local government officers.

However, by the mid-1970s the economic crisis brought cuts in public expenditure, which fell most acutely on the inner cities (Higgins *et al.*, 1983: 154). Local authorities made strenuous efforts to revive their economies independently of central government with employment creation schemes (Chandler and Lawless, 1985) and by wooing national and multinational firms (Massey, 1985). Various enterprise boards were formed, the most ambitious being the Greater London Enterprise Board of the GLC, though others were established in Labour-controlled London boroughs and in the West Midlands, Lancashire, West Yorkshire and Merseyside.

The New Right cometh

When the Conservative government came to office in 1979 it did not look kindly upon these ventures. Local authorities were seen not as instruments for reviving capitalism but as part of the problem. The new approach was to freeze out councils and bring in local businessmen without the inconvenience of any close encounters with the ballot box. In 1980 the Local Government Planning and Land Act created urban development corporations (UDCs) for the London and Merseyside dockland areas. A further five were created in 1986–7, followed by several 'mini-UDCs'. The UDCs became high-profile agencies, their achievements much praised. However, they offered more to the 'yuppie' generation than to the real victims of capitalism's desertion of the cities. Yet by the end of 1990 even this enterprise was collapsing in bathos and disillusionment. A former chairman of the Royal Town

Planning Institute pronounced it a missed opportunity of monu-
mental proportions, the result of proceeding 'with no guiding
framework, only market-led opportunitism' (*Sunday Times*, 18
November 1990).

Conclusion – local authorities in a hostile environment: an endangered species?

The administrative environment of elected local government, a
bewildering miscellany of agencies, boards and committees appointed from the ranks of the great and the good, is by no means
healthy for local democracy. Like any ecosystem, it involves relationships which are symbiotic, competitive and predatory.

Symbiotic
Symbiotic behaviour occurs when other bodies act in partnership
with local authorities. Promotional agencies and voluntary organisations may be seen in this light. In the latter case the authority
provides funds and the association helps with service delivery.
However, although it may take two to quango, much partnership
rhetoric is spoken with a tongue in the official cheek. Sometimes
the actual use of the term can be a legitimating mask for something
more sinister, rather like the partnership between the butcher and
the lamb.

Competitive
Competitors fight for resources, often grants from central government (opted-out schools and council tenants, voluntary associations), many of which would previously have gone to local
government. Thus, for example, while restricting the housing role
of local government, the Thatcher government showed increased
commitment to housing associations, with a funding rise from £580
million in 1986–7 to £1328 million by 1991–2 (Spencer, 1989: 95).
The London Docklands Corporation managed to attract investment commitments of over £3 billion by 1988.

There is also competition for legitimacy. While the national
media continue to mock left-wing councils with 'loony left' jibes,
citizens are assailed with stories of the great wonders wrought by
private-sector-led development corporations such as the exotic
creation in London's docklands.

Predatory

Predators threaten to take over elected local government. There are many of them, though the UDCs have the sharpest teeth. Thus, in its Meadowhall retail and leisure centre, the Sheffield Development Corporation produced a veritable alternative city, a megalithic Creditsville built with enough concrete to fill Wembley stadium to a depth of eight metres (though not a house in sight). Its estimated annual sales were greater than those of Leeds, Nottingham, Leicester, Bradford and, of course, the city of Sheffield itself.

An endangered species?

In this chapter an environment has been mapped out that is hostile to the institutions of local democracy. Moreover, it is one that the central government can manipulate by feeding one species rather than another, introducing new predators and even exterminating certain life forms. Local democracy, frail at best, lives in dark times. After the 1982 Toxteth riots, Environment Secretary Michael Heseltine actually proposed as part of the solution the abolition of the Merseyside County Council (*The Times*, 15 January 1983). The increased use of *ad hoc*, non-elected agencies destroys local accountability, the essence of democracy. The problem was highlighted when the chief executive of the Sheffield Development Corporation compiled a dossier documenting how its multimillionaire chairman had displayed a 'lack of understanding of the whole concept of public accountability'. An independent inquiry confirmed that he had failed to keep 'a clear distance between his public and private duties' (*The Independent*, 8 September 1990).

The metropolitan counties and the Greater London County disappeared in the 1980s and all local authorities had just cause to feel themselves an endangered species.

5

Mapping Local Democracy

This chapter examines the boundaries which define the local government areas, beginning with some basic considerations including the origins of the boundaries, area size and the way the map was drawn in the nineteenth century. Following this the problems of the post-war era and the reforms which were supposed to deal with them are addressed. The next section considers the implications for the local government map arising from new settlement patterns imposed by new forms of production. The great industrial cities developed in what is sometimes termed a 'Fordist' era (after the famous motor car manufacturer), when giant industries based on mass production and mass consumption of a limited number of standardised products demanded great urban settlements to feed their voracious appetites for labour. Today Britain has entered a 'post-Fordist' era of production where small flexible business, catering for limited specialist markets, often prefer to locate outside the old cities. Bearing these developments in mind, the conclusion speculates on the local government map of the future. These issues are not dry questions of public administration; the areas are not shaped by pin-striped cartographers in Whitehall, they are the outcome of social and political forces.

Who draws the map?

Local government boundaries arise in two broad ways: they may be drawn with a ruler and pen by some constitutional master architect or may evolve organically, reflecting physical features such as rivers, valleys and ridges as well as naturally occurring patterns of communal and economic life.

The evolutionary mode can be said to be part of the general process of organic development much praised in the British constitution. There is an emotional dimension to the issue, for people develop a profound sense of territorial attachment and will fight hard to preserve the integrity of an ancient boundary. It can be argued that a real sense of community, what German sociologist Ferdinand Tönnies (1855–1936) termed *Gemeinschaft*, can only emerge in a natural territory; an artificially imposed area will engender a form of impersonal association or *Gesellschaft*. When the Normans advanced across the country they were careful to preserve ancient boundaries which survived to become the shires of today. In contrast, European colonial powers often imposed boundaries for their own administrative convenience, cutting insensitively across ancient patterns of life with the unyielding verticals and horizontals which score the maps of Canada, Africa, the United States and Australia today.

Area size

The size of an area is a key factor in the boundary debate. It is generally believed that a sense of community can only be engendered in relatively small areas. Conversely, it is argued that large areas are associated with greater efficiency. Such a view was put forward by Whitehall in evidence to the Royal Commission on Local Government (Redcliffe-Maud, 1969: vol. III, ch. 12). Thus there appears to be a basic trade-off: community or efficiency. However, the dilemma is open to question. The alleged efficiency of larger areas is not supported by conclusive empirical evidence. It is more probable that large areas are seen by a central state as a way to dominate local government (Dearlove, 1979), although Newton (1982: 191) argues that they can be as democratic as small ones.

Time for tiers

However, the solution to the issue has been found in some form of tiered system, with large areas subdivided into smaller ones. The

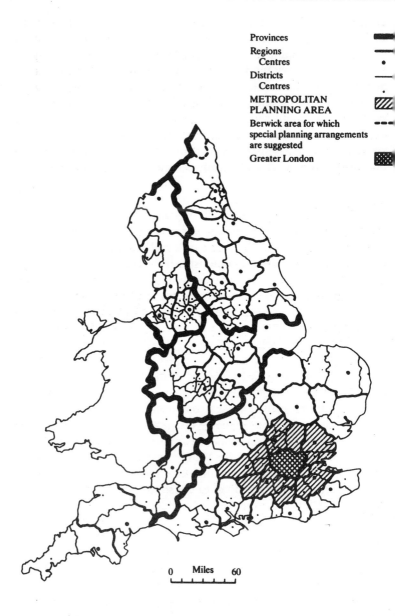

Figure 5.1 Senior's city region model. Source: Redcliffe-Maud, 1969 (maps for vol. II).

possible divisions and subdivisions can stretch almost to infinity, producing a hierarchy including province, region, county, district, parish, community, even a group of houses in a street forming for the purposes of neighbourhood watch. Britain has long had such a structure based on a top tier of counties, each incorporating a number of districts. However, this in itself produces a new set of problems relating to apportioning functions between tiers, co-ordination, inter-authority friction and a baffling complexity of structure. The alternative is a unitary system with only one level of authority, each responsible for all functions.

The city region

While people cherish a historic sense of community, patterns of life can change so that the real space in which one lives may bear little relation to formal boundaries. Once people lived, worked and died within the confines of the village, but the modern passion for commuting means that we may have our home in one area, work in another and socialise in a third. Hence, it can be argued that the natural local government unit today should reflect the commuting way of life. Using 'journey-to-work' areas it is possible to divide Britain into 228 functional urban regions (Coombes *et al.*, 1983), 115 of them self-contained and the remainder linked in complex commuting patterns within twenty dense metropolitan regions. This leads to the concept of the *city region*, an area typically comprising one large town or city, a few smaller towns and the surrounding rural hinterland, all welded by a complex matrix of communications. It is a concept which features in much debate on the subject of local boundaries and reflects the essential unity of urban and rural in modern life in a way that the present structure does not (see Figure 5.1).

Rival maps

As noted in Chapter 4, a range of non-elected bodies operate on a territorial basis, scoring the country with various alternative boundary patterns. Public utilities such as railways, electricity and gas supplies were organised regionally; water areas largely followed the watersheds. Some maps divide the country into very small areas, such as the tax districts of the Inland Revenue. Some-

Figure 5.2   Standard regions of England and Wales. (Standard regions are the eleven economic planning regions of the UK. They are also classified as 'level 1' regions for the purposes of the EC.)

times maps are shared; the 1974 NHS reorganisation explicitly set out to make its areas coterminous with those of local government. Moreover, the regional planning areas established in the 1960s continue to be used as Standard Regions (see Figure 5.2) by a number of Whitehall departments and regional tourist boards, although the planning authorities themselves have vanished.

The changing landscape

In Britain organic evolutionary development is cherished: counties, boroughs, towns, villages and parishes all have long histories. In some, annual ritualistic walks are taken to reaffirm ancient boundaries. Even the great Victorian cities arose in an unplanned way, resulting in the amalgamation of small parishes which chanced to be the sites of the factories.

Of course, the nineteenth-century Philosophical Radicals favoured rational rather than evolutionary change. The 1834 Poor Law reforms forced parish amalgamations to form the large Poor Law Unions. Further rationally based boundaries were staked out in the great public health movement forming the urban and rural sanitary districts. Later the 1888 Act established a nationwide

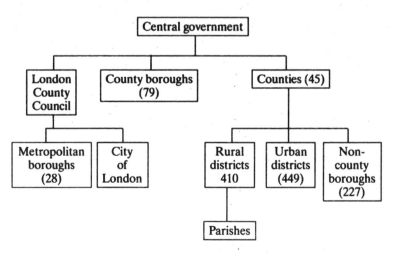

Figure 5.3 The late nineteenth-century local government structure (actual numbers varied).

two-tier system within a framework of administrative counties, though these were not entirely new, being based on the areas of the Quarter Sessions (Keith-Lucas and Richards, 1978: 12–13). Moreover, as Chapter 2 showed, municipal corporations remained outside as independent county boroughs (see Figure 5.3). Although this reform is said to have set the modern pattern, it contained no effective mechanism for change in the light of demographic developments and, with the passage of time, it began to resemble the ruins of a monastery, tracing the architecture of a bygone age.

The twentieth century

The most important of the forces for change were economic and technical. Industrial growth led to increased urbanisation with more towns able to claim county borough status. The number had risen from the original sixty-one to eighty-two by 1923, at which point the government put an effective stop to the trend by making promotion more difficult.

Improved transport led to urban sprawl around the cities. More than 4 million houses were built between the two world wars so that by 1939 over one-third of all British houses were less than twenty years old. Critics argued that a city region model was the appropriate unit for local government in the twentieth century, yet little was done to redraw the map and the following ill-effects ensued:

(1) *Inter-authority friction.* This generally restricted effectiveness in the planning of services such as transportation which required a broad perspective.

(2) *Fragmentation of services.* In the counties the two-tier system, with different types of second-tier authority, led to confusion and wasteful divisions of responsibilities.

(3) *Suburbanisation.* In the dormitory towns residents leeched themselves onto the host cities, sucking their blood in the form of salaries and facilities while contributing nothing to their rates.

(4) *Central domination.* The weaknesses gave the centre ample grounds for interfering. Chapter 4 showed how some functions were assumed by central government or given to newly created *ad*

hoc bodies. Others were subject to increased regulation and control by ministers, so that local authorities seemed mere outposts of Whitehall.

(5) *Loss of morale.* All these developments were said to have contributed to a loss of morale by those involved – councillors and local officials.

(6) *Democratic failure.* It was also claimed that local authorities were not serving their democratic functions, low turnout figures at elections representing an overwhelming vote of 'no interest'.

Explaining inaction

The aging system lay in a constitutional oxygen tent while journalists, academics and boundary commissions debated how deeply the reformer's scalpel should cut. Yet, despite energetic post-war reconstruction on many fronts, no significant changes were made. The following reasons can be advanced to explain this:

(1) *Overload.* Post-war reconstruction covered a major education reform, nationalisation of industry, creation of the NHS, implementation of the Beveridge Report, a major housing programme and rearmament. Government was obliged to prioritise its programme, and local government was ignored.

(2) *Political opposition.* All proposals for reform carried threatening implications for one or another type of authority. It was a tug-of-war in which contestants remained in a state of purple-faced immobility.

(3) *Indecision.* There was no agreed reform formula. Differing schools of thought on the goals to be pursued (localist democracy or centralist efficiency) and the means of promoting them (large or small authorities, single or multi-tier, simplicity or complexity and so on) produced unresolved debate. Boundary commissions made recommendations which were either considered too radical or too piecemeal to make any serious impact.

(4) *Whitehall strategy.* The erosion of local power in favour of the centre was welcomed by the mandarins. They feared that reform might produce legitimate claims for a restoration of power to local government.

(5) *Social justice*. The post-war Labour government had rejected municipal socialism for a centralised social democratic state (Sancton, 1976). Equality in the provision of services had to take precedence over local rights to diversity.

(6) *Capitalist production*. National and multinational capitalism had replaced locally based enterprises. Capitalists no longer needed the local state.

A further explanation for delay was the cumbersome machinery. In 1945 a Local Government Boundary Commission was created, a brainchild of the wartime coalition. Its terms of reference were strictly limited; it was obliged to work within the existing framework, able only to modify but not remodel. However, the problems seemed to require more drastic treatment and after four years the Commission was wound up. In 1958 two new Commissions were established to consider England and Wales separately. These were to conduct piecemeal surveys of different areas, taking evidence from various interests, including the local authorities themselves. Once again they were restricted to preserving the broad status quo. Changes could only be marginal. The Commission wound its weary way with little sense of inspiration or indeed perspiration until, in 1965, a new Minister for Housing and Local Government mercifully put it out of its agony.

Mapping metroland

The first real moves towards reform came in the 1960s. As is often the case, London led the fashion.

The municipal government of London had long posed unique problems. The city grew particularly rapidly in the sixteenth century; by 1600 its population of 200,000 vastly exceeded that of any other town, reaching over half a million by 1700. The key to its dramatic growth lay outside the country altogether; London stood at the centre of a world trading network and the avaricious fingers of its merchants and financiers encircled the globe. At home, its monopoly of trade and commerce led it to dominate all other towns regardless of the scale of their production. Although the industrial revolution spawned new cities without the aid of London finance, the wealth and population of the capital maintained its importance as a source of domestic demand.

The 1888 reform met the special needs of the huge conurbation by creating an entirely new administrative county (based on the boundaries of the Metropolitan Board of Works which had exercised jurisdiction over abutting parts of Middlesex, Surrey and Kent) under a London County Council (LCC). The area contained a second tier of districts and three autonomous county boroughs.

In the post-war era the problems of London continued to be the most acute in the country. Most new urbanisation was concentrated in the south-east; between 1921 and 1951 more than a million people emigrated from other parts of Britain. Most were in managerial and professional jobs and they settled in a salubrious suburban 'metroland' in the leafy home counties, tied overground and underground to the metropolis with tarmac and steel. The result was severe housing problems and hardening sclerosis of the commuting arteries.

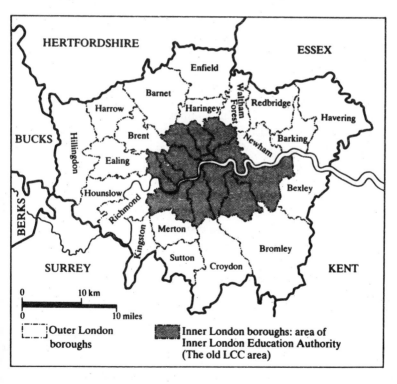

Figure 5.4 The Greater London reforms.

The LCC area was too small to manage the problem and, in 1957, the Conservative government set up a Royal Commission under Sir Edwin Herbert. This had to drive through a wall of intransigence erected by the local authorities and the Labour Party, which feared the loss of the control it had been able to establish over the LCC. The commission declared:

> The primary unit of local government in the Greater London Area should be the borough, and the borough should perform all local authority functions except those which can only be effectively performed over the wider area of Greater London. (Herbert, 1960)

It recommended a radical redrawing of the 1888 boundaries, massively expanding the LCC area from 75,000 to 510,000 acres and raising the population from just over 3 million to well over 8 million, engulfing parts of Kent, Surrey and Essex and the whole of Middlesex. The newly staked territory would be divided into fifty-two boroughs. The corporation of the City of London, with a long history of insularity, had proved a continuing thorn in the side of reform and was to be left untouched.

The government, deaf to loud Labour opposition in Parliament, pushed the legislation through and the new system came into operation in 1963 (see Figure 5.4). There was some slight modification to the Herbert scheme: the number of boroughs was reduced to thirty-two and the LCC education department, which had many defenders, was preserved as the Inner London Education Authority (ILEA). Elsewhere education remained with the boroughs. The new Greater London Council (GLC) was to be responsible for those functions requiring coordination over a wide area (housing, major roads and traffic management) and, before long, gained public transport. The reform provided important pointers for the rest of the country.

1974 and all that – *plus ça change?*

When Labour came to office in 1964 Richard Crossman, Minister of Housing and Local Government, found local government a boring subject (Keith-Lucas and Richards, 1978: 211). However, reforms suggested by the Boundary Commission threatened Labour constituencies and he decided that drastic medicine was needed. His permanent secretary, Dame Evelyn Sharp, counselled inaction; the mandarins were happy presiding over an enfeebled system. However, while she was on holiday Crossman, in true *Yes, Minister* spirit, delivered an unexpected speech promising to erase the archaic boundary pattern (Crossman, 1975: 441).

The result of this cavalier intervention was a Royal Commission chaired by trusted Whitehall mandarin Lord Redcliffe-Maud. The membership included Dame Evelyn herself, along with a variety of individuals with a known interest in reform. The report, published in 1969, was critical of what it saw as a complex maze of over a thousand authorities, recommending that it be swept away and replaced with a simple system of fifty-eight unitary authorities. There were to be only three exceptions: in the large conurbations around Liverpool, Manchester and Birmingham a GLC-type model would operate. The threatened remoteness of the new, very large authorities was to be mitigated by community councils (see Figure 5.5).

The commission declared this to be 'local government in its simplest, most understandable and potentially most efficient form' (Redcliffe-Maud, 1969: 68). The plan was indeed radical and would have had far-reaching political and administrative implications. The large uniform authorities suggested a Benthamite orderliness redolent of efficiency rather than democracy. However, in a

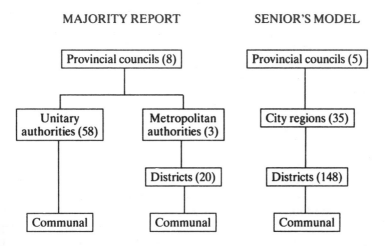

Figure 5.5 The Redcliffe-Maud recommended structure.

forceful note of dissent, one of the commission's members, jour-
nalist Derek Senior, argued for a city region solution, with thirty-
five top tiers divided into 135 districts (Figure 5.1).

The government showed every intention of going ahead but the
general election of 1970 gave unexpected victory to the Conservatives, who smelled a political rat. The integration of urban and
rural districts with the old county boroughs might easily see the
new authorities swamped by the Labour-supporting urban masses.
There were also dangerous implications for Conservative MPs
(constituencies being linked to local government boundaries).
Hence the resulting legislation preserved the two-tier principle.

Under the Local Government Act 1972 the fifty-eight counties
of England and Wales, along with their districts and the county
boroughs, were recast in the form of forty-seven *shire counties* and
six *metropolitan counties*. The former, largely reincarnations of the
administrative counties, contained populations ranging from
100,000 to 1.5 million and were divided into 333 districts. Here the
top tier was the most vital, responsible for area-wide functions
(planning, roads, public transport) as well as social services and
education. The county boroughs had been dealt a mortal blow;
they were to be no more.

The metropolitan counties covered the major conurbations of
Greater Manchester, Merseyside, Tyne and Wear, West Yorkshire, South Yorkshire and the West Midlands, with populations
ranging from 1 million to 2.7 million. They followed the GLC
model, their thirty-six districts having greater operational importance, including responsibility for education and social services. In
both types of county, provision was made for a form of communal
government such as parish councils, meetings, or community councils, in symbolic deference to the traditions of localism.

In Scotland, the Wheatley Commission had concurred with
Redcliffe-Maud's diagnosis but the prescription had been for two
tiers from the beginning, with nine regions based on the journey-
to-work principle, fifty-three districts and more than 1,000
community councils. These top tiers, the largest of which was
the Strathclyde Region with a population of 2.5 million, were the
most important, with a wide range of functions including water
supply. In addition, because of geographical factors beyond even
the scope of parliamentary supremacy, there were three autonomous island councils (see Figure 5.6). This was closer to the

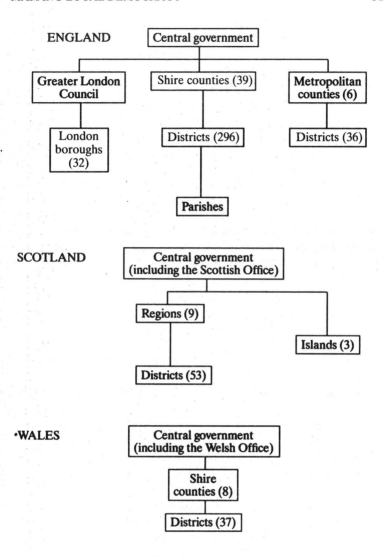

Figure 5.6   The local government structure after the 1974 reform.

Redcliffe-Maud model and demonstrated the falsity of any claim that it could not work. However, Britain was placed in the anomalous position of having two contrasting boundary patterns standing side by side.

Evaluating reorganisation

It is common to speak of the 1972 Act as a *reorganisation* rather than a *reform*, and for those favouring radical nostrums it was a sadly missed opportunity, open to the following criticisms:

(1) *Timidly incremental.* The new pattern of county boundaries made few significant innovations. There was no serious attempt to match the pattern to contemporary life.

(2) *Remote.* The new counties were too large to establish close relationships with the community.

(3) *Anti-city.* A host of proud county boroughs such as Bristol, Hull, Leicester, Nottingham, Plymouth, Cardiff, Exeter, York, Edinburgh and Glasgow were reduced to the level of, for instance, Cheltenham Spa or Tunbridge Wells, leaving an after-taste of smouldering resentment.

(4) *Bureaucratic.* Contrary to official assurances, the reforms provided an opportunity for increased domination by officials, with a bonanza of new highly paid positions (see Chapter 11).

(5) *Constrictive boundaries.* The boundaries circumscribing the metropolitan counties were, like Victorian ladies' corsets, drawn too tight to permit natural expansion. This prevented comprehensive planning and effective housing overspill policies. It also allowed the suburban middle classes to continue evading city rate contributions.

(6) *Functional depletion.* The rhetoric of Redcliffe-Maud had sung of an increasing role for local government, expressing hope that eventually the NHS might be taken over. However, far from this, the reform stripped away the vitally important functions of water supply, sewerage and personal health.

(7) *Centralisation.* The reduction in the number of authorities promised to make central control easier.

The whole reform saga was by no means an exercise in cool rationality. The various participants were more concerned to serve their respective interests than to improve the system. The Conservatives had the good fortune to be sitting in the chair of power when the music stopped. Their two-tier model served party advantage by preserving the integrity of their suburban and rural strongholds, and general centralisation favoured the elite power structure against the socialist challenge from councils. It could be seen as gerrymandering; it was estimated that some 16 per cent of the population in Labour county boroughs awoke to find themselves in Conservative shire counties. In the end, some 58 per cent of the population were assigned to safe Conservative wards while only around 20 per cent were in safe Labour wards (Dunleavy, 1980). However, both major parties, as well as officials, favoured the greater uniformity and larger authorities conducive to easier central control. Few shed tears for any loss of community and local democracy.

Death by 'streamlining'

In the new system the metropolitan counties proved the least loved. They began life with few functions and something of an identity crisis, and sought to develop new services by sponsoring activities such as the arts and community projects. Strategic planning was made difficult by the fact that the districts were responsible for most of the important services and friction between tiers was intrinsic to the arrangement.

They also found themselves in conflict with their Conservative creators as a result of the increasingly strong hold gained during the 1980s by the left. After a prolonged series of engagements central patience with local democracy snapped, and a White Paper, *Streamlining the Cities*, delivered the death sentence (Department of the Environment, 1983). The events revealed much about the British constitution. Being unwritten, amendment requires nothing more than the normal legislative process, but convention has demanded some kind of debate and consultation, usually in the form of a Royal Commission. Yet the government revealed itself innocent of constitutional nicety. Had there been a referendum (Ken Livingstone, GLC leader, was adjudged an easy winner of the propaganda battle – Patrick Jenkin, the government's champion, being quietly 'retired hurt'), or a separation of powers (the House of Lords opposed the abolition bill), then matters might have been resolved differently. As it was, the 'enemy at home' went down as certainly as the *General Belgrano* in the Falklands War (Figure 5.7).

Figure 5.7 Counties of England and Wales, 1989. Source: *Regional Trends*, 1988.

Continuing trends – counter-urbanisation

The processes of settlement change did not, of course, stop with the reorganisation of 1974. The direction of developments characteristic of the first half of the century have, to some extent, gone into reverse so that Britain can now be said to be in a period of *counter-urbanisation* with the drift to the south-east less significant than a movement away from the cities into the smaller towns. The process is found in many advanced economies and represents the most recent stage in urban development. Between 1961 and 1981 the population of Britain's six largest conurbations fell by some 2 million, while that in rural areas as remote as districts of Cornwall, Wales and Scotland grew (Perry *et al.*, 1986). Reasons for the new trend include the following:

(1)   *Deliberate policy.* Starting with the Town and Country Planning Act of 1947, it has been government policy to limit further growth of cities by dispersing populations into 'new towns' and 'greenfield' developments. The Thatcher government pursued land release policies, and in February 1987, in the face of opposition from a range of pressure groups including the National Farmers' Union and the Council for the Preservation of Rural England, lifted building restrictions on agricultural land.

(2)   *Unintended policy effects.* The 1974 reorganisation had the effect of reducing the power of the cities to control their territory. In transport policy, a concentration on roads for haulage purposes opened up lines of escape from the cities as well as links between them. Indeed, counter-urbanisation occurred in countries with no deliberate policy of restricting urban growth, such as the US and Japan (Sundquist, 1975).

(3)   *Information technology.* Modern telecommunications make it less important to congregate together. Telephone meetings can be held, information can be 'faxed', people can work from a home base in a new kind of cottage industry.

(4)   *The rural idyll.* A strong tradition in British social culture, stimulated by revulsion felt for the social effects of industrialisation, places great spiritual value on the rural life. This is reflected in the Romantic tradition in art and literature, as found in the work of Constable, Wordsworth, D. H. Lawrence and so on (Williams, 1961).

(5) *Economic determinism*. People cannot live where they please; they are locked into a lifestyle determined by the mode of produc tion. Factories created the nineteenth-century cities. Coal mag nates did not take their mines to the male-voice choirs in search o workers; miners settled around the pits and sang to make life bearable. The British economy may now be said to have moved into a post-Fordist era, with small firms operating away from the major repositories of labour power. Capitalism may have brough the industrial city into existence but now it is killing it.

Of course, not everyone can follow the capitalist Pied Piper into the hinterland, and the development bequeaths to the cities a resi due of unemployment and poverty while depriving local author ities of the income increasingly needed to provide social services The result is the urban crisis that became so familiar from the 1970s.

Conclusion – mapping the future

It is clear that the local government map of today is a mosaic beneath a pattern of social and economic life no less volatile than that of the nineteenth century. If it is to remain a relevant base for local administration and democracy it must remain able to change The future pattern of settlement could develop in one of two poss ible directions. Continued urban decay and counter-urbanisation could reach the point that the old pattern of a relatively few major centres set in a sparsely populated rural hinterland is replaced by a more even spread of the population, with many medium-sized towns. The alternative scenario is a process of re-urbanization, a conscious policy of economic regeneration: rehabilitation of the housing stock, improvements of infrastructure, pedestrianisation and so on to promote a phoenix-like revival of the city (Van Den Berg, *et al.*, 1982).

The cards are stacked against the latter solution. There are many positive advantages for profit-maximising firms in the small towns. The rural work-force, although socialised into a regime of wage labour, has been conditioned by a long history of decline; traditions of unionisation are weaker, inequalities of wealth and income are traditionally accepted and there are fewer oppor tunities for alternative employment. There is also a greater tradition of deference among the rural working class, more likelihood of a Conservative-controlled council and lower local taxes. This development is in certain respects analogous to the exploitative penetration of the Third World by multinational conglomerates. For these reasons the Conservative government's initiatives towards inner city revival may be seen more in terms of legitimation than real intent.

How might the local government map be redrawn to take account of the shifting sands of the capitalist economy? If the city and its municipal institutions were to be restored it would be necessary to expand the boundaries on the city region model. This would bring the newly prospering small towns into the same area as the city authority. However, it would lead to the domination of the rural by the urban areas, making it politically unattractive to Conservatives.

The alternative is to redraw the map to recognise a more even dispersal of the population, with a pattern of single-tier (district-sized) authorities all with equal powers. In 1987 the Association of District Councils produced a report entitled *Closer to the People* which argued for a unitary system of all-purpose authorities, effectively a take-over of the counties by the districts. This would leave the old cities as empty husks to grow white in the sun (an approach accepted in the United States) but would allow the growing towns the freedom to manage their affairs. After the abolition of the GLC and metropolitan counties, the London boroughs and metropolitan districts assumed independent status to the envy of other major cities. By the late 1980s there was talk within the Conservative Party of abolishing the shire counties as well (*The Independent*, 16 March 1988). The central government onslaught on county responsibilities in the late 1980s, particularly on education (see Chapter 3) began to make this an increasingly real possibility.

The regional dimension

An alternative future for the boundary pattern lies in a move towards regionalism. The rival administrative maps discussed above reveal that there already exist a number of regional divisions of the country. Some reformers would see a great increase in the regional dimension based largely on political and administrative devolution from the centre. A model could entail approximately twelve regions under the control of directly elected assemblies with power to raise money through taxation. They could take responsibility for the work of many of the present regional quangos as well as certain functions devolved from Whitehall (rather on the model of the Welsh and Scottish offices). Many would argue that the region would be the natural area for economic planning and development today. The Royal Town Planning Institute (RTPI, 1986) suggested the following set of major functions for such authorities:

Regional economic development
Strategic physical planning
Major sub-regional problems (for example, inner cities)
Regional housing policy
Regional health policy
Water supply and sewerage
Public transport and highways
Police and fire services
Specialised further education
Tourism and education
National parks
Strategic minerals policy
Regional resource reports for public expenditure planning

It is clear that such a reform of the territorial map of government would have radical implications for local government. An immediate threat would be an encroachment on the remit of local authorities (Jones, 1988). Certainly such a development would add further nails to the coffin of the county.

6

Choosing Councillors

This chapter considers the formal mechanism of local democracy: electing members of the community to the council. Elections are essential to the legitimacy of any system of modern government, so local elections are of profound political significance. The great constitutional lawyer, Dicey, attributed the supremacy of Parliament not to any abstract principles of sovereignty but to the popular election of MPs. Local councils are constitutionally unique in being the only public bodies outside Parliament to be popularly elected and, for this reason, have a greater moral right to challenge Westminister than any other state agency. Hence, local elections are much more than a convenient means of establishing community opinion; they are key elements in the pluralist state, protecting freedom against a central government unfettered by a constitutional separation of powers or a written constitution.

The chapter begins with a brief examination of the coming of the local franchise, noting the reluctance with which the ruling establishment welcomed mass democracy. Next it outlines the main features of today's electoral system, observing some of its principal defects and considering the case for local proportional representation. After this local electoral behaviour is examined and the chapter concludes with an assessment of the value of elections for local democracy.

Representative government

As outlined in Chapter 2, early parish government was often populist in nature, with community decisions taken by an assembly of
citizens. However, this cannot work once a population expands
beyond village size. The alternative to this direct democracy is
some form of representative government, with small groups making decisions on behalf of the mass. Indeed, parish government
itself often saw the large gathering giving way to the small secretive 'closed vestry' under a local oligarchy. For representative government to be democratic the people must be able to choose and
control the rulers. This is achieved by the principle of elections,
giving everyone an equal (and secret) say in the choice of representatives, who are permitted only limited terms of office. This
remains the principal basis for modern forms of democracy.

However, it will be seen in Chapter 8 that representation can
mean various things in practice. Before the extension of the franchise there was a belief in what was termed 'virtual representation',
in which it was supposed that the interests of ordinary people were
taken into account by the the ruling elite. As the franchise was
extended this theory was modifed by Edmund Burke to interpret
representation as meaning that the one elected had no responsibility
to advance the views or interests of constituents, the responsibility
was only to exercise personal judgement on public matters, a view
much favoured by the establishment elite in Britain.

The coming of the local franchise – votes for
some

The nineteenth century was a period of far-reaching constitutional
reforms with major extensions to the parliamentary franchise
(right to vote). These concessions were gained as a result of pressure by the rising bourgeoisie and the threat of a radical uprising
by the working class. They were never made willingly by the political elite, which feared democracy almost as much as revolution.
The simple logic of mass democracy promised an end to the privileged lifestyles enjoyed by the landed interests for centuries.

The bourgeoisie were not against privilege as such; they merely
wanted a little of the action for themselves. Although it was fear of

radicalism which brought them to power in 1830, they showed no more desire for full democracy than had the Tories. The Reform Act of 1832 parsimoniously extended the franchise to middle-class property owners only, increasing the parliamentary electorate from around 500,000 to some 700,000. Subsequent pressure, including the formation of the Chartist movement in 1836, led to further grudging extension, first to the urban male working class in 1867 and then, in 1884, to the rural areas.

This ethos of parsimonious democracy influenced the development of the local franchise. The very real possibility of radical forces in control of the municipalities deeply alarmed the establishment, which is partly why Bentham preached his message of central control and limited local discretion.

Some go-ahead independent boroughs had used various limited forms of popular election and, in areas where guilds had assumed a political leadership role, their electoral practices had permeated the municipal institutions established in the guild halls. In addition there were often elections to the *ad hoc* boards. However, major reform of the local franchise was a result of the quest for municipal power by the nineteenth-century industrial bourgeoisie.

Popular election was an ideal way for the new moneyed class to wrest control from the *ancien régime* of landed interests, thereby gaining authority to shape the new cities in accordance with their industrial wants. Early reforms came in the Sturge Bourne Acts of 1818 and 1819, which aimed to extend the principle of representative government with a system of plural voting based upon the ownership of property (to exclude working people). Those rated £50 gained one vote, while increments of £25 would secure further votes up to a maximum of six. However, the parishes were not compelled to adopt the provisions and many declined. In 1831 John Cam Hobhouse secured the passage of an Act to extend voting rights to all ratepayers and to force annual elections.

However, it was the Municipal Corporations Act 1835 which laid the foundations for widespread local election in the towns, though this was by no means full democracy; as with the 1832 Reform Act, the right was restricted to the propertied (remaining so until 1894). The 1888 Act, following the 1884 Reform Act, extended electoral rights to the rural areas.

The early franchise saw councillors as guardians of the public purse rather than as service providers. Since votes were accorded in proportion to rates paid the wealthy could have as many as six, while non-payers were effectively disenfranchised. This condition remained long after it was abolished for parliamentary elections. Indeed, it was not until after the Second World War (when local elections were restarted after a period of suspension) that a Speaker's Conference recommended the placing of the local franchise on the same footing as the parliamentary. This was no minor change; another 8 million were added to the electoral registers. Yet certain privileges endured; businessmen with premises in areas where they did not live were allowed an extra vote. Most were Conservatives and in 1969 the Labour government ended the practice.

Votes for women

The local franchise was extended to women almost as grudgingly as the right to vote for MPs. Ironically, women had been able to vote and stand as candidates for *ad hoc* bodies so that reform of the municipal franchise had actually reduced their rights. Unmarried women who fulfilled the property qualifications gained the vote in 1869, and in 1882 this was extended to married women. It was not until 1918, when the parliamentary franchise was extended to women after their long struggle in the suffragette movement, that women were generally permitted to vote in local elections. Even so, in both cases the right was restricted to those over thirty for fear that dizzy factory girls might act without due reverence, might even prove a dangerously radical force. A further decade was to pass before the rights of the sexes became equal.

The wards

One very significant principle established was that of the small electoral district or ward, the effect of which was to fragment an area and emphasise pockets of political homogeneity. Tories were worried that the large industrial towns would be dominated by Liberals, but a judicious set of electoral divisions could ensure that enclaves would be protected. Hence they successfully pressed for the preservation of small ancient areas as electoral districts. Indeed, the division was based not merely on numbers of voters but on total rateable value, which meant that fewer rich people were required to elect a candidate. The drawing of ward boundaries gave continuing opportunities for gerrymandering by local politicians who had the right to advise the Home Secretary. This was removed in the 1972 Act which transferred the responsibility to the independent Local Government Boundary Commission.

The aldermanic system

The 1835 Act placed a further blot on the democratic landscape in the form of the aldermanic system, which allowed councillors to elect some of their fellows to serve for further periods regardless of the feelings of the electorate. It was introduced as a result of a compromise between the Tories (in opposition) and the Whig government, its purpose to preserve some of the power of the old ruling elites in the face of advancing democracy. The practice meant that it was quite possible for unpopular councillors to evade electoral nemesis. Indeed, sometimes they were appointed at the very moment they were being rejected by the voters! It became a useful means for a majority party to cling to overall control against the wishes of the electorate and was preserved until 1972. In certain authorities the title lingers on, like that of Privy Councillor, an honour with no executive power.

Local electoral systems today

The conduct of the election is in the hands of a Returning Officer, who organises the polling stations, election publicity and the count. He or she enjoys a moment of celebrity when announcing the result to the thronged party supporters, and sometimes the television cameras.

The voters
Subject to certain disqualifications, the local franchise today is universal: electors must be over eighteen and of sound mind. Those convicted of felony or treason are barred, as is anyone guilty of electoral malpractice. All voters must be entered on the Electoral Register, which is updated annually.

The candidates
A candidate must be a British (or Irish) citizen, registered as a voter in an area in which he or she has lived for twelve months

prior to nomination. It was not until a private member's bill of
1907 that women became eligible. Another barred category were
the poor; under the harsh nineteenth-century Poor Law ethos
paupers were not regarded as full citizens until 1948.

There are various disqualifications relating to bankruptcy and
convictions for crime. Moreover, candidates must not be paid employees of the authority for fear that they might feather their own
nests. This restriction can penalise the working and lower middle
classes, many of whom are employed by local government, while
placing no obstacles in the way of estate agents and other local
businessmen, who may have much to gain from council membership. In 1989 the Thatcher government increased these restrictions
(see p. 169).

Today parties dominate the process; relatively few candidates
standing as independents. Within each ward a formal selection
procedure is followed, sometimes involving all ward members
but often controlled by local oligarchs. The certainty of outcome
in many wards means that this is tantamount to electing the councillor, although in the less-winnable seats the process is more one
of arm-twisting than selection. In his study of Sheffield Hampton
notes how, in 1967, Labour was unable to fight all eighty-one
seats. 'When it came to select the last twelve candidates only
three people were left on the list and the ward members present
considered two of these unsuitable' (Hampton, 1970: 14). The
highly centralised nature of the party machines in most areas
demands that prospective candidates be expected to stand in any
ward.

Each candidate must appoint an election agent with responsibility for ensuring that the campaign is conducted within the
rules; expenses must not exceed statutory limits.

The electoral process
While the date for a parliamentary election is effectively chosen by
the Prime Minister (by dissolving Parliament), the local contest is
set more democratically, occurring like constitutional clockwork
on the Thursday of the first full week in May.

However, the clockwork varies. In the Scottish regions, London
boroughs, shire counties and most shire county districts, councils
are elected *en bloc* as in a general election after a four-year term.
This is the most common method, used for some 5,000 seats in

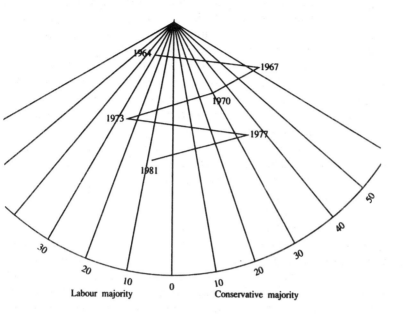

Figure 6.1 The swing between Labour and Conservative on the GLC.

201 authorities in 1990 (March, 1990: 11). Under this system it is possible for the majority party to be turned out in a single fell swoop. Figure 6.1 shows that between its creation in 1963 and its abolition in April 1986 the GLC swung regularly between Conservative and Labour domination.

Metropolitan districts and the remaining shire county districts (which have a choice of either method) follow a different pattern, with only a third of the seats contested each year (partial renewal). Usually there are three councillors for each ward, which means that it is very difficult for the electorate to rid itself of an unpopular council.

The ballot is secret and the essence of simplicity: the voter is merely required to place an 'X' against the favoured candidate or party (both named on the ballot paper) and the winner is the one 'first past the post'. This curiously British method of election arouses much controversy. In a three- (or more) horse race, the victorious candidate can be comfortably returned with well below 50 per cent of the vote. The system is unduly hard on third parties with support spread evenly throughout the area, but excessively kind to those with concentrated support. As in parliamentary elections, the system can produce ruling parties, returned time after time, with below 50 per cent of the vote, sometimes with even fewer votes than one of the defeated parties. Sometimes parties have gained all seats on the council, leaving just under half the electorate entirely unrepresented. It is a curt denial of one of the most essential principles of true representative government: proportional representation.

Proportional representation
Proportional representation (PR) in local government elections would mean that each authority would have a council with party strengths reflecting the pattern of community allegiance; if 30 per cent of citizens vote Labour then 30 per cent of the council would also be so. The case for PR is stronger in local than in central government since the greater homogeneity of the wards (middle class areas, council estates, ethnic ghettos) can result in greater distortions. The existence of housing classes within areas, where birds of a feather flock together, adds to the effect. In 1910 the Royal Commission on Electoral Systems made such a recommendation, to be endorsed by the Speaker's Conference. However, a later bill introducing PR for local government was narrowly defeated in the House of Commons in 1923, even though it had successfully navigated the House of Lords.

PR could revitalise local politics; parochial issues would assume greater salience and one could expect the formation of a large number of small parties (ethnic minorities, cause groups, the women's movement and so on). Hence, it is not surprising that establishment interests fight shy of such a reform. Indeed, the great Redcliffe-Maud Royal Commission, treating the issue as one likely to disturb those of a nervous disposition, paid it no heed at all.

Local electoral behaviour

Knowledge of an electoral system cannot in itself tell us much about the real world of politics; the important questions relate to the way people behave. This section addresses one of the most persistent issues of local electoral behaviour – the low turnout (the proportion of the eligible population voting), followed by a consideration of how those who vote make their choices. Finally, the chapter examines the behaviour of the politicians by turning to the electoral campaign.

Why people vote – or why they don't

One of the most frequently discussed features of local elections is the low turnout; 40 per cent is relatively good, yet in parliamentary elections one expects around 70 per cent. For opponents of local democracy, this is invariably taken as evidence of lack of demand. However, there are other possible reasons.

(1) *Size of electorate.* In local government the larger the population the greater the likelihood of a low turnout (Stanyer, 1971). Turnouts are higher in rural areas than in cities.

(2) *Social composition.* However, the size of the electorate may reflect the fact that the large populations found in the cities are predominantly working class and less likely than their middle-class counterparts to vote (Lipset, 1959: ch. 6). This reflects a political culture which has long discouraged working-class participation. Working-class black people are even less likely to vote.

(3) *Sense of community.* Another, more fundamental, reason for the low turnout may lie in the nature of the boundary structure. It may be argued that the areas of the towns and cities of Britain are too large to engender any sense of community spirit (*Gemeinschaft*). Goldsmith and Newton revealed that while there is one councillor for between 250 to 450 citizens in Western Europe, a UK councillor represents a population of around 1,800 (Widdicombe, 1986e: 141). The rural–urban differential can be explained in these terms. Similarly, turnout in Wales and Scotland is higher than in England.

(4) *Impregnable majorities.* The foregone nature of the result in many wards provides little incentive to leave the warm television set for the polling booth. Hence turnouts tend to be higher in marginal seats (Hampton, 1970: 14–15). An extreme case is the non-contested seat (though these have declined since 1974), where there is a zero

incentive and the candidate may confidently anticipate success by relying only upon a spouse and/or mother for support.

(5) *Central dominance*. The fact that local government exists in a centrally dominated state cannot be expected to increase interest in local elections. If people see their local authority constantly frustrated in its policy designs by Whitehall and Westminster they will feel that local democracy is a charade, unworthy of a vote.

(6) *Rival local governments*. It was shown in Chapter 4 how the local administrative environment contains a variety of public bodies which, while assuming important community responsibilities, steer clear of the ballot box. Their presence reduces the area over which the voter can exert influence and hence reduces the need to vote.

(7) *Democratic surfeit*. Though democracy may not be the food of love it is sometimes argued that the British have an excess of it. In some districts there is an election every year and the appetite becomes cloyed.

The apathy agenda

The issue of whether or not people vote is of immense political significance; the price of freedom is eternal vigilance and, where people are apathetic, democracy is in peril. Britain has evolved a deferential political culture which is not conducive to mass participation. When the franchise was extended the old ruling establishment worried late into the night on the likely effects. The political essayist Walter Bagehot posed the key question: will the masses defer to their betters? Edmund Burke propounded his elitist theory of representation and the Philosophical Radicals argued for central control.

Part of this culture is the belief that government is something best left to the natural leaders of society; those who try to lead trade unions, or become active in local government, are in some way rocking the boat, not playing the game. Deference helps explain why generations of working-class people have (as 'working-class Conservatives') rejected the party formed specifically to represent their interests.

Once franchise extension was conceded, many other ploys to limit working-class participation were applied, including multiple restrictions on trade unions, prohibitively high electoral deposits (payment to be allowed to participate as a candidate), no payment for MPs and councillors, domination by the old elite parties, lack of PR and so on.

It can be in the interests of the powerful if the masses keep out of government. Low working-class turnout is functional to class rule in a capitalist state, and much is done to encourage it. Hence, in popular rhetoric and media reporting there is the suggestion that local government is something of a joke, a bore, fair game for derision, to be ranked with mothers-in-law and English cricket. When working-class forces do become actively involved, as in the 1980s, it becomes necessary to resort to draconian measures with finance cuts, loss of functions and ultimately abolition. Yet when the carefully constructed wall of apathy crumbles, as it did over the introduction of the poll tax, matters can be rather different. In the local elections of May 1990 turnouts of over 60 per cent were recorded (*The Guardian*, May 1990), and major concessions were forced from the government (see p. 183).

How people vote – the local general election

One of the most significant aspects of local electoral behaviour has been the extent to which it is influenced by the politics of central government (Newton, 1976: 16). Voters in local elections tend to use the occasion to express their feelings about the party in power at Westminster. The mass media do much to accentuate this by reporting local results in national terms, even using them to extrapolate a hypothetical parliamentary scenario. Central politicians also promote the tendency, dominating campaigns, appearing on television results programmes and using local verdicts as a basis to pontificate on national issues. This is not entirely new; in the 1870s the dynamic Liberal Party organisation of Birmingham under Joseph Chamberlain used local elections as a means of alerting voters to central matters.

This tendency works regularly against the government of the day, the local vote being largely in the nature of protest (see Figure 6.2). The Conservative government of the 1980s saw its local support sink to hitherto unplumbed depths. In the 1986 elections Labour made an enormous 484 net gain, yet four years later they

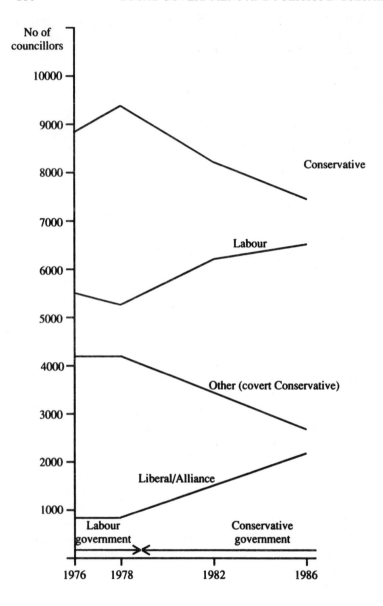

Figure 6.2   The protest effect. Source: data from *Social Trends*, 1977, 1988.

were able to go on to add a further 303 seats, and could claim to
have more councillors, and control more councils, than ever before
(March, 1990; 10).

This central domination makes it difficult to analyse local electoral behaviour in terms of any other factors. However, to ignore
them would result in oversimplification; thus the effects of class,
sector and rational choice are considered next.

Class explanations

The presence of characteristic urban Labour strongholds and Conservative shires demonstrates the underlying class factor in the
local electoral landscape. Indeed, class loyalty has remained the
most enduring explanation of British voting behaviour. However,
it has by no means told the full story; there is much evidence of
significant cross-class voting.

In particular, the phenomenon of working-class Conservatism
has given the political right a hegemony not anticipated by either
the reforming radicals or the worried Tories of the nineteenth
century. Yet this is not entirely surprising when account is taken of
the political beliefs of many working-class people, which do not
match the elevated vision of radical intellectuals. Popular attitudes
towards nuclear weapons, the monarchy, capital punishment,
European integration and so on show that many working-class
people were speaking New Right prose long before it became
fashionable. Indeed, the policy of unilateral nuclear disarmament
consistently proved a major vote-loser for Labour. Some policy
areas arousing right-wing working-class sentiments are particularly
salient in local government, including race and immigration, council house sales, law and order, arts sponsorship, social service
'scroungers' and gay rights. The media make much of this, and
feeling can be particularly strong in local elections owing to the
more extreme nature of some of the candidates.

Moreover, the British class system itself has changed through a
process of *embourgeoisement* whereby working-class people acquire middle-class values and characteristics. During the 1970s voting patterns became more volatile and political scientists began to
speak of class dealignment; by the early 1980s over half the
electorate appeared to be rejecting the class imperative (Crewe,
1986: 620). This was stimulated by the emergence of the Social

Democratic Party and the revival of the Liberals. Labour was the main casualty and in the south of England it became possible to identify a 'new working class' living in owner-occupied accommodation, non-unionised and employed in the private rather than the public sector (Crewe, 1987). The London Borough of Wandsworth became a Thatcherite utopia.

Sectoral explanations

It has become increasingly possible to explain voting behaviour in terms of the public–private sector dichotomy, those working in (or dependent upon) the former being more likely to support Labour, the party of social democratic state intervention (Dunleavy and Husbands, 1985). This is particularly relevant to local government, because its dedication to collective consumption services promises large-scale support for Labour, especially in the cities. Accordingly, the Conservative attack on the functions of local government may be seen as a party strategy.

Rational explanations

An alternative explanation of voting behaviour comes from 'consumer voting' models (Downs, 1957; Himmelweit *et al.*, 1985: 70), which characterise voters as shoppers in an electoral supermarket, choosing policies as they would washing powder. This model emphasises the idea of the local party manifesto (a set of promises prior to the election), although central domination of local elections reduces its applicability to local government. Moreover, the extent to which local parties can make promises is limited by the principle of *ultra vires* and the power of central government to override local initiative. This was the fate of various cheap bus fares policies which local electorates had apparently supported and, in the GLC 'Fares Fair' case, Lord Denning in effect ruled in the House of Lords that a local manifesto was not worth the paper it was written on.

The local campaign

Although, given the class and sectoral imperatives, the idea that voters behave like discerning shoppers is rather fanciful, politicians nevertheless act very much as if it were true. The pre-election period can see much frenzied activity designed to entice and persuade that this or that policy will reach parts that others cannot. Today this is largely a party matter; members will distribute leaflets, trudge the streets canvassing, hold meetings in draughty halls, feed information to the media and generally try to stimulate interest in the election and their party.

Again, we find much centralisation as the national machines roll into action. To a great extent the campaign is conducted in the national media, Westminster leaders dominate and local politicians are banished to the sidelines in much the same way as the run-of-the-mill parliamentary candidates during a general election. Increasingly campaigns take on a hi-tech character, with slick party broadcasts betraying the skills of Madison Avenue rather than those of the hustings of old. The general effect of technology is to reduce the level of popular participation; television offers no opportunity to question and heckle and national presentation takes little cognisance of the politics of this or that area.

Conclusion – do local elections work?

The problems with local electoral systems, including the absence of PR, partial renewal, low turnout and the overwhelmingly centralist orientation of the process, suggest that local accountability is little more than a sham. There is much in this. Yet it can be argued that the position is mitigated by the fact that those who serve on councils cherish some belief that the system works.

This idea was explored in an important study of the councillors of Birmingham, Britain's largest city outside London. Here Newton found that, while councillors were worldly enough to recognise the importance of central government policies, many believed that local variables mattered (Newton, 1976: 17–18). The significance of this is not whether or not their belief is correct, but that they held it at all. It means that councillors can be expected to behave in a manner calculated to win local votes, seeking to act in the interests of their political supporters. The councillor 'does his best to manipulate . . . local factors with an eye to their electoral consequences' (Newton, 1976: 19). When behaving in this way councillors may be said to be following the law of anticipated reactions; believing oneself to be watched is almost as good as being watched (Kingdon, 1967). Thus it is possible to argue that democracy enters the local electoral process as a result of psychology.

However, this is democracy via the back door. For local government to remain responsive to its community and encourage participation, reforms are clearly needed. These could include provision for local referendums, a system of recall, the selection of councillors in the same way as juries, or the creation of smaller areas which would generate a genuine sense of community. Alternatively, the antique 'first-past-the-post' system could be be carefully polished and placed on the top (most inaccessible) shelf of the constitutional curiosity shop where many feel it belongs.

7

Political Parties

Although not constitutional bodies like, for instance, Parliament or the town council, political parties are essential units in modern politics. They orchestrate the life of the municipality. This chapter begins by identifying various kinds of local party and party system. It also considers the development of the modern local parties from their nineteenth-century origins. Analysis of the operation of parties in local politics today notes their impact in the community and in the town hall, and examines the question of internal power structure and party orientations towards policy. The conclusion assesses the impact of parties on local democracy and finds that, although crucially important to the local polity, they are deeply enmeshed in the wider political system of the central state.

Introducing the local party

A political party is typically defined as an association established for the purpose of gaining political office by constitutional means; that is, by fighting elections. Local parties do this at local level, their object being to win seats on councils. However, the idea that parties wish to do nothing more than gain office is simplistic. Characteristically they aim to shape society in line with some vision; they represent an ideology. Broadly speaking this may be said to be of the left or the right, and will imply both concrete policies and a general orientation towards government. These they set out in their electoral manifestos.

It is surprising how many textbooks have ignored local political parties. Indeed, an official inquiry into management in local government (Maud, 1967a,b) regarded them as so unimportant that, although it asked whether councillors were party members, it did not bother to inquire 'which one?'. The Bains Report on the same subject went so far as to denigrate parties for undermining the efficiency and morale of local bureaucrats (Bains, 1972: 37).

This neglect and disdain in part reflects an establishment conviction that parties are out of place in local government. They have been accused of distorting the community will and bringing an unwarranted ideological dimension into an arm of the state which should be concerned with efficiency of service delivery rather than political debate.

There are various reasons for anti-partyism. It derives in part from the Benthamite centralism which is suspicious of a local policy dynamic. Further antipathy stems from the disquiet felt within the ruling establishment. Local parties can mean working-class involvement in decision–making, an unwelcome prospect for those seeking to preserve patterns of privilege.

Party types

There are various kinds of party active in local politics which may be broadly classified as follows.

Local national parties

Intuition might suggest that local parties are autonomous and unique to their areas but this would be mistaken. The major parties in local arenas are mere appendages of the mighty organisations dominating the Westminster stage. These consist of three basic elements: a parliamentary cadre composed of MPs, a central bureaucracy concerned with the large task of administration and a great mass membership in the country of voluntary workers and activists. A key unit of local organisation is the constituency association, which is divided into ward associations with a direct concern with local government. Local organisations are welded together through nationally organised federal associations.

In the Labour Party the National Executive Committee (NEC) is the fount of all authority and has the power to discipline local organisations. As Labour began to win seats on councils efforts were made to create a secure bond between the local organisations and national headquarters. After the First World War a Liaison Committee was created, to be replaced in 1932 by a Local Government Sub-Committee of the Policy Committee of the NEC. In 1930 Model Standing Orders were circulated to local party associations to increase central standardisation.

Conservative Central Office is headed by a powerful Party Chairman appointed by the leader, but is less forceful than the NEC in its centralising influence. This is mainly because Conservatives are generally more compliant by nature. The landslide post-war victories of Labour in central and local government caused panic within the establishment and, under Chairman Lord Woolton, the Conservatives began to rebuild at all levels to restore their position as the country's natural ruling party. Although much rhetoric lamented the evil intrusion of party politics into the tranquil world of the parish pump (Hoffman, 1964: 68), a Local Government Advisory Committee was created and local Conservatives were encouraged to copy the electioneering and organising methods of Labour.

Local forces of the third kind

In some local authorities, such as Liverpool, the Liberals remained virile and have made a point of relating to localities with a manifesto of 'community politics'. Thus, gaining control over the London Borough of Tower Hamlets in 1986, they divided the area into seven units under teams of bureaucrats and councillors in order to promote community access. The formation of the Social Democratic Party in the early 1980s saw a general revitalisation of the 'third force' in British politics that was particularly evident at the local level, especially in the shire counties, where it had the effect of increasing the number of hung councils (where no party enjoys a clear majority) (Widdicombe, 1986b: Table 2.4). In the 1989 merger of the centre parties as the Social and Liberal Democrats, the Liberals, with more activists and councillors, remained the dominant element.

Local splinter parties

Sometimes the local members of a national party become dissatisfied and break away to form a separate party. The reasons for the discontent can be infinitely various, but are likely to reflect a feeling that the national party is ignoring local factors. In a celebrated case Lincoln MP Dick Taverne broke with Labour at national level and successfully fought a parliamentary election as an independent. His supporters formed a local splinter party, the Democratic Labour Association, espousing local issues, that went on in 1973 to win control of the council (Ramsden and Jay, 1973). In urban areas racist movements have emerged, such as the Campaign to Stop Immigration formed in Bradford – a largely Conservative splinter party led by a former councillor (Bentley, 1972: 47). In West Oxfordshire eleven Conservative councillors resigned over the poll tax prior to the 1990 elections and regained their seats as independents.

Local parties – the real thing

The dominance of the central machines does not mean that genuinely local parties are entirely extinct. Citizens may organise themselves to fight local elections, although it is unlikely that they could ever contest all seats like the giants. Such parties often focus on a single issue (pedestrianisation, city-centre parking, school discipline, anti-fluoridation, nuclear dumping and so on) rather than ideological vision, and in this respect they resemble pressure groups. They are often concerned to resist change, such as invasions of aging conquistadors into the salubrious environs of the south-east coast which scar the landscape with bungalow settlements and convert ancient manorial buildings into nursing homes and hospices (Grant, 1971). Such parties usually have a short life, during which they will either achieve their objectives or give up in despair. Some local parties are not all they seem to be; this is particularly true of ratepayers' groups, and Central Office has repeatedly encouraged them to 'come out' as consenting adult Conservatives.

Party systems

Parties do not exist *in vacuo,* they stand as interacting elements in a system. Systems are conventionally characterised in terms of the number of parties. At national level Britain has traditionally been seen as a two-party system, but locally we find more variety:

(1) *Multi-party.* Three or more parties fight with equal chances of success. This can often result in a hung council. Thus, after the 1990 elections, Portsmouth, Gillingham, Torbay, Gosport, Bath, Harrogate, Haven, Tandridge, Rochford and Kingston-upon-Thames all went from Conservative to 'no overall control'.

(2) *Two-party.* Two parties each have a viable chance of gaining a council majority. They expect to take turns as the dominant party.

(3) *Single-party-dominant.* One contender can usually count on a bigger seat-share than its rivals.

(4) *Single-party.* One party maintains long-term hegemony. Conservatives traditionally dominate in the shires while Labour's strongholds are in inner London and the northern industrial cities.

(5) *No-party.* Political activity is unsophisticated and most candidates see themselves as independents. It is largely a rural phenomenon, most likely in parish politics.

Chapter 6 showed that the electoral system tends to promote two-partyism, which is why there are fewer minority parties in British local government than might be expected. In the long term, most minorities find it best to ally with one of the giants. In the 1980s, to the alarm of traditionalists, Labour became a haven for women's groups, ethnic minorities, gays and others.

The party's moving on – evolution

Those deploring the presence of parties in local government cast atavistic eyes at some halcyon age when they are supposed not to have existed. However, since the beginning of the nineteenth century there have been groups contesting municipal leadership, seeking control of the *ad hoc* bodies, and most boroughs after the Municipal Corporations Act of 1835. These were not recognisable as modern parties but the same ideological orientations were present. There were 'improvers', keen to develop local services, and 'economisers', dedicated to keeping the rates as low as possible.

These sometimes (but not always) coincided with the parliamentary groupings of Whigs and Tories, the former representing the thrusting bourgeoisie who needed efficient local services to maintain their mammoth work-forces and the latter the old landowning interests. In addition there were the two great religious groupings of Non-Conformists and Anglicans which again tended to reflect the Whig–Tory divide; indeed, the Anglicans were seen as the Tory Party at prayer. In London, tight party control was evident from the inception of the LCC, although Labour did not win control until 1934.

The Liberal Party was particularly significant in the early development of local party politics. It was largely the party of the industrial bourgeoisie, responsible for creating modern local government. In Birmingham a particularly strong organisation (the Birmingham caucus) provided a legendary period of local government under the dynamic leadership of Joseph Chamberlain. Before the Labour Party reached maturity, a number of working-class candidates were grateful to stand under the Liberal flag.

However, it was the rise of Labour after 1900 which marked the emergence of the modern local party. The local elites who rubbed well-padded shoulders at numerous social, religious, business and ceremonial functions spoke the same language of wealth and power and were easily endowed with the skills and knowledge to operate the municipal institutions. Working-class candidates possessed none of these advantages; formal organisation was their only means of political leverage and the political party was the key to social change.

Although control of Parliament was the ultimate goal (the party was first named the Labour Representation Committee) initially this could only be a pipe dream. Under the intellectual dynamic of the Fabian movement, the party made early gains on the local front, particularly in the industrial cities and in London. This is hardly surprising. The new cities were from the start potential land-mines for the right. As dormitories for the vast labour forces assembled to serve the factories they afforded opportunities for workers to meet, talk and act collectively. Their political potential was enormous. The city was the crucible for amalgamating the coherent working class predicted by Marx and dreaded by the bourgeoisie. Long working hours, a newly invented militaristic police force and repressive legislation could only delay the advent of working-class action in the cities.

However, it was the First World War which provided the stimulus for the most dramatic advances. In the 1919 elections Labour won almost six hundred seats on the London boroughs and made voracious gains in the provincial cities and even in some of the counties. The inter-war era saw Labour replacing the Liberals as the second major political force in the country. On the eve of the Second World War the party had majorities on four county councils, eighteen county boroughs, twenty-four non-county boroughs, seventeen London boroughs and a hundred district councils (Keith-Lucas and Richards, 1978: 114).

Alarm at developments often led the old Liberal and Tory factions to bury political hatchets in an effort to construct anti-socialist caucuses, piously avowing a distaste for party politics, but fighting under such flags of convenience as 'Progressives', 'Citizens', 'Moderates', 'Independents', the 'London Municipal Society' and so on. In addition, they developed an ethical theory which lingers today: that party politics should be kept out of local government. What they really meant was that working people should be kept out. When a number of allegedly non-party alliances amalgamated as the National Union of Ratepayers' Associations, their true colours were revealed.

The Second World War provided yet another stimulus to Labour when a landslide in Parliament was matched by some 1,600 seats on councils (Cole, 1948: 445–58). In the post-war era party politics received a further injection of constitutional insulin through the local government reorganisation of 1974, when the more politically active urban areas were merged into the wider territories. This resulted in a steady decline in the number of independent candidates and in the number of uncontested seats. The 1980s marked a new high for party activity at the local level with the rise of Labour's New Urban Left (see pp. 234–9).

Local parties in action

Parties provide the pulse of modern politics, to be felt throughout the community and in the town hall.

Parties in the streets

Political life in the community would be a lot duller without parties. Prior to the extension of the franchise, activity was muted; the power-sharing elites had little desire to publicise their doings, but the need to mobilise a mass electorate forced them to court the community.

A prime function of the modern party is the aggregation of interests into an election-winning coalition. This process has been more apparent in the case of Labour than the Conservatives. The latter are welded with strong bonds of property and wealth, with little need to entice members from outside the ranks of the comfortable middle classes (though of course they rely upon working-class support). Labour, on the other hand, has been described as a broad church and this became particularly evident in the 1980s with a wide New Urban Left coalition of social interests and underprivileged minorities. Particularly evident in the London boroughs, it was not welcomed in all its facets by traditionalists in the northern working-class heartlands where sexism, racism and anti-gay machismo are deeply ingrained into popular culture.

However, parties do much more than aggregate. They stimulate interest in local affairs and provide an avenue for political recruitment (particularly important for the working class, whose education and life chances are not intended to bestow leadership skills or aspirations). A number of prominent national politicians have had their first taste of political excitement and intrigue through the local party. Ken Livingstone, Bernie Grant and David Blunkett, all prominent in the local politics of the 1980s, went on to pursue Westminster careers. It is not only Labour MPs who enter politics via the local party; a number of Conservatives, including headline-catching Edwina Currie, have travelled the municipal route.

Parties in the town hall

In modern urban government one finds a form of control reminiscent of Westminster when the majority party becomes the government. This phenomenon is not new; the London boroughs saw majority leadership as early as 1900. Indeed, there had been a Labour majority in West Ham in the nineteenth century and during the inter-war years Herbert Morrison presided over the LCC like a veritable prime minister. Neither is it entirely uniform across the country; in the 1960s Manchester was maintaining a tradition of bipartisan politics (Bulpit, 1967: 76). However, party domination has spread appreciably since the reorganisation of 1974 (Widdicombe, 1986b). The tendency is matched by minority parties' willingness to accept a self-denying ordinance, refusing policy-making positions to become 'the opposition'.

The party group

A key factor in town hall dominance is the party group, the local equivalent of the parliamentary party, in which councillors from a single party meet regularly to plan strategies. These can be highly organised, with policy sub-groups, various positions of seniority and even whips to maintain discipline, a discipline sometimes sterner than that at Westminster. The Widdicombe Committee found that Labour and Conservative members voted on the party line for over 90 per cent of the time in full council meetings and around 80 per cent of the time in committee (1986b: Tables 2.3, 2.5).

The committee system

Party dominance is further enhanced through one of the principal instruments of local policy making: the committee system. Traditionally each important service has been controlled by a committee of councillors enjoying a high degree of autonomy. The model has come under fire in the post-war era (see Chapter 10) but committees remain key units in the town hall power structure. The majority party is able to ensure that its numerical advantage is reflected on each committee and can also appoint its own members to key positions. By the 1980s, over 90 per cent of party-dominated authorities saw the majority party taking all chairs, vice-chairs and even those of the sub-committees (Widdicombe, 1986b: Tables A.13, A.14, A.15). Parties can also increase their control by using the right to coopt outsiders. Originally intended to bring in expertise, this was used to include political sympathisers.

Corporate management

A further potent form of control came by default as a result of the corporate management movement of the 1960s and 1970s (see Chapter 10). This introduced a very special committee, a small group of senior councillors known as a management board, or policy committee, to make over-arching policy. These were reminiscent of

Westminster-style Cabinets and offered undreamed-of power to majority party leaders who could become, in effect, local prime ministers. Indeed, pursuing the Westminster analogy further, the senior bureaucrat (chief executive) can be induced to work hand in glove with the council leaders rather like the Cabinet Secretary. These developments mean that the ideal of the council as a decision-making body is quite bogus; like Parliament it is reduced to dignified status, a rubber stamp, with back-benchers mere lobby fodder.

Politicising the bureaucracy
Finally, party domination can be enhanced through politicisation of the bureaucracy. In the way that Mrs Thatcher secured commitment from Whitehall mandarins by enquiring 'Is he one of us?', ruling groups have sought, through judicious appointments and promotions, to ensure a sympathetic ideological disposition from officials. Thus, for example, in Lambeth in 1974, the Housing Director was 'a person that the new chairman had a hand in appointing' (Cockburn, 1977a: 84). Moreover, some councils have sought to heighten the general political consciousness of all employees (Blunkett, 1984: 248). Though employed increasingly throughout the 1980s, these tendencies are not unique to the urban left; a nod, a wink or a quiet masonic handshake can easily identify a friend, and many an anonymous Conservative bureaucrat has rendered loyal service in the shires and leafy suburbs. There has also been an increased tendency for leading councillors to appoint political advisers rather like ministers in the Thatcher government.

The developments were not welcomed by the Conservative central government, which saw them as inappropriate 'politicisation'. Not sure what to do, it acted uncharacteristically and set up a committee of inquiry, the Widdicome Committee, which reported in 1986 (1986a). The government subsequently issued a White Paper outlining various proposals to curb political behaviour which formed the basis of legislation in the form of the 1989 Local Government and Housing Act. The overall intention was to curtail majority party groups by extending opportunities for minority parties. There was to be a pro rata requirement for committee membership and minor parties were to be given rights to shape the agenda and raise issues in full council. Advisers were to be limited to one per party, regardless of size. There was even a proposal for the imposition of a centrally prescribed core of standing orders

(Department of the Environment, 1988). In addition, there were various proposals aimed at increasing the power of non-elected officers over their putative political masters (see p. 168). A similar package for central government would seem ludicrous; it would be like allowing members of the Opposition to sit on Cabinet committees! The motivation and effects were nakedly political, all part of the attack on the left.

Leaders and followers – an iron law of local oligarchy?

The party group is only the tip of an organisational iceberg upon which it depends for loyal support, advice, canvassing and fundraising. The mass membership looks to the top for leadership but it can also expect to have its own views expressed in the council chamber. Establishment fears that the rise of the modern mass party would lead to such domination was voiced in a celebrated study of political parties by Ostrogorski (1902). However, in the same period the contrary view was advanced by sociologist Robert Michels (1962 edn), who argued that any mass party would succumb to what he termed the 'iron law of oligarchy', whereby the natural advantages of the leaders would lead inexorably to their omnipotence. The question raises ethical issues: should the elected representatives be seen as delegates of the party membership, or do they have a wider responsibility to the electorate?.

The Conservative Party, with what can be termed a 'sleeping membership', has displayed a tradition of passivity before the leader (Gamble, 1979: 40), but Labour has evolved a more democratic constitution and leaders have often had to fight to get their way. Hugh Gaitskell's epic battles in 1960 over nuclear disarmament and Clause 4 (the historic commitment in Labour's constitution to public ownership) stand as cautionary tales for his successors.

The local version of the debate sees the same postures, Conservative associations being far more passive than their Labour counterparts (Gyford, 1976: 70). Although the Labour constitution is silent on local organisations, there was an expectation that democratic principles would apply. Internal wrangling in the 1920s led to intervention by the central party organisation and the 'Model Standing

Orders' enshrined the views of one of Labour's great local government figures, Herbert Morrison, who declared that councillors should not be seen as 'marionettes' of the local membership. However, Morrison was a political puritan (Donoghue and Jones, 1973: 76) and the reality in the boroughs and counties remains contentious. In Birmingham, for example, the local association fought a long battle to influence the party group over comprehensive education policy (Isaac-Henry, 1972). Generally Labour has accorded more authority to members, and it is usual to hold 'caucus' meetings when they can put their views to the party group (Wiseman, 1963). In Sheffield during the mid-1980s, Labour manifestos 'were the product of elaborate discussions between members of the Labour Group and the District Labour Party'; moreover 'party activists . . . [would] monitor the progress of the city council in honouring manifesto commitments' (Seyd, 1990: 337). Of course, the problem is lessened by the fact that many leading party figures are themselves councillors. However, by 1990, after the defeat of the New Urban Left, more oligarchic tendencies emerged as the party accepted the need to work with local capitalists.

Ideology

The fact that parties fight local elections and gain council majorities leads to the intuitive expectation that they will make distinctive policies for their areas. Certainly local issues can arouse intense feeling; for example, in 1902 and 1903 the method of propelling the city's trams was to inflame the passions of Wolverhampton's councillors (Jones, 1969: 40–1).

However, the general climate of centralisation means that local party views largely reflect the national party line. In Wolverhampton Jones (1969: 321) found predictable attitudes toward rates: dislike from Conservatives but acceptance from Labour as a means of income redistribution. Dearlove's study of the London Borough of Kensington and Chelsea revealed Conservative councillors extolling the virtues of self-help and decrying collectivist solutions to social problems (Dearlove, 1973: ch. 10). More generally, Davies (1972: 110) was able to demonstrate a clear positive relationship between Labour control and spending on welfare services.

Where local parties stray from the national line there is likely to be friction. This is more common in the Labour Party, with a generally greater propensity towards fratricide and, during the early 1980s, the rise of the left aroused considerable misgivings at headquarters. In 1985 a nine-person inquiry team descended upon Merseyside to investigate the local party and, amid allegations of witch-hunts, recommended expulsion, a sentence duly executed.

Even the divisions within local parties reflect national debates and the 1980s saw increased friction between moderates and extremists (Widdicombe, 1986b: 197). Changes in the Labour constitution (compulsory reselection) gave more power to the left but this was promptly reduced in 1989 when the centre instigated selection on the basis of voting by all local members. In the local Conservative associations the national wet/dry cleavage was reflected. Indeed, in some areas groups of 'dries' emerged determined to prove themselves *plus royaliste que le roi*. In 1988–9 Conservatives in Bradford gained control of the council by breaking the impartiality convention of the position of the Lord Mayor, and with this flimsy legitimacy embarked upon a New Right crusade (attacking the welfare structure with raised school meals charges, fewer social workers, increased council house rents, the sale of thirteen old people's homes and so on).

Conclusion – local parties and democracy

Party politics in local government experienced a decline in the immediate post-war decades. This was the era of consensus politics when both major parties accepted the broad premises of the mixed economy, Keynesianism and the welfare state. The Labour Party, secure as a party of government, no longer talked of municipal socialism; indeed the egalitarian ethic of social democracy implied a centralised state. However, the fracturing of the consensus during the Thatcher years saw a recrudescence of local party politics. This period revealed that, though a party may enjoy unchallengeable supremacy in the council chamber it cannot be said to be in the driving seat like the majority party in the House of Commons; it must go on to meet the greater, twin-headed dragon of Whitehall and Westminster.

Yet the ability of local authorities to resist the insidious virus of centralism from the early 1980s was largely a function of the strength of the local parties as antibodies in the bloodstream of the political body. Councils consisting of independents could never have mustered the strength of the New Urban Left. Hence, parties in local government can represent one of the last lines of defence of pluralist democracy; in resisting the centre they are also resisting tendencies towards totalitarianism.

Although there can be little doubt that parties are key actors on the local political stage, they are by no means the only ones. Local politics involves the professional officers of the local authority as well as a wide variety of pressure groups representing various interests in the community. Like central government, these limit the space in which parties operate. More will be learnt about them in subsequent chapters.

8

The People's Representatives

This chapter places the microscope on the 26,000 or so elected members sitting in the council chambers of England, Wales and Scotland. It is their presence which makes local government unique among public bodies outside Parliament. All others are under the day-to-day control of mysterious figures appointed by arcane and elitist processes conducted well away from the public gaze and innocent of the ballot box. In contrast, any citizen may stand for the council, penetrate the cold armour of the state and gain some control over the decisions which shape our lives. Hence, it is not surprising that there are those within the state who eye them with considerable unease; they can stand, rather like trade union leaders, in dangerous political territory.

The chapter begins by considering the nature of representative government and the roles played by councillors (drawing the distinction between front- and back-benchers). Motivations for council work and the calibre of those who do it are then considered, noting a political dimension to these debates not usually stressed. The following section looks at the characteristics of councillors in order to assess the extent to which they resemble those they represent. Also examined are the new breed of councillors who emerged in the 1980s. Next is a consideration of the question of whether councillors should be paid. The conclusion notes how central government can extend its tentacles into the council chamber to inhibit the behaviour of the people's representatives.

Representing the community

The fact that councillors are the chosen representatives of the community does not actually reveal much about how they may be expected to behave. There are conflicting theories on the relationship a representative can be said to have with constituents which vary in the degree of freedom he or she is permitted. Consider the following:

(1) *Typical case.* Here the person is chosen to resemble those represented. Thus, opinion pollsters select people for questioning on the basis of their membership of class or occupational groups. On local councils Labour members are often of working-class origins and Conservatives from the middle classes. In this view of representation the council is a microcosm of the community.

(2) *Delegate.* Here the representative is expected merely to report the views and opinions of others. At the TUC conference, for example, delegates are said to vote as their members have instructed. We can find this kind of representation in local government; because wards are small it is possible for constituents to ask their councillors to present their case to the council.

(3) *Mandatory.* Here the representative may be said to have entered into a kind of contract, trading promises for votes through the medium of the manifesto. Party domination makes this appropriate to local elections through the doctrine of the mandate.

(4) *Advocate.* Here the representative is seen as one with particular skills of advocacy. This is analogous to representation in court by a barrister. Many councillors see their main role as arguing for their constituents.

(5) *Statesman.* This is the highly elitist Burkean view in which the representative, though elected, owes no particular allegiance to constituents, being concerned only to exercise personal judgement on matters of state. Leading councillors making city-wide policy operate in this way.

Role types

Although councillors in the real world do not generally muse upon theories of representative government, they must establish a view of their role. In his study of the city of Birmingham, Newton (1976: 136–42) identified five role types; as follows:

(1) *Parochials* are mainly concerned with their constituents, seeing themselves as social workers or ombudsmen. They are not highly ideological and avoid the party battle, though their lack of strong commitment means that they rarely fail to toe the party line. They tend to enter politics relatively late in life.

(2) *People's agents* are similar to parochials but concerned with general problems and injustices on a city-wide basis. They tend to show an 'aggressive and ideological individualism' in protecting the ordinary citizen, rather like Batman of fabled Gotham City.

(3) *Policy advocates* are more interested in governing the city as a whole rather than helping individuals and tend to be ideologues. They are highly partisan, though likely to vote against their parties if ideologies clash. They seek the chairs and vice-chairs of the council's committees.

(4) *Policy brokers* resemble policy advocates in their commitment to policy but are more pragmatic, willing to compromise and more moderate. They serve to 'oil the machine' and reduce friction.

(5) *Policy spokesmen* are similar to parochials but see the solutions to problems more in terms of shaping broad policy than pursuing particular cases.

Clearly, representation can have various meanings and it is not possible, or desirable, to set up a single normative model. However, this typology enables us to identify clear representational problems such as might occur when a councillor refuses to speak for constituents, breaks a manifesto promise or lacks the skill to articulate his or her case. There is also the question of how closely councillors should resemble those represented; this is examined later in the chapter.

The self-seekers

The idea that all councillors are working for the community according to their own lights is of course fanciful. It has a normative tone; while saying what is the case, it is also implying what *should* be the case. In real life there are less noble role-types, such as the following:

(1)   *The personal careerist.* This is one concerned with using a position on the council to advance his or her own interest. The nineteenth-century bourgeoisie had much to gain from council membership and today some members of the *petit bourgeoisie* (shopkeepers, estate agents) show interest in council work.

(2)   *The interest group representative.* This is one who is deeply committed to some particular sectional interest. At local level this kind of representation (termed functional representation) may range from a concern with handicapped children to a deep commitment to the sale of council-owned property for the development of supermarkets and filling stations.

(3)   *The drone.* There are some councillors with no particular interest other than the social life. To these the council is little more than a club. They are the free-loaders to be found in most walks of life.

What councillors do

Figure 8.1 shows how the 1986 Widdicombe Committee report broke down the official duties of a mythical average councillor. Overall Labour members, averaging ninety-two hours a month, tend to work hardest but Liberals, with a greater commitment to community politics, devote more time to constituents.

The demands have increased over recent decades (Widdicombe, 1986b: 51). This is not surprising, since the 1974 reorganisation reduced the number of councillors in the country. Moreover, the greater volatility of the electorate called for more political activity to meet the challenge of the centre parties. There have also been socio-demographic developments (an aging population, the growth of ethnic communities, unemployment, inner city decline and so on) placing greater strain on local services. The Thatcher era posed further problems; paradoxically, cuts did not lessen the work of councillors because not only was much effort expended in resistance, but the management of decline proved more complex than that of growth. New burdens were imposed on the districts of the abolished GLC and metropolitan counties. There were also side-effects of economic policy in the form of increased pressure group activity by voluntary organisations, more social problems

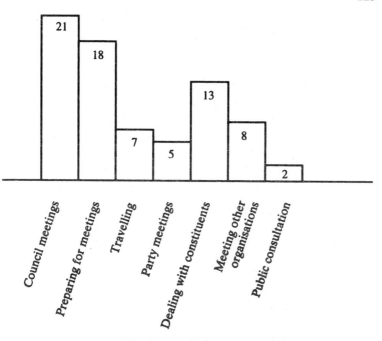

Figure 8.1 Average hours per month spent on council work.
Source: data from Widdicombe, 1986c, tables 5.5, 5.8, 5.10, 5.11,
5.12, pp. 46–53.

associated with unemployment and more demands for protection
against the ravages of the unfettered market.

Front-benchers and back–benchers

Of course, it is misleading to speak of average work-loads and
there is no single job description for a councillor. Newton's cat-
egorisation suggests a fundamental dichotomy between serving
constituents and operating in the more heady stratosphere of policy formation, pointing to an important back-bencher/front-
bencher distinction. Both roles can be onerous.

Constituency work entails receiving and answering mail and
meeting people in surgeries and in other formal and informal
settings. Moreover, councillors are generally 'joiners', tending to
belong to other organisations (sometimes *ex officio*) such as voluntary associations and pressure groups.

The front-bencher role demands attendance at numerous meetings in and around the town hall, either in full council or, more
commonly, in committee or subcommittee. In addition, there is the
preparation of discussion papers, the study of documents drawn up
by officials and incessant lobbying before and after the meetings.
Throughout, there are complicated dealings with council officials
(see Chapter 9) and pressure groups (see Chapter 12). As well as
this, there are demanding party leadership duties involving further
meetings and a range of related activities such as fund-raising,
recruitment and publicity.

What makes them do it?

Many orthodox studies pose the question: 'Why do people become
councillors?'. This is not an unreasonable query, but carries a suggestion that such behaviour is rather odd and needs explaining.
This attitude can be traced back to the late nineteenth century,
when working people began to enter the local political arena, previously the preserve of elites.

It was shown in Chapter 2 that the principal motive of the bourgeoisie, who dominated nineteenth-century town halls, was self-
interest; urban power propelled the process of profit maximisation
as much as steam power. Working-class participation saw
councillors driven by different class interests, an ideological quest
for municipal socialism. This was never welcomed by those in
power and part of the defence has been to impute rather unflatter-
ing motives, such as the following:

(1) *Ideology*. This motive is associated particularly with the
Labour Party and was reaffirmed with the rise of the New Urban
Left. In contrast, the Conservatives have long been a largely non-
ideological party, seeking office in order to govern in the broad
interests of a particular class (Ingle, 1987: ch. 2). This began to
change under the 'conviction politics' of Margaret Thatcher, and
some New Right councillors emerged every bit as 'wild-eyed' as
the alleged 'loonies' of the left. The modern Liberal Party has not
been particularly ideological (it has certainly not espoused classic
liberalism) and the ill-fated Social Democratic Party (SDP) began
life in order to reject an increasing ideological commitment within
the Labour Party, particularly at grass-roots level.

(2) *Power*. Although politics is pre-eminently about power, that which any one councillor can achieve is limited. Only a few front-benchers can expect to make things happen and even they will be circumscribed by factors beyond their control, notably central government and their own officials. However, council membership can also confer the next best thing to power: its illusion, and an accompanying sense of prestige. Critics sometimes portray working-class councillors as self-important poseurs, although the ornate town halls of the nineteenth-century bourgeoisie testify to the enormous pomp, if not pomposity, with which they adorned their own municipal activities. Yet it would be absurd to imagine that all councillors thirst for power or prestige. The Maud Committee found that most were content to serve quietly on committees rather than strut like prima donnas (Maud, 1967b: 40).

(3) *Satisfaction*. Many who indulge in politics do so because they find the intrigue and cut and thrust intrinsically pleasurable. Moreover, altruistic satisfaction can be derived from the pursuit of an ideal, helping the weak and generally performing public service.

(4) *Specific policy interest*. For some council membership is a means of achieving some specific goal, such as the prevention of a road development. This kind of motivation is more usually present in the case of independents or small parties better described as pressure groups.

(5) *Self-interest*. Although the great age of bourgeois control over local government has passed, there is still scope for personal advantage. Some professions, such as estate agents and property developers, have much to gain from council membership although, where appropriate, they must declare an interest and leave any relevant meeting. This prudent rule does not, however, extend to informal soirées at the golf club the evening before. Similarly many Members of Parliament have business and commercial links, which is why there is a voluntary register of MPs' interests. In 1989 the government established a statutory register of councillors' pecuniary (financial) interests. However, this does not cover the more shadowy area of non-pecuniary interests.

(6) *Ambition*. A number of national figures began their political careers in local government, although the route has been most important for Labour. One of the party's greatest figures, Herbert

Morrison, served a long and distinguished apprenticeship in the government of London.

The general tenor of much writing on the subject of councillor motivation implies something disreputable in the desire of ordinary people to pass through the hallowed portals of the state. The Maud Report suggested that they sought membership in order not to pursue any genuine ideology or to improve the lot of their fellows, but to enliven their own drab and talentless existences (Maud, 1967b: 163). However, middle-class councillors can also gain social enrichment. For some the council is a kind of club, generally an all-male one, and membership can serve as an entrée to a wider social life encompassing golf club, freemasons lodge and directors' dining-room. This debate is closely related to another dominant theme in much orthodox writing, which laments that the calibre of councillors has fallen during the twentieth century.

The calibre of councillors

One ex-local government officer claims that 'many people coming into contact with councillors have expressed surprise that people obviously of such modest abilities should be . . . exercising considerable power over a wide range of complex matters' (Henney, 1984: 326). Case studies such as that of Glossop by Birch (1959) link the decline with changes in British capitalism. The industrial 'natural rulers' disappeared with the rise of the joint stock company, owned by an anonymous and amorphous body of shareholders and controlled by a new, geographically mobile managerial class with no sense of local identification. At the same time the fledgling Labour Party began to field its own candidates, with alarming prospects of working-class community leadership. The Poplarist movement of the early twentieth century (see p. 230) confirmed establishment fears. There has also been a sexist dimension to the debate. The intrusion of 'middle-class housewives' with time on their hands has been alleged to impair the efficiency of municipal life.

Another strand in the attack stems from the Benthamite mistrust of local autonomy. This was the thinking that led to the nineteenth-century centralist reforms and the Northcote-

Trevelyan Report which established the civil service as a national centralised elite. J. S. Mill argued in his great work, *Considerations on Representative Government* (1861), that councillors must inevitably be of a lower intellectual standard than MPs. This refrain has been echoed in various official reports, including Maud, Redcliffe-Maud, Mallaby, Robinson, Bains and Widdicombe. Research for the Maud Committee reported that 'councillors were unable to grasp any issues of complexity' and were 'at sea with the complicated financial matters'. The report bewailed 'abysmal standards of discussion' and even 'vulgar abuse' (Maud, 1967b: 43).

Jones, in his study of the councillors of Wolverhampton, argues that a dispassionate appraisal of calibre is extremely difficult to make. Outstanding figures were found to come from all classes (Jones 1969: ch. 7). Moreover, the quality of representation 'is not susceptible to measurement' (Jones 1969: 162). The essence of democracy is that ordinary people remain in control of their lives. The fact that councillors may appear unexceptional to civil servants and technically minded local government officers is a matter of complete irrelevance. The essence of democracy is that the people govern themselves. The argument that they will be too stupid to do so is as old as democracy itself and will always be put by its opponents. When stripped of its gloss, the criticism that the calibre of councillors has fallen looks rather like an expression of a middle-class fear of working-class participation.

How representative are the representatives?

The microcosmic view of representation holds that councillors should be like their constituents. There is frequent criticism that this is not the case. The following sections examine the question in terms of age, class, race and gender.

Age

Figure 8.2 shows that councillors are generally older than those they represent, a disparity noted by the Maud Committee in the 1960s (1967b: ch. 2). This means that they will have different life experiences and in particular will be innocent of the youth unemployment which became part of working-class culture in the 1980s. Nor will they have endured the social tensions impacting on

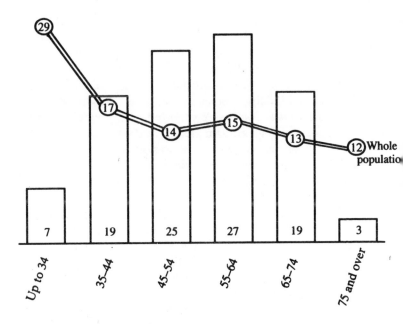

Figure 8.2 Age distribution of councillors in 1985 compared with the whole population (per cent). Source: data from Widdicombe, 1986c, table 2.3, p. 21.

today's adolescents, such as heavy policing, racial tension, riots and industrial disputes.

However, age can confer wisdom and experience. In politics those below the age of fifty are regarded as young (few ministers are younger) and MPs are expected to gain lengthy experience in some other walk of life (business, academia, trade unions and so on) before earning the right to stand.

Class
Notwithstanding the rise of Labour, councillors continue to display a disproportionately large endowment of middle-class characteristics such as home ownership, educational attainment (Figure 8.3), salary level and occupation. This is true even in predominantly working-class areas such as Sheffield. Although only a small proportion of Labour councillors are university educated (Rose, 1980: 58), the Maud Report revealed that manual workers comprised only 27 per cent of councillors and by the 1980s the Widdicombe

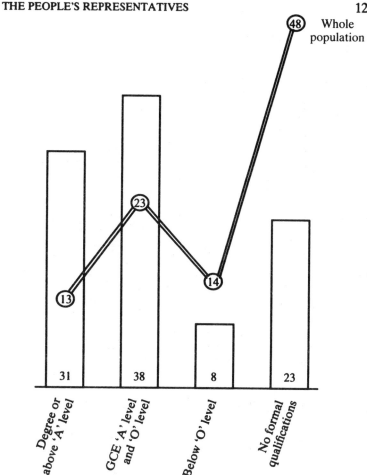

Figure 8.3 Educational attainment of councillors compared with the whole population (per cent). Source: Data from Widdicombe, 1986c, Table 2.8, p. 24.

Report noted a fall to 21 per cent (Widdicombe, 1968c: Table 4.5). Predictably, most working-class councillors belonged to the Labour Party and 8 per cent were unemployed (Widdicombe, 1986c: 39).

Race
Although there has been a gradual growth, the proportion of black people on councils remains, at some 1 per cent, well below

their national presence (4.2 per cent in the 1981 census). Britain has a racist political culture in which voters are disinclined to vote for black candidates and parties are disinclined to select them. Not surprisingly this contributes to a reluctance among black people to seek office. It is in the areas of highest black concentration that most black councillors are found, including inner London and the central wards of the decaying Victorian cities. Most belong to the Labour Party (Anwar, 1986) and, in spite of working-class and trade-union prejudice, they tend to see socialism as the philosophy most likely to promote racial equality (Ben-Tovim *et al.*, 1986: 72).

Gender

Although it may be decidedly cold comfort, the proportion of women found on local councils is higher than in Parliament.

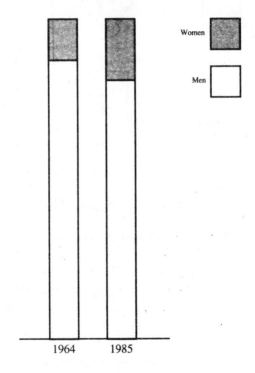

Figure 8.4 Proportion of women councillors in 1964 and 1985. Source: data from Widdicombe, 1986c, table 2.1, p. 19; Maud, 1967b, ch. 1.

Figure 8.4 shows a slight improvement since the Maud Report but, at 19 per cent, the representation of women remains lamentably below the logical 50 per cent. Scottish and Welsh authorities have a worse record than the English.

A distorting mirror?

It is apparent that the typical councillor is middle class, middle aged, white and male. However, is microcosmic representation all-important? The Burkean view insists that what matters is good judgement. The uneducated and under-privileged may well get a better deal if their case is presented by the articulate middle classes. The Maud Report reasoned:

> It is neither possible, nor in our opinion is it desirable, that councils should in some way be representative of all the varying interests, economic groups, income or educational levels in the community. (Maud, 1967a: 143)

In the final analysis, however, one must ask whether representatives can really understand the conditions of their constituents without direct experience. Does a white man know what it is to be a victim of prejudice; is a middle-aged stockbroker able to empathise with an unemployed youth; how many earnest intellectuals from the polytechnics and universities understand the demoralization of the unskilled; what men can imagine the fears of women alone in the city centre? Aristotle argued that the wearer of the shoe knows better than the cobbler where it pinches. Without microcosmic representation the most altruistic of policies will carry the odour of paternalism. Yet the alternative is to open the council doors to the poor, unemployed and despised, as well as the well-heeled and politically street-wise. This is not a prospect that the establishment views with equanimity, which helps explain why local government is seen as such a problem for the central state.

The new breed

By the mid-1970s a new post-war generation had reached maturity and the 1974 reorganisation had seen increased political dynamism from urban councils. At the same time, a crisis developed within the Labour Party arising from the dissatisfaction felt by the left with the performances of the Wilson and Callaghan governments at Westminster. The idea grew that local government might become a more vital part of the political system, a vehicle for social change. These factors led to the emergence of a new kind of councillor, particularly in the Labour ranks: younger (generally below forty-five), more articulate, more self-confident, better educated and more assertive. Although they were generally white and male there was some improvement in the representation of women and, at twenty-three, Merle Amory of Brent Council was remarkable for being the youngest ever black woman councillor. The new councillors were able to form the vanguard of a New Urban Left movement which united a diverse collection of interests under a common banner, fighting for the welfare state and for local democracy (see pp. 234–9). A number of them became national celebrities, better known to the public than most MPs.

With the advent of the Thatcher government of 1979 and its declared intention to roll back the frontiers of the state, it became clear that local and central government were set on a collision course with no one in the signal box (see Chapter 14). The developments were alarming to the centralist establishment, including the media and both major parties. To the right the new breed constituted the 'loony left', wild-eyed zealots to whom 'politics is an obsession and a power game' (Henney, 1984: 323). Labour moderates were also embarrassed, the young turks even being likened to 'Nazi storm-troopers' (Gladden, 1987). However, as we shall see in subsequent chapters, the new breed was to influence all aspects of local politics in the 1980s.

Tools for the job

Britain makes notoriously poor provision for its elected representatives. Conditions for MPs in the House of Commons compare unfavourably with those of other European assemblies and those in the US (Batty and George, 1985). Councillors fare even worse, only 56 per cent of authorities providing the council leader with an office, and only 14 per cent providing one for committee chairpersons. A mere 40 per cent make accommodation available for councillors' surgeries. Although the position is better in those authorities where more assertive political styles prevail, councillors generally lack both secretarial services and research and library support, and receive little training. There are even problems with simple things such as access to headed notepaper, photocopying facilities, filing cabinets and coffee-makers (Association of Councillors, 1987). The issue here is not that certain individuals are denied the finer things in life; it is that local democracy is devalued by a culture which does not conduce respect for the people's representatives. Nothing illustrates this problem better than the issue of salaries.

Remunerating the representatives

Unlike MPs, local representatives are expected to operate as amateurs. This is not merely a minor inconvenience, it is a matter of deep constitutional significance. Such payments as are made to councillors come in the form of allowances to compensate for loss of earnings and for subsistence (travel, meals and so on). The 1974 reorganisation introduced attendance allowances for approved duties (meetings, seeing constituents and so on) and the 1980 Local Government Planning and Land Act provided discretionary allowances for special responsibilities such as committee chairs or council leader. Yet the average annual attendance allowance claimed in 1984–5 was £852, a mere 0.1 per cent of total local authority expenditure. Claims were higher in the metropolitan counties (£1,853) and their districts (£1,306) (Widdicombe, 1986b: ch. 3).

Not only are the allowances derisory, they have actually fallen behind inflation, and the proportion allocated to dealing with electors' problems and attending party meetings has fallen, even though these are among the most important aspects of the work. Moreover, allowances are liable to taxation and can adversely affect rights to welfare benefits, as well as holiday and pension entitlements.

Some urban councils have sought to circumvent the problem. The judicious use of attendance allowances enabled councillors (allegedly hundreds: Grigsby, 1985), to function in a virtually full-time capacity (though very low paid for the level of responsibility). To this was added the practice of 'twin-tracking', whereby councillors of one authority would be 'employed' in another (see

p. 167). However, such methods are essentially undignified, placing councillors in a position of poachers rather than gamekeepers. Even a system of allowances, however generous, is fundamentally different to the idea of a positive right to payment.

The case for the amateur

A number of rather unconvincing arguments have been advanced to justify non-payment. It is suggested that payment would, in some way, attract the 'wrong sort'. The issue was addressed directly by the Robinson Committee on the Remuneration of Councillors (1977), which rejected the idea of the fully professional councillor on the grounds that it would compromise the cherished 'voluntary principle' and harm the relationships of councillors with both electors and officers. Yet we do not hear the suggestion that payment of company directors, brain surgeons, stockbrokers or even government ministers will attract the wrong sort.

The Widdicombe Committee also pondered the question, but feared that payment would make councillors too involved in the work of the authority: 'Councillors . . . should seek to leave the day to day management of . . . services as far as possible to officers' (Widdicombe, 1986a: 127). Moreover, it was recommended that leave from work for council business for public sector employees be restricted to no more than twenty-six days a year. The argument was expressed in terms of saving public money (Widdicombe, 1986a: 136), a helpful indication of the price placed by the establishment on democracy, and was accepted by government as a means of curbing twin-tracking (Department of the Environment, 1988: 9).

However, Widdicombe (1986a: 132) conceded that 'current levels of allowance are substantially below what they should be'. It recommended a system comprising two elements: first, a basic flat-rate allowance to replace the attendance and earnings-loss elements with a variable rate ranging from £1,500 for a small shire district to £4,000 for a large urban area, and secondly, a statutory rather than a discretionary special responsibility allowance. The government response was to argue for the preservation of the voluntary spirit (Department of the Environment, 1988: 6). However, the flat-rate principle was accepted as a replacement for the attendance and financial loss allowances, payable to all councillors regardless of activity level. The special responsibility allowance remained, but was to be restricted by a refusal to increase the total level paid out, thus reducing the possibility of the emergence of 'full-timers'.

The case for the professional

It was the Wheatley Royal Commission on Local Government in Scotland (always more generous in the operation of the allowances system) which admitted the case for salaried councillors. This would be 'the simplest, least invidious and generally most satisfactory way of dealing with the real problem' (Wheatley, 1969: 214–15).

On occasions the state seems more than willing to concede the principle of payment. Chairmen of nationalised industries have received huge salaries on the grounds of attracting the best person for the job. Indeed, those given non-elected policy making roles in rival local state agencies can be paid. Chairpersons of district health authorities receive salaries, and the Chairman of Sheffield Development Corporation received £16,000 per annum for one-and-a-half days' work a week (*The Independent*, 8 September 1990).

Payment of councillors could transform local democracy out of all recognition. It could be expected to encourage more able people to come forward, increase representation of the poorer classes (manual workers, women, ethnic minorities) and stimulate greater public interest in local affairs. The ultimate effect could be a significant decentralisation of power from the Whitehall–Westminster hothouse. Why is reform resisted?

Amateurs only

The official attitude is quintessentially an English one where, in many walks of life, amateur status is an indication of superiority. Professional cricketers and tennis-players, for example, have had to fight for self-respect and, to this day, rugby league attracts sneers from rugby union, where players remain amateurs. The insistence that an activity be labelled 'amateurs only' is one of many social exclusion rites practised to preserve the 'English way of life'. The continued hegemony of the lordly Whitehall generalists over the specialists from the non-Oxbridge universities vividly illustrates the process at the very epicentre of the state (Ponting, 1986: 70). It creates enclaves which those without means cannot enter and impedes mass entry as effectively as the officials positioned at the gates to the Ascot Royal Enclosure. Indeed, until as recently as 1964 even MPs received only the equivalent of part-time salaries.

Exclusion represents a fundamental threat to democracy; working-class people do not stand because they cannot afford to. Moreover, where they do appear on councils, they are obliged to work with middle-class people on very high salaries (officers, civil servants, pressure groups representatives and so on), placing them at a psychological disadvantage and reducing their authority.

Conclusion – the private public state: trespassers will be persecuted

It is clear that, although councillors are the key figures in local democracy, they labour under many impediments. This is not surprising in a state which is highly centralised and elitist. The beleaguered history of the trade unions and Labour Party testify to the problem of working-class penetration of the state. The establishment sees local government as its Achilles heel. Hence it is not surprising that it takes place in a political culture constantly dismissive of the role of the councillor.

Councillors do not stand alone on the town hall stage. Behind them moves a vast chorus in the form of a permanent bureaucracy without which they can make few moves. This will be examined in the following chapter.

9

Municipal Mandarins – The Local Bureaucracy

Local government and administration is traditionally a labour-intensive activity. Today local authorities are large-scale employers of almost 3 million people. The town hall bureaucracies may be seen as local civil services; employees are permanent, technically apolitical and engaged and promoted on the basis of merit. However, the bureaucratic role is by no means merely technical; like the senior civil servants, who rub pin-striped shoulders with ministers of Her Majesty's Government, the senior officers inhabit a political world of intrigue and power. They may be aptly dubbed the 'municipal mandarins'.

This chapter starts by considering the structure of local bureaucracy and then examines the role of those who inhabit its upper reaches. Some key debates are addressed, including the effects of professionalism, the specialist–generalist dilemma, the extent to which bureaucrats share the characteristics of the community they serve, and their relationship with their Whitehall cousins. It concludes with a discussion on the internal politics of bureaucracy.

Implementing the community will

From earliest times parish government entailed more than the making of collective decisions; there was work to be done. The fabric of the church required maintenance, roads and bridges had to be built and repaired, paupers needed assistance, law and order was to be maintained and so on. Initially members of the local community would take turns to play their part but before long it became expedient, particularly for the wealthy of the larger towns, to pay others to do things for them and the idea of a municipal labour force developed. The upheavals of industrialisation dramatically increased the scale of the operation, promoting a professionalisation which was to become a hallmark of municipal employment. Lawyers, civil engineers, accountants and so on found themselves in rapidly enlarging professional empires, investing them with power and prestige as junior partners of the bourgeoisie.

Departments galore

One of the most characteristic features of local authorities is the way they are divided up into separate departments, each responsible for clearly defined functions. These departments may be broadly dichotomised as *vertical* or *horizontal* (or line and staff). The former deliver services directly to the community (education, housing or social services), while the latter are essentially parasitic, serving not the public but other departments (finance, personnel, or estates) (see Figure 9.1).

There are two reasons for the departmental organisation. Historically many key services developed independently, administered variously by *ad hoc* bodies, voluntary societies and even private undertakings, so that a tradition of separateness was woven into the culture of the system even as the model of the all-purpose authority was fashioned. Secondly, because Parliament has often wanted to ensure that a new service will receive due attention, legislation has demanded separate dedicated machinery. As recently as 1968 the Seebohm Report on local authority and allied personal social services recommended that each authority have a social services department (Seebohm Report, 1968). Alternatively, statutes may lay down that there should be a chief officer or a special committee (for instance, for police) and such demands imply a separate department.

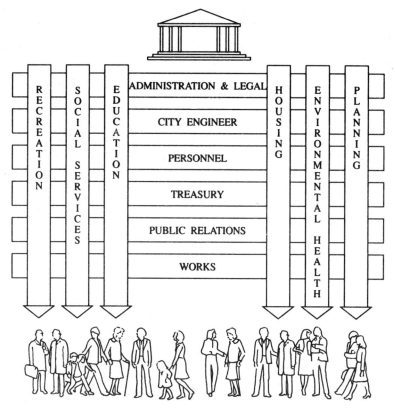

The community as voters, citizens, clients, customers and so on

Figure 9.1   Vertical and horizontal departments

Local government by committee

Wedded to the departmental structure is the council committee structure, another long-standing tradition. At the beginning of the century two great chroniclers of English local government wrote:

> An English town council is . . . a deliberative body, too large and unwieldy for the work of administration. Therefore let it be divided in order that it may govern . . . The Town Council forms itself into standing committees. (Redlich and Hirst, 1903)

The fragmented management structure can give a number of advantages: it provides a focus for loyalty which would not be so easily given to a huge organisation (the departments often field football and other teams); it produces a sense of *esprit de corps* for members of professions; it provides a career avenue for those wishing to specialise in particular policy areas; and it gives the public clear points of access.

Inside the departments

Like all bureaucracies, departments are organised hierarchically, individuals being accorded different status levels. At the top sits the chief officer, supported by various layers of assistant chief officers and lower professional grades, through a blue collar range to the clericals. Not all employees are located in the town hall; there are large armies in the field, including the police, social workers, teachers, park-keepers, manual workers repairing roads and buildings and so on (see Figure 9.2).

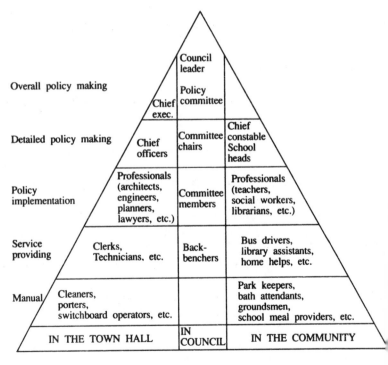

Figure 9.2 Working for the local authority.

Municipal mandarins

The focus of this chapter is on those occupying the top left quadrant of Figure 9.2. These are the senior officers (known as the administrative, technical and professional grades) whose working life brings them into daily contact with the putative masters of local government: the councillors. At the very top of the local bureaucracy stands a lone figure, the chief executive. Below him (rarely her) are the heads of the various departments.

The chief executive

This term has been in common currency since the reorganisation of 1974. The formal role is that of bureaucratic supremo, one who oversees and directs the entire work of the authority. The position has evolved from that of the town or county clerk, a Dickensian figure who rose to prominence in the nineteenth century when one of the most important municipal professions was law. His art was to ensure that the authority would not stray onto the treacherous swamps marked *ultra vires*. However, the passage of the twentieth century was to render this cautious servant an anachronism, cutting a poor figure against the dynamic 'city managers' of the US. The cry of reformers was for a more entrepreneurial view of the role, analogous to the image of a private sector managing director.

The call of the Maud Report on management (1967a), to be echoed by the Bains Report (1972), was for an end to the lawyers' monopoly and, after the 1974 reorganisation, most authorities appointed a chief executive of some kind. Indeed, some permitted the combination of the post with that of treasurer, creating a position with enormous potential. In 1986 the Widdicombe Report (1986a: 144) went even further in the call for a strong, private-sector-style manager, but central government resisted this for fear that the power would be hijacked by the ruling party groups. In practice the power exercised is often more modest than the 'Chief Executive' nameplate on the door implies. Though the quill pen has been superseded by the fibre-tip, the occupant of the municipal room at the top is not so different from his nineteenth-century forebear.

Chief officers

Like chief executives, the officers heading the departments are characteristically middle-class, middle-aged, white males. Each will have worked his way up from the lower ranks within a single functional area, although as 'cosmopolitans' they will probably have moved through various authorities across the country in a promotion-seeking spiral. Their work is complex, involving policy formation, public relations, departmental management and liaising with other departments, local authorities and central government. In addition, they work closely with councillors: advising, providing information and interpreting policy. Chief officers do not necessarily enjoy co-equal status, their standing tending to reflect the nature and importance of their departments. Heading them all is the treasurer, overseeing all other departments through expenditure implications; similarly, the voice of the head of the legal department rarely goes unheeded. It will be seen later that the Thatcher strategy of weakening local government placed certain chief officers in a particularly vulnerable position as their budgets and functions were cut.

Professionals' paradise

Local government bureaucracy is characterised by an exceedingly high level of professionalism, which has profound implications for local democracy. A profession is an occupational community with certain characteristics, including a monopoly of esoteric knowledge, control of recruitment and training, powers to exclude those defined as 'unqualified', a central association administering rules of conduct and an ethical code usually stressing the responsibility of members to clients and the public at large (Wilensky, 1964). The political result of these factors is great power for the professions as pressure groups.

Professionals in large organisations have dual obligations. In addition to loyalty to the organisation itself they have a loyalty to the profession generally, usually expressed in the form of membership of an association (Johnson, 1972). In local government, professions can be placed in two broad categories: those with a well-developed structure extending beyond the town halls, which may be termed the *autonomous professions*, and those largely confined within the municipal sphere, the *dependent professions*. This has political implications for their respective roles and power.

The autonomous professions

These are well established and include the venerable professions bestowing great social status such as law and accountancy, as well as newer ones such as architecture and surveying. Members are in a strong bargaining position for the following reasons:

(1)   Their associations, such as the Law Society and the RIBA, are very effective pressure groups.

(2)   They have an external reference point in wage and conditions-of-service negotiations.

(3)   They have a private-sector bolt-hole to escape to if municipal life gets tough. Indeed, architects and lawyers are loath to work for local government and have to be enticed.

(4)   In decision making they can refer to wider professional–technical considerations which may be argued to override municipal contingencies.

As a result, these professions enjoy high status in local government (matched by high salaries). They must be treated with kid gloves, their personal self-interests duly considered in all decision making.

The dependent professions

Some of the traditional professions have specialised local government sections such as the Chartered Institute of Public Finance and Accountancy (CIPFA). However, for a number of professions local government, with its characteristic functions, provides an administrative ecosystem without which they would perish. Thus, for example, there are no town planners in the private sector since the function has been exclusive to the state. (The existence of the UDCs questions this tradition.) Similarly, local government is the near-exclusive employer of social workers, public health inspectors, municipal engineers, teachers, police, inspectors of weights and measures and so on.

Members of this category are more vulnerable in political terms. They are generally unable to claim the protection of well-established elite groups; the National Union of Teachers, for example, cannot aspire to the authority of the Law Society. Individuals unhappy with their lot cannot easily abandon ship for the private sector. The result is that they tend to have less status, receive lower salaries, are obliged to endure inferior conditions of work and generally lack security in their working lives. They are certainly the most queasy when the language of redundancy is being spoken. It is a cruel irony that these professions tend to be those reflecting the social, caring role which has given local government its essential character in the post-war era.

On top or on tap – specialists and generalists

A long-standing debate in public administration concerns the distinction between the role and status of specialists (qualified professionals) and generalists (well-educated individuals without particular professional qualifications). Whitehall has a tradition of domination by generalists from the public school–Oxbridge establishment but, in local government, the opposite is the case. Here tradition reserves the elite positions for specialists. The reasons for this are partly historical in that nineteenth-century municipal growth was geared to the provision of technical services needed to keep the pistons and wheels of industry running smoothly. In addition, the Benthamite centralist view saw local government as *implementing* centrally determined policy, rather than *shaping* it. Thus the local–central relationship becomes a spatial manifestation of the specialist–generalist relationship within Whitehall – central government proposes, local government disposes.

Yet the tradition poses serious problems. The fact that chief officers are professionally qualified does not necessarily ensure they will be good managers, policy makers or leaders; indeed, the reverse is likely. Specialists are by definition blinkered, unlikely to appreciate the goals of other departments and may lack a wider communal vision. The problem was recognised by the Herbert Commission which argued:

> The view of the expert can become too narrow. Professional enthusiasm can carry the expert beyond the bounds of good judgement. (Herbert, 1960)

A further problem is that experts can be 'blinded by their skill' (Hill, 1974: 89), seeing problems in technical (rather than political) terms, which leads to a belief that all can be solved if only people will harken to their Delphic utterances. This amounts to professional arrogance, an arch enemy of democracy; the natural inclination of experts is away from popular involvement. They become elitist 'urban managers', paternalistically shaping the lives of the ordinary people they are supposed to serve (Dennis, 1972; Pahl, 1975).

In 1966 the problem was addressed by the Mallaby Committee on staffing in local government, which recommended that a position of 'lay administrator' be recognised, affording similar status, promotion prospects and opportunities as the professionals. Lay administrators would come from universities, with degrees in the arts, humanities and sciences. This led in 1967 to the setting up by the local authority associations of a Local Government Training Board to encourage the training of lay administrators. In addition, generalist courses have developed in institutions of higher education, including degree programmes in public administration in polytechnics. At the University of Birmingham, an Institute of Local Government Studies was established to offer high-level courses in management and administration.

Of course it is possible, with training, for specialists in top positions to experience conversion; to cast off their professional blinkers and widen their vision. However, this cannot be guaranteed to solve the problem because the remaining professionals within the department continue to form the dominant culture and press the technocratic imperatives in policy formation (Malpass, 1975).

Representative bureaucracy?

Because local government officers have a major responsibility in providing for the collective consumption needs of ordinary people it might be argued that they should be expected to have some empathy with the recipients. However, the professional bias militates against representative bureaucracy. Recruitment and promotion is formally based on the principle of merit, with much emphasis on the passing of examinations.

Class

Unlike the civil service, local government has not skimmed its recruits from the *crême de la crême* of society. Before the Second World War recruitment was from schools and those appointed would work towards some specialist qualification. The effect of the 1944 Education Act was to make grammar schools the main avenue to a municipal career but, with increased university opportunities for lower-middle-class children from the 1960s, this source dried up. Consequently, there was an increased recruitment of graduates, who expect to enter at relatively high grades, thereby reducing the promotion prospects for those coming directly from school.

Hence, today local government administration lies in the hands of the lower middle classes, those from 'respectable' backgrounds who have 'made it' in individualistic terms. Many of these deliberately break their links with those they left behind on the great meritocratic ladder. Even those who retain a sense of commitment may betray the paternalism which can lend the welfare state something of the cold touch of charity.

Gender – *homo municipalis*

Women are particularly high consumers of the services of local government. While they may not populate the artificial pistes or municipal golf courses, they are the mothers of the millions of children in the schools, they care for the elderly in need of social services, they are the euphemistically named 'single parents' and they bear the brunt of the social upheavals attendant upon family sickness, unemployment and crime. Accordingly, there is a strong case for their representation at the highest bureaucratic levels. Yet, while in the nether regions of the clerical grades the keyboards of the word processors vibrate beneath feminine fingers, and while the splendid municipal offices are kept clean by vigorous female arms, the seats around the important meeting tables are warmed predominantly by male buttocks. The decisions affecting the lives of women in the community are made by male minds, shaped by male perceptions. Although authorities nominally pursue equal opportunities policies, the organisation of work in local government remains geared to the idea of the family (Cockburn, 1977b), with the male hunter/worker freely available from nine to five, and guaranteed to be in working order by an unpaid nurse/cook/mistress/nanny.

Not surprisingly, this male municipal world has been slow to take the medicine it needs in the form of crêches, maternity leave, flexible hours, job-sharing and so on. The women's movement, often working through local authority Women's Committees, has begun to press for fairer policies and some, particularly those in inner London, have endeavoured to respond with special appointments to deal with women's issues (Goss, 1984). However, within Britain's patriarchal society, they have been dubbed the 'loony left', mocked and described as sexually inadequate, unattractive, lesbian and so on. This derision is one of the main weapons of the English, class-based establishment; it comes from the same source, and serves the same purpose, as the mockery of working-class councillors, trade union leaders and so on. Encouraged by the media, the working class itself is among the worst offenders, their women continuing to believe that office cleaning and clerical work is somehow as natural for them in the municipal world as is childbirth in the biological world.

Race

Britain has a racist culture with strong anti-black sentiments evidenced variously in the euphoric support for the proclamations of Enoch Powell, racially motivated violence, and in voting behaviour. An important manifestation is institutionalised racism, and local government is one of its major sites. Before the 1970s it was blatant. Black people were denied rights to health care, social services, housing and education (Ouseley, 1984), though latterly progressive Labour authorities have begun to improve opportunities. Yet professional officers have a natural tendency to resist race initiatives in policy since these will be seen as politically, rather than technocratically, motivated. They will find it easy to dismiss them as 'flavour-of-the-month' gimmicks which must not be allowed to disturb their grand strategies. In the meantime black people in the inner cities form a new underclass marked by poverty and demoralisation (Ouseley, 1984: 135; Benyon and Solomos, 1987).

Although black people feature prominently among the clientele of the welfare state they are not represented proportionately in local bureaucracies. In Liverpool, for example, with a 7 per cent black population, there were 272 black employees out of a total work-force of some 30,000; that is, just 0.9 per cent (Ben-Tovim *et al.*, 1986: 42). Even where black unemployment is high there are few black careers officers. And where black people are employed by the local authority, they are less likely to be designing one-way systems and shopping precincts than digging or sweeping them. It is of course natural that the highly professionalised nature of local administration will legitimate the exclusion of black people; educational disadvantages prevent them acquiring the vital certificates which are the keys to the door of the bureaucratic world.

Ideological disposition

It might be argued that the non-representative nature of local bureaucracy is compensated by a commitment to social democracy. However, the fetish of professionalism tends to screen out those who have studied arts, humanities and social sciences in favour of architects, civil engineers, accountants, lawyers and so on, so that the idea that public administration can have an ethical mission is largely submerged, leaving an ever-present threat of overbearing, insensitive local officialdom. The reality of this is recognised in the creation of special officials to deal with citizens' complaints: Local Commissioners for Administration.

The citizen and the local administration

In 1967 Parliament established the office of Parliamentary Commissioner for Administration (PCA), or Ombudsman, to deal with citizens' complaints of what was termed maladministration by the hand of the state. During parliamentary debate on this, there were arguments for placing local government as well as the civil service within the jurisdiction of the PCA but these were rejected on the grounds that Parliament was not directly responsible. However, the climate gradually changed so that a local system came into operation in 1974. The Local Commissioners for Administration, three for England (each responsible for defined regions) and one for Wales, are appointed by the Queen on the advice of the Environment Secretary. In 1976 a commissioner for Scotland was added.

Aggrieved citizens may approach commissioners directly or through a councillor. When the investigation is completed, reports are sent to the complainant and the authority concerned, which is obliged to make a copy available to the public for three weeks. The commissioners are granted various powers and immunities. They can employ experts as advisers and can call for any persons and papers deemed relevant. It is an offence to hinder them in any way and they cannot be sued for defamation of character. However, there are various 'no-go' areas, including the conduct of courts in criminal proceedings, actions taken in the prevention of crime (freeing much police activity from scrutiny), commercial transactions, transport operations, docks administration, industrial establishments, entertainment administration, markets, personnel matters and certain aspects of education. The effect of these is to confuse the average citizen and undermine confidence in the system (Lewis *et al.*, 1986: 25).

Perhaps the greatest restriction lies in the elusive concept of maladministration itself, which defies precise definition. The general effect is to focus on questions of procedure rather than the main cause of grievance, the nature of a decision reached; indeed, only approximately 10 per cent of complaints are eligible for full investigation. In 1977 a report from the prestigious association of jurists, Justice (Widdicombe, 1977), recommended that the definition be extended to include 'unreasonable, unjust, or oppressive decisions', but this was stoutly resisted by the ever-defensive bureaucrats.

In the final analysis the local ombudsmen have no power (other than a second admonishing report) to compel an offending authority to comply and in a significant number of cases redress is not given. The Widdicombe Report recommended that the findings be legally enforcible (1986a: paras 5.76–99) but this was rejected in favour of the less compelling injunction that reasons for non-compliance be published.

Public knowledge of the system remains low. Moreover, those most vulnerable to the cold shoulder of officialdom are likely to be among the less articulate: the old, young, poor, handicapped, members of ethnic minorities and so on. There is no way of knowing how great is the mountain of suffering caused by the insolence of office and the law's delay before this white, male, middle-class face of the local state.

Municipal village – the politics of bureaucracy

Town halls are not the tranquil tea-drinking havens of popular myth. Local bureaucracies are like villages dominated by gossip, rumour, petty jealousies and a knife-in-the-back political subculture in which the inhabitants vie with each other for resources, power and prestige. Municipal village life is about who gets what, when, how. The combatants can be organisations, including the departments themselves, or individuals. We examine each below.

Interdepartmental wars

The departments are very visible rivals. They will battle for the resources of finance and personnel, growing fat by assuming new responsibilities, and even taking each other over with voracious acts of bureaucratic cannibalism. This competition can be seen either as a healthy demonstration of the free-market spirit or as wasteful. Most management writing has passed the latter verdict. 'Departmentalism' has been portrayed as one of the great evils of local administration, generating enervating internal strife and duplication (for example the social services and education departments may both collect the same data on families), and precluding an integrated, or corporate, strategy (see Chapter 12). Departmentalism is usually bad for policy outcomes; a study by Davies (1981), for example, showed how competition for control over industrial policy damaged the overall programme by dissipating responsibility.

Various factors fuel interdepartmental conflict. There is professional jealousy as well as the search for security of jobs and income. This became particularly acute in the 1980s, when centrally imposed cuts led some departments (those concerned with education, housing and social services) to feel particularly vulnerable while others (such as finance and law) could relax, smug in the knowledge that accountants are needed whether one is spending or saving, hiring or firing.

Intradepartmental wars

Rather less documented than the interdepartmental battles are those enacted behind closed oak doors. Of course individuals working together will always find cause for disagreement as a result of petulance and personality clashes but, beyond this, there are certain conflict-producing structural features including the following:

(1) *Structural fragmentation.* The departments are by no means seamless. The giant social services empires, for example, were formed from a number of smaller departments which retain old traditions and values. There are various reasons for departmental subdivision (decentralised administration, professional specialism, and so on) and the sections develop a kind of mini-departmentalism, with all the symptoms of the full-blown variety of the disease (Young and Mills, 1983).

(2) *Ideas versus hierarchy.* The high degree of professionalisation runs counter to the formal model of bureaucratic hierarchy (Dunleavy, 1980: 119). It is an organisational truism that the wrong people get to the top, either because they disliked the real work of the department or, more usually, because they were incompetent and wished to escape to less-exacting work. At the same time their colleagues, the good teachers, social workers, architects, accountants and so on, happy in their work, do not apply for top administrative jobs. Consequently, when ideas are required, those occupying the senior positions are obliged to turn to those below, or press their own inferior solutions. Either way there is cause for friction and tension.

(3) *Contraction pains.* In the boom years, or even during the reorganisation period from 1974, rapid promotion to heady heights could be gained by promising, or lucky, newcomers. However, the political pressures of the late 1970s and 1980s changed matters. Some in the dependent professions (social workers, teachers, housing managers, planners and so on) were faced with the bleakly beckoning finger of redundancy. Tensions arose when their colleagues in the safer professions took upon themselves the function of Thatcherite hatchet-persons in looking for cuts in their services.

(4) *Intraprofessional rivalry.* A characteristic of the professions is a lack of homogeneity in attitudes and ideas; it is in their nature to contain various competing schools of thought. In addition, there are differences between the generations; the old guard find their orthodoxies challenged by the young turks from the colleges and universities.

Conclusion – professionalism under a cloud

Life in the bureaucratic villages was subject to some rude shocks from the mid-1970s. The post-war consensus had seen substantial agreement over social and economic policy. Crosland's *The Future of Socialism* (1965) was a paean to a brave new social democratic world in which the state had all the answers. Educational equality for all was an accepted goal, the need for mass public housing was beyond dispute, roads (including urban motorways) were necessary arteries for a new car-owning democracy, the nineteenth-century slums should be cleared and flats could mushroom in the cities to create a futuristic high-rise Utopia. At the same time, society's losers were to be cushioned with a comprehensive welfare state.

Within this broad area of harmony the professions were largely free to peddle their technological nostrums. As arch-priests of the welfare state, they could feel wanted, with jobs and salaries as secure as the foundations of the Victorian municipal cathedrals they inhabited. However, clouds had been gathering on the bureaucratic horizon.

Doubting the technological fix

In 1968, to the horror of the nation, high-rise flats at Ronan Point collapsed, and with this deeply symbolic tragedy confidence that the state could deliver the technological fix to society's problems also began to crumble. It became apparent that a housing boom, involving every major house-building authority, had littered the physical and social landscape with hundreds of thousands of hideous, hated, expensive, high-rise, low-amenity dwellings (Dunleavy, 1980: 122–3), while at the same time decimating inner-city communities with a brutality surpassing the efforts of the German Luftwaffe. The result was a legitimacy crisis in public housing and a loss of public confidence in experts in general. In a number of highly publicised cases social workers were castigated for failures to protect children at risk. Black Papers adduced widespread illiteracy as evidence of failures in education. The television drama documentary *Cathy Come Home* stirred the national conscience about the plight of the homeless and the 'rediscovery of poverty' by Peter Townsend and colleagues detailed appalling conditions in the inner cities where multiple deprivation mocked the social engineering skills of the professionals. Analyses of the impact of town planning generally concluded that the proposed solutions were always tending to be in the economic, social and political interests of dominant social groups rather than the great urban masses (Castells, 1977: 44).

With a mood of disillusionment about, the mass media were happy to fan the flames with alarmist stories from the streets, schools and old people's homes. Senior bureaucracts entered a crisis with pressures from below and above.

Pressure from below

Changing recruitment patterns since the 1960s had led to new attitudes from staff lower down in the departmental hierarchies. The increased proportion of graduates meant that they were generally better qualified than their superiors who had worked their way up on the basis of long service. The new generation was more assertive and self-confident and generally less amenable to top-down (authoritarian) management styles. Matters reached a head in the 1980s with an increase in union activity. Although the actions of the manual workers' unions attracted much attention, particularly during the 1977 'winter of discontent', teachers and social workers also waged bitter struggles. Even the hitherto staid National and Local Government Officers Association resorted to industrial action, working to rule and taking to the streets.

Pressure from above – the New Right assault

New Right thinking, which provided much of the ideological underpinning of the Thatcher strategy, was strongly opposed to bureaucracy *per se*. William Niskanen (1971) was one of the most vociferous on this theme. For him there were two sets of actors in the process of providing state services, corresponding to the sellers and buyers in the economic market: the bureaucrats supplying, and the politicians demanding. The former are driven by a desire to maximise their budgets and the latter their votes. The outcome is a dizzy, uncontrollable, upwards spiral towards 'over-supply'. Local officials were seen as drones, placing their own career prospects before those of their clients and the beleaguered taxpayers. Hence, though the party may not have ended in the mid-1970s, the pretty balloons were certainly bursting by the early 1980s (Laffin and Young, 1985). Cuts in funding and resources, a reduction in functions and general disparagement of local government left officers with diminished career prospects, reduced self-esteem, lowered motivation, and eroded self-confidence.

This chapter has shown that municipal mandarins have great potential to affect the lives of ordinary citizens. Yet they are unrepresentative of them and have no acquaintance with the ballot box. In theory this is no problem for local democracy because they are neutral instruments of the political will, under the control of the elected representatives. Or are they? Constitutional prescriptions are often mocked by reality. This chapter has not said the last word on the place of bureaucrats in local politics. The full picture cannot be seen without a deeper inspection of their relationship with their putative masters, the councillors. This is the issue to be addressed in the following chapter.

10

Power in the Town Hall

The officers and councillors examined in the preceding chapters do not act in separate corners delivering solitary monologues; they share centre stage and conduct dialogue which lies at the heart of the drama. The key issue is where the power lies. The chapter begins with a consideration of Weber's 'dictatorship of the official' thesis and its application to local government. It then examines the growth of official power in the post-war era, from the heady days of the social democratic consensus to a darker era of fiscal crisis. It also considers the power implications of management style. Next the chapter outlines how the rise of the New Urban Left in the 1980s sought to increase the power of councillors and examines the central government response to this. In the final section, an uncertain future is pondered.

Official threats

A hallowed principle of Britain's constitution is that state officials will be the compliant instruments of elected politicians. In 1960 the Herbert Commission declared: 'The control of the expert by the amateur representing his fellow citizens is the key to the whole of our system of government'. Without this condition representative democracy is a sham. It would be not democracy, but bureaucracy in its most pejorative sense of 'rule by officials'. Around the turn of the century, the great liberal sociologist Max Weber (1864–1920) observed with some anxiety: 'It is obvious that technically the large modern state is absolutely dependent upon a bureaucratic basis' (Weber, 1978: 971). There are good grounds to fear the power of full-time career bureaucrats for they possess the following potent resources:

(1) *Permanence*. This brings experience, an unchallengeable familiarity with the administrative machine and a detailed historical knowledge of policy.

(2) *Expertise*. Officials are generally better educated than the politicians, particularly when the latter are from working-class backgrounds.

(3) *Size*. They vastly outnumber the politicians and can work together within and across departmental boundaries.

(4) *Social status*. Officials are often of a higher social class than the politicians (more likely with working-class representatives).

(5) *Information*. They control the flow of one of bureaucracy's most valuable currencies: information.

(6) *The executive role*. Their formal function of putting policies into practice affords an opportunity to influence policy outcome and gives irresistible grounds for a say in policy making, since they understand the limits of feasibility.

Controlling officials – an ideal bureaucracy

As a liberal (favouring limited government) Weber was instinctively opposed to the 'big government' characteristic of the social democratic state. However, while others feared the dictatorship of the proletariat predicted by Marx, Weber feared a 'dictatorship of the official' (Gerth and Wright Mills, 1957: 50). His mission was to find a way of curbing such power and his method was to propose an 'ideal-type' model of a bureaucracy as a guide for behaviour in the real world. In this, members would be placed within a structure of constraints designed to keep them on the constitutional straight and narrow. They were to be permanently employed by the state (rather than the government of the day), recruited and promoted entirely on the basis of merit (rather than nepotism or political allegiance), bound by clear rules, expected to play rigidly defined roles and placed within a hierarchy of discipline channelling all authority to the elected representatives at the very top. The 'ideal-type' bureaucrats would be politically neutral servants.

Today modern bureaucracies do approximate to this ideal type. Much orthodox liberal democratic writing, as well as many declarations by actual practitioners, pays tribute to the real-world impartiality of state servants. It is a necessary part of the modern theory of the democratic state. How true is it?

Who makes policy?

The theory of the compliant bureaucracy is based on the idea that politics (that is, policy making) and administration (that is, policy implementation) are distinctive and separate activities. This politics–administration dichotomy lies at the heart of much writing and thinking about politics and the state. As a normative principle it has been extremely useful in eliminating corruption in Britain (the Northcote–Trevelyan reforms), America (the Pendleton Herring reforms) and elsewhere.

Though not always explicit, it can be found in much official writing on local government. The Maud Report stated: 'It is the members who should take and be responsible for the key decisions on objectives . . . It is the officer who should direct and co-ordinate the necessary action . . . ' (Maud, 1967a; vol. 1, para. 145), while the Bains Report (1972) was underscored by an insistent drumbeat calling for maximum delegation of implementation to the lowest possible levels of bureaucracy. In June 1990 the Thatcher-created Audit Commission, in a draft of advice to local authorities, urged that members 'concentrate on major policy issues and keep out of operational management, which should be mostly delegated to officers' (Hedley, 1990: 1).

If we can believe in the politics–administration dichotomy we can feel confidence in modern democracy. However, as a description of what actually happens in the real world it is essentially naïve. Although much of the formal rhetoric acknowledges the distinction (such as meetings in which the councillors officially 'make' decisions), informal processes ensure that the two activities are entwined like stems of dense bindweed. In the process of implementation, policy directives must always be interpreted in the light of particular contingencies on the basis of the judgement and discretion of officials. This in itself amounts to a policy making role. Moreover, policy cannot be made without knowledge of implementation. David Blunkett, one-time leader of Sheffield City Council, argued that 'changing policies is about knowing whether they're working and being able to monitor and evaluate the success of what's taking place' (Baddeley and James, 1987).

Hence the reality of the policy making process in local government is that councillors and senior officers must work together. One of the most critical relationships is that between the committee chairs and chief officers, replicating many of the features of the minister–civil servant relationship at Whitehall. At the very apex of the organisational structure is the relationship between the chief executive and the council leader, which can be likened to that between Prime Minister and Head of the Civil Service.

'Yes councillor' – the member–officer interface

The upper echelons of the British civil service have been said to constitute 'one of the most powerful oligarchies in existence' (Gladden, 1967: 199), yet there are grounds for believing that local government officers exert even greater influence over their constitutional masters than the silken–tongued 'Sir Humphrey Applebys' of Whitehall.

The predominantly professional backgrounds of the senior officers mean that they have more specialist knowledge than the generalists who inhabit the Whitehall terrain, and membership of professional associations lends added authority to their technical arguments (Dunleavy, 1980: 117). Moreover, councillors, as part-time amateurs, lack the advantages of ministers who are full time, highly paid and served by sophisticated party machinery.

A committee chairperson can be virtually powerless before an uncooperative chief officer. The problem is intensified in the case of working-class councillors, professional arrogance leading some officers to resent them as managers *manqué*, intellectually out of their depth (Henney, 1984: 321–41). Officers can also use their affinity with Whitehall as a resource, appealing to the centre for support in disputes. This is particularly the case where central and local governments are of contrasting political persuasions.

Swamped and lost

The informal means whereby the local mandarins can frustrate the councillors are legion. One Labour councillor graphically told researchers of 'a subtle blend of bullshit and flannel' entailing writing, rewriting and reprocessing reports and advice until councillors feel swamped and lost (Newton, 1976: 156–7). Reports can be made too long to read or too numerous to handle and can be filled with obfuscating jargon, or may introduce deliberate error to waste time and divert attention from the key points. Wily officers can pack a committee agenda with insignificant matters to submerge controversial items, flatter councillors, withhold information, present advice in such a way that one favoured course of action appears irresistible, and complain that however brilliant the councillors' ideas may be they are too expensive or technically infeasible.

These are not new tricks, nor are they unique to municipal life: they were known in Chaucer's day, are used at Whitehall and even in the White House. They are standard gambits in the game of bureaucracy. However, the ordinary men and women who become councillors may not be prepared for them and may unwittingly become tame poodles rather than guard-dogs of the community interest.

Are they neutral?

The excessive power of officials is less of a threat if we can accept the neutral-state arguments that they will not favour one ideology, or class, over another. However, it can be argued that they are forced into roles which are essentially ideological. The nature of their training produces a cast of mind favouring a certain kind of policy. They are naturally inclined to shy away from 'extremes', and are loath to engage in 'political' unpleasantness, seeking smooth cooperation with central government, other public authorities and certain interests regarded as 'respectable'. All this adds up to a position located within a range from 'moderate conservatism to moderate Labourism' so that in their relations with councillors they will tend to push a line of caution and conservatism (Miliband, 1984: 140). However, this moderate tendency is itself a political position; indeed, it is one favoured by the English establishment which, under a guise of reasonableness, will resist any attempt to shift the status quo – a status quo favouring inequality and generally more sympathetic to the needs of capital than those of labour.

However, there are pressures to lean to the left as well as the right, and these are particularly strong in local government, with a large corps of bureaucrats dedicated to the provision of social services and committed to the 'big government' characteristic of social democracy. It was the recognition of this by thinkers of the New Right which contributed much to the dynamic of the Thatcher assault on local government in the 1980s (pp. 250–1).

Councillor power

Any idea that councillors are totally impotent in the politics of the town hall would be entirely wrong. Though apparently at a grave disadvantage they are not without their own resources. In the first place, they have the constitution on their side; as the representatives of the people their right to power is highly legitimate. Moreover, there is a closer relationship between politicians and officials than is found at the centre. While back-benchers at Westminster experience considerable frustration in trying to scrutinise the comings and goings of civil servants, councillors have ample opportunity to peer into day-to-day town hall matters on an informal basis. In addition, formal meetings bring chief officers and ordinary councillors together on a regular basis. Moreover, while ministers rarely remain at a department for longer than two years, senior councillors can devote a political lifetime to some particular policy area.

Councillors' resources were utilised to the full when the collapse of the social democratic consensus and the Thatcherite assault on the welfare state threatened the *raison d'être* of local government. The Widdicombe Report (1986b) chronicled some far-reaching changes in the officer–councillor relationship.

Party control
Perhaps the most important and effective way in which councillors can exert their authority *vis-à-vis* the officials is through the

dominance of a majority party on the council (see pp. 112–14). This can ensure the following:

(1)   *A clear policy manifesto*. This leaves little room for doubt on the part of the officers as to what they are expected to accomplish.

(2)   *Moral authority*. This is derived from an electoral mandate.

(3)   *Mutual support*. Councillors, usually as a party cohort, can stand together in their dealings with officers.

(4)   *Political leadership*. This can come from front-bench councillors and, perhaps, a strong individual council leader operating 'prime ministerially'.

A changing balance

Although it is possible to detail the respective resources of councillors and officers, their relationship is not static. From the high point of the nineteenth century councillor authority diminished. The next sections examine the relationship in the post-war era.

The consensus years – efficiency and to hell with democracy

The decades of post-war consensus saw a relatively tranquil relationship between officers and councillors. Society's faith in the power of reason and the technological fix gave officer-power an unchallengeable legitimacy. A number of case studies (Jones, 1969: 269–75; Brier, 1970; Hampton, 1970; Dennis, 1972; Dearlove, 1973; Newton, 1976; Cockburn, 1977a) testify to a techno-bureaucratic heyday.

Officers avowed their political impartiality and generally stood aloof from councillors. Where the two did meet, it was in a controlled and formalised way through council and committee meetings, pre-arranged audiences granted by officers or formal pre-meeting briefings. Moreover, the audiences were confined to senior officers; councillors could not communicate with those labouring in the bowels of the town hall hierarchy. Councillors were not even permitted to walk in and out of the municipal offices as and when they pleased; they would wait obediently to be summoned by the officers.

Officers remained as ostentatiously innocent of overtly political behaviour as the three monkeys who see, hear and speak no evil. They did not join political parties, draft manifestos, write speeches or attend party group meetings. Indeed the formal APT code of practice majestically declared: 'the officer should not be called upon to advise any political group of the employing authority . . . neither shall he be required to attend any meeting of any political group'. They also, like their Whitehall cousins, shrouded their activities in dark secrecy: councillors knew only what officers wished them to know.

The policy-making procedures were largely run by the officers, acting in solemn conformity with standing orders. Councillors could not call spontaneous meetings or inconveniently amend agendas at the eleventh hour. Officers determined what the council would talk about beforehand and in effect decided what it had said by writing the minutes.

Consultations with local interests were largely conducted by the bureaucrats, meeting representatives of 'respectable' commercial and professional bodies where they would talk the language, not of politics, but of technicalities. The officers conducted the relationship with central government on the same basis, seeking generally to act as loyal technical specialists dedicated to the efficient implementation of Whitehall edicts. The content of policy largely reflected technical imperatives, councillors following the advice of 'urban managers'.

Not all councils followed this pattern. In some, strong party domination ensured more policy-making power for councillors. Yet the above model might be described as the traditional officer–councillor relationship. For most councillors the attempt to shape policy was a Sisyphean task. Bureaucratic supremacy was celebrated in a long-running movement to enhance their power *vis-à-vis* councillors by reforms in the process of the internal management of local authorities.

Celebrating bureaucracy – management and managerialism

Contrary to the impression often given, management in local government is no mere question of techniques and technicalities; its implications for the councillor–officer relationship go to the heart of the operation of local democracy.

Local authorities are unlike private-sector organisations in that management cannot be a simple matter of profit maximisation; an efficient use of resources must be secured within an ethic of public service. In addition to value for money they must offer public accountability, and these twin goals can be antagonistic. However, movements for reform emanating from Whitehall and from the officers themselves have tended to favour efficiency (of a private sector kind) at the expense of democracy. These have been based upon two alleged weaknesses of local government:

(1) The low calibre of councillors.

(2) Administration based on separate departments directed by specialist council committees.

The call was for the end of the traditional departmentalism; everything from road-sweeping to sponsorship of the arts should be centralised under the control of a single supremo, a non-elected 'city boss' with awesome power. This was a model drawn not from the Greek city-state where democracy was nurtured, but from the capitalist world of big business.

The gospel of corporatism

Early moves towards managerial reform came in municipalities with particularly strong and ambitious leaders (Cockburn, 1977a: 19–24). In 1965 Newcastle Corporation, led by the dynamic T. Dan Smith (later to be disgraced for his part in the Poulson scandal), appointed Frank Harris, a senior executive from the giant US multinational Ford motor company, as a veritable managing director of the city. The committee structure was demolished so that the effective leaders of all departments were to be chief officers led by Harris himself and a small team of senior councillors forming a kind of board of directors. The majority of councillors were relegated to the sidelines.

So impressive were these developments to the Whitehall establishment that a committee of inquiry into the management of local government was established under civil servant Sir John Maud. Its extensive research supported the 'declining calibre of councillors' thesis and a Newcastle model was endorsed. The report stated baldly: 'The local administration of public services is

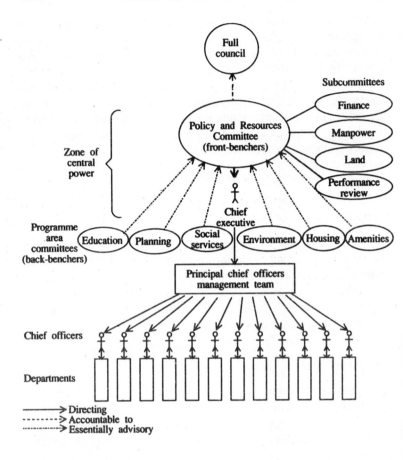

Figure 10.1 The Bains-style management structure. Source: based on Bains, 1972, p. 99.

essential, that the organs of administration should be democratically elected bodies is not' (Maud, 1967a: 68).

Officers felt warmly towards the model and a number of academic institutions picked up the scent and began to offer courses and seminars to celebrate the new buzz term, 'corporate management'. Yet, although his efforts were rewarded in the time-honoured manner (elevation from plain Sir John to Lord Redcliffe-Maud), councils accorded a frosty reception to this blueprint for government by middle-class bureaucracy. There were some experiments but no managerial revolution.

However, opportunities for re-emphasising the corporate message came with the promise of major reorganisation in 1974. The officers, with the connivance of central government, decided to strike while the iron was hot with yet another committee of inquiry. Councillors were completely excluded from this small cohort which comprised top local government officers and a representative from ICI. The Bains Report of 1972 reiterated the private-sector nostrums. The fount of all power was to be a high-powered (and highly paid) chief executive, a Policy and Resources Committee of leading councillors and a management team of senior officers (see Figure 10.1). The report was a hymn to bureaucracy, arguing that 'the skilled professional officer is not just a servant who is paid to do as he is told' (Bains, 1972: 8). It was aptly described by critics as an 'officers' charter' (Hambleton, 1978: 56).

Following reorganisation almost all the new authorities established Bains-style management structures. Chief executives were installed in plush offices and in some cases their power was amplified by combining the role of treasurer. The effect of the reforms was to create a structure which made officer domination natural. There were profound implications: officers began to develop closer links with local capitalists, planning in their interests rather than those of ordinary people (Flynn, 1982). Issues were increasingly presented in terms of esoteric technical jargon and depoliticised to freeze out the politicians (Bennington, 1976: 19–23). Yet even as this high point was being reached the political climate had been changing.

The end of the party

The consensus era had accepted officer dominance as part of the price of a technically controlled, egalitarian, social democracy. However, the crisis of confidence in the technical fix (see pp. 152–3) was compounded by the collapse of the long boom, signalling the end of the 'party' for local government (see pp. 233–4). All this was underlined throughout the 1980s by the New Right, anti-social-democratic agenda of the Thatcher government. The events were to challenge the traditional councillor–officer relationship in various ways. Not only were officers to lose confidence, but the new breed of councillors were to assert their role in local government more aggressively. The New Urban Left councillors (see pp. 234–9) used their resources in the following ways.

Using the corporate structures

Although the corporate management model was often operated in the interests of officers rather than councillors, it was not necessarily undemocratic. This depended on who held the reins – chief executive or Policy and Resources Committee. Councillors began to use their political authority to re-establish control (Greenwood *et al.*, 1980). Some chief executives were retired while others remained only as symbolic figureheads. The management structures became a basis for centralised political control; Policy and Resources Committees became mini-Westminster-style Cabinets.

Meetings, bloody meetings

Councillors increased their power through the formal meetings of the council and its committees. Discussion here can determine the political agenda and a strong chairperson can relegate officers to the status of mere information providers, demanding that technical jargon be demystified (as in a court of law), a fundamental condition of effective popular democracy. In pre-committee briefings officers were challenged more aggressively, and technical recommendations were no longer revered as gospel.

Sailing close to the legal wind

In the politically charged atmosphere of the 1980s councillors, under attack from the centre, became bolder (if not foolhardy) and officers were asked to sail close to the legal wind and invent various resistance strategies, such as the buccaneering practice of 'creative accounting'. Under these circumstances the impact of official caution was severely diminished.

Politicising the bureaucracy

Officers themselves became more political with the breakdown of many traditional conventions. Attendance at party group meetings became common and officers were even involved in drawing up party manifestos and other forms of overt political activity (such as canvassing and party meetings).

Twin-tracking

Councillors would technically become employees of a neighbouring (and sympathetic) local authority. They would then take liberal amounts of time off for their council duties so that they became in effect full-timers, with offices in the town hall and secretarial staff. In this way they were able to develop greater expertise and understanding of the various policy areas. They were also able to involve themselves deeply in the work of the officials, discussing policy, scrutinising and directing.

Political advisers

It was possible to counter the official line by appointing politically sympathetic experts to advisory positions. This expedient mirrored developments in central government; advisers had been used during two world wars and had been dramatically advanced by the post-1979 Conservative governments.

Political appointments

Councillors were able to ensure a more compliant bureaucracy by becoming involved in appointments (Widdicombe, 1986b: 132). Press advertisements for positions from principal to chief officer specified the need for sympathy with council ideology. Special units in areas such as police monitoring, race or women's matters were established, staffed by sympathetic ideologues.

Broadening access

Councillors refused to accept limited access to officers, entering town halls when they desired and speaking to whom they wished. Thus they were able to bypass chief officers to work with those with greater political sympathy.

Mobilising the lower echelons

It became possible to appeal to ordinary employees as a weapon against their seniors. David Blunkett, when leader of Sheffield City Council, stressed the need to 'develop within our own employees some perspective on what it is we are trying to achieve'. This led to clashes with the local mandarins fearful 'that their traditional management prerogatives were being undermined' (Blunkett, 1984: 248).

Local goose, central gander?

Central government looked with extreme disfavour at the changing balance of power in the urban authorities. This is hardly surprising since it was in large measure occasioned by its own anti-local-government stance. Yet, ironically, many of the changes in the official–politician power balance at local level were directly paralleled by developments under Mrs Thatcher at Whitehall. The Prime Minister was taking an unprecedented interest in senior appointments (asking 'Is he one of us?'), the Number Ten policy unit was beefed up, and a legion of personal ministerial political advisers, such as Sir Alan Walters, marched in to strengthen the politicians in their dealings with the mandarins. Moreover, the machine became centralised around the office of the Prime Minister as never before. However, a battery of legislative measures sought to reduce councillor power in the town halls.

The central response

The Widdicombe Committee was set up to examine 'politicisation' of the municipalities. However, its recommendations, in some ways supporting the increased political role of councillors, were not all the government had hoped for, and a White Paper (Department of the Environment, 1988) and subsequent legislation departed from them in certain respects.

Chief executives

Widdicombe argued for increasing the authority of the chief executive, with an overall responsibility for 'the propriety of council business' (1986a: 144). On the face of it this might be expected to increase officer control but, in the new climate, the government was wary of the possibility of the office being controlled by the ruling party. Instead, the White Paper proposed separate officers for three specific watch-dog functions: *financial probity*, *legal propriety* and *management coordination*. Significantly, the Local Government Finance Act 1988 laid down that the legal and financial monitoring responsibilities could not be held by the same officer, thereby preventing chief executives combining the position with that of Treasurer.

Cheap advice
Widdicombe took a favourable view of local political advisers
(1986a: 151–2) but the subsequent Local Government and Housing Act 1989 laid down that only one per political party was per-
missible, to be paid no more than a modest £13,500 per annum.

Curbing the twin-trackers
Although Widdicombe had acknowledged the case for full-time
councillors, the Act banned all officers earning salaries above
£13,500 from standing for any council. In addition, it was made
considerably more difficult for councillors to subsist entirely on
their allowances (pp. 134–5).

We can't go on meeting like this
Changes to the allowance system were designed to avoid the 'pro-
liferation' of meetings (Department of the Environment, 1988: 10).
A draft of advice published by the Audit Commission in September 1990 argued that too much time was taken up with committee
meetings discussing things which should be left to officers (Hedley,
1990: 1).

Pour encourager les autres
Various provisions in the White Paper promised to reduce the
power of majority party councillors by increasing that of minority
parties (such as access to agendas, use of political advisers, and
rights to raise issues in council meetings) (Leach, 1989: 113).

However, the impact of the New Right policies for the town hall
power structure did not end with these piecemeal moves. The
underlying Thatcherite mission to redraw the contours of the state
promised far-reaching implications. This chapter concludes by gaz-
ing into a crystal ball.

Conclusion – from managing to enabling

The managerial basis of local government up to the 1980s was built
upon the idea of the local authority as a provider of services. The
direct implication of this was enhanced power for officers; when it
came to supplying services they were the unchallengeable experts.
However, the policies of the 1980s (compulsory competitive

tendering, care in the community, contracting out, privatisation, opting-out, local management for schools and so on) meant that local government was to supply fewer services directly, while acquiring the new function of facilitating, or enabling, other agencies to do so. What would be the future for the town hall power structure? There are various possibilities.

Councillors on top

One scenario envisages a strengthening of the hands of councillors. Officers skilled in the art of providing a service lose their claim to authority. Many technical decisions will be made by the non-local-government agencies supplying the services.

It may be argued that local authorities will enjoy greater freedom to clarify their policies in terms of community needs rather than professional dictates. There is also a monitoring function which will similarly be made on the basis of effectiveness of service rather than professional satisfaction. Hence, the policy may lead local authorities 'to change in ways that support their role as local government' (Stewart, 1989: 177). It can also be argued that something of a reborn corporate management approach may evolve to counter the fragmentation and loss of accountability. This may involve rejuvenated chief executives and Policy and Resources Committees, able to develop and sustain community strategy and a public service ethic (Stewart, 1989: 183).

However, it was by no means part of the Thatcher agenda to enhance councillor power, and the enabling role poses immense managerial difficulty. Rather than managing its own work-force, the authority is faced with the intractable problem of working through a dense network of public, voluntary and private local agencies. This offers only a limited basis for control and accountability. There will also be rigidity since contracts, once negotiated, will freeze a service for up to five years or more (that is, for the length of the contract). Moreover, the private sector does not take kindly to regulation. The Thatcher government showed little stomach for it in its privatisation programme and the reception to the contract compliance policies of the GLC and others was hostile. The overall effect of this bewildering fragmentation of provision must cloud any holistic community perspective. There will be great difficulty in dovetailing services to reflect the sense of overall strategy which genuine local government requires.

Officers on top

An alternative vision would be one where the awarding and monitoring of contracts is seen as a largely technical matter, to be placed under the control of officials, mainly lawyers and account- ants. The immense difficulty of finding mechanisms of political accountability and control makes this bureaucratic scenario ominously possible. Official power in the community is also in- creased through the growth of non-elected administrative agen- cies. In the case of hived-off operations, ex-employees inevitably enhance their professional autonomy (see p. 252).

Towards a complete picture

Today councillor–officer relations are far more messy and politi- cally charged than in the days of consensus. Yet, regardless of structural reforms, the basic problem of bureaucratic power under democracy remains a key question of political analysis. We have not yet fully explored the policy-making terrain of local govern- ment, for there remains the financial dimension and a shadowy world of interest groups. There is a lot more to the making of government policy than meets the eye; these darker political re- cesses are explored in the following two chapters.

11

Paying for Local Government

The study of local government finance is no aimless ramble through a monotonous landscape of municipal ledgers and account books. It is a crucial site for political struggle, with outcomes affecting the lives of everyone. This chapter begins by placing it in the larger context of state finance generally. Next it examines the main sources of funds: fees and charges, local taxes, central grants and borrowing, noting in each the surrounding political debate and the long arm of central government stretching sinuous fingers into local coffers. The chapter also examines the audit process whereby central government peers inquisitively into municipal ledgers. The conclusion assesses the way the financial processes affect the balance of power within the state and the implications of this for local democracy.

Local finance in context

Like most aspects of local government, finance can only be understood in terms of its location in the totality of the state. Local expenditure is *ipso facto* public expenditure, comprising around one-third of the whole. It is part of a mighty universe of public finance moving in accordance with mysterious laws. The modern system has passed through several periods.

The nineteenth century – the cheeseparing state
In the nineteenth century the key to public expenditure was the

notion of a balanced budget, a natural desideratum of the prudent capitalist. Governments would raise, in tax, enough to finance their expenditure and not a penny more. Coupled with this was great parsimony; expenditure was necessary but evil. Gladstone himself said that a Chancellor of the Exchequer should aim to save 'candle ends and cheese parings in the call of the country' (Hirst, 1931). One of his first acts as Chancellor was to compel the Foreign Office to use thinner notepaper (Magnus, 1963: 112). The same parsimony applied in local government; most elections would find some candidates termed economisers, whose principal political aim was to protect the ratepayers from profligate spending on the poor. For the bourgeoisie the role of councillor was guardian of the public purse.

The early twentieth century

The municipal socialism of the early decades of the century saw a movement away from economising, with the Labour Party pursuing social justice through tax-funded local services. In addition, the Liberal government at Westminster began to intervene in social life with legislation for pensions and national insurance.

The world wars

Two world wars had a profound effect on attitudes towards public expenditure. The state intervened in social life on an unprecedented scale so that the liberal idea of the minimal state could never be completely reasserted. Expenditure rose during both wars, never to return to the pre-war levels.

The post-war consensus – spend, spend, spend

The long boom of the post-war decades saw an entirely different approach. Public expenditure was no longer merely a process whereby government paid its way. Orthodox opinion accepted the Keynesian doctrine that the state should use its huge expenditure muscle to influence the economy in pursuit of full employment. The concept of the balanced budget was replaced by the idea of a budget deficit aimed at stimulating the economy in times of slump. In addition, social democracy was in the ascendant and, in a unique period of consensus politics, high spending on social services was acceptable to both parties. Local government was a main piston in the new welfare state machine.

The end of the party

All was to change with the international collapse of the long boom and the oil crises of the 1970s. Lack of profitability produced a fiscal crisis in which the private sector became unwilling to meet the costs of state welfare (O'Connor, 1973). In 1976 Labour minister Tony Crosland (along with singer Shirley Bassey) warned local government 'the party's over'. Indeed, the popular singer showed further prescience to add that 'the piper must be paid'. The piper was the US-controlled International Monetary Fund, and the cost of a loan was a symbolic renunciation of social democracy with welfare state cuts.

The New Right – full circle

For the Conservative government of the 1980s the answers to Britain's problems lay in a return to the nineteenth-century ethos. Keynesianism was to be replaced by monetarism, a doctrine which decreed that governments should keep out of the economy and concern themselves only with regulating the rate of increase in the money supply (quantity of money in the economy) to control inflation. The free market would do the rest. In this new climate local expenditure was seen as evil but by no means necessary. It was alleged by the New Right to have created a dependency culture, a post-war funk, in which wasteful councils, elected by non-ratepaying voters, served by empire-building bureaucrats, dispensed lavish patronage to working-class scroungers. The scene was set for some bloody political confrontations with no aspect of local government finance left untouched.

No free lunches – defining local finance

Local government finance is essentially the means whereby local authorities obtain and spend money. Much of politics comes down to issues of money. There is no such thing as a free lunch; whatever local government does must be paid for, and local government does a considerable amount. Local authorities are mega-spenders, often the biggest in their area, and their financial behaviour has far-reaching repercussions. The services provided are expensive because they tend to be labour intensive, offering no easy technological routes to savings. Television sets and motor cars can be made by robots, but social services and education need people. The meals may come on wheels, but the lonely, aged or handicapped may want to talk as well as eat. Computers teach spelling but they cannot bandage the knee of a child in the playground or counsel a troubled adolescent.

The local authority accounts

Local authorities keep two accounts: a *current account* (from which they pay salaries and other running costs) and a *capital account* (for the purchase of capital assets such as schools, roads and buses). This distinction has important implications for the way money is raised. Figure 11.1 shows that there are four linked sources: fees and charges, taxes, grants from central government and borrowing. The first three fund the current account while the capital account is largely financed by borrowing and capital receipts (income from capital sold). Ultimately all finance comes from the private sector, to which it returns. We will find that central government is a powerful intermediary in all local government's financial processes.

Municipal marketplace – charging for democracy

Many local government services offer potential for charging. However, unlike private firms roaming in the anarchic world of the free market in search of profit, local authorities pursue more complex goals and use the following charging policies:

(1) *Deterrent charge.* The purpose is to limit use (for example, high parking charges in city centres and library fines).

(2) *Market charge.* Price fixed to maximise profit. The service is received only by those willing and able to pay.

(3) *Full cost charge.* Users are asked to pay the full cost of the service but no more.

(4) *Zero charge.* Many services are provided by local government because the technical difficulties of charging mean that private

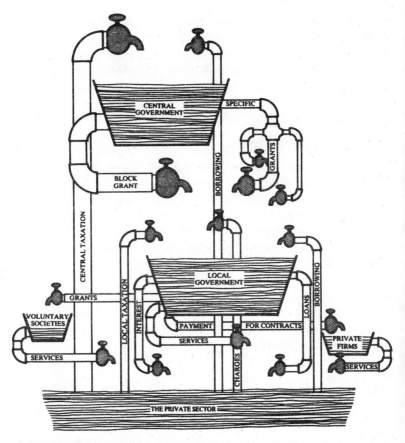

Figure 11.1   Local government finance in context.

firms are not interested (street lighting or clean air which all can enjoy).

(5)   *Social charge.* Price set lower than market value or cost in order to pursue social objectives (for example, council house rents). A social charge can be zero, as in education.

Of course no authority relies exclusively on any single one of these principles, neither can they always be expected to work in a single prescribed manner. Thus, though not intended as such, a market charge can also be a deterrent to the poor. On the other hand, what is actually designed as a deterrent charge can have the effect of producing a service reserved for the rich. The zero charge usually arises from what economists call the problem of 'non-excludibility'. For example, if you pay for a record on a juke-box, others can enjoy your choice as 'free loaders'. Many public services are of this kind.

The pattern of development

In the nineteenth century local authorities were able to raise funds by charging for services such as water, electricity, gas, roads, public transport and so on. This ended in the era of municipal socialism and in the post-war decades of the social democratic consensus the idea of free access became a cornerstone of the welfare state. People were seen as citizens, with rights to services regardless of their ability to pay. However, the era of Thatcherism questioned this view.

Central government and local charges

Prima facie it might seem that central government would have little interest in this area. However, if a service is offered below cost, a subsidy is required from some other source and total public expenditure rises. Consequently, a government wishing to limit public expenditure will be concerned and the Thatcher government argued for a great expansion in local charging.

The New Urban Left movement resisted the pressures and ran certain services deliberately as loss-makers (school meals, housing, public transport and leisure activities). As a result of its attempt to reduce London Transport fares, the GLC was pursued through the courts by the Conservative-controlled London Borough of Bromley (encouraged by the central government). The case went for a final judgement to the House of Lords where the policy was outlawed. In the wake of this came the 1983 Transport Act, subjecting all transport subsidies in metropolitan areas to a limit prescribed by the Transport Secretary. The result was wholesale fare rises.

The highly successful, and locally popular, cheap public transport system of South Yorkshire (which could hardly be said to pose a threat to the exchange rate – Duncan and Goodwin, 1988: 109) had to be abandoned, precipitating increased congestion, road wear, pollution, traffic accidents and more general frustration to the users who had thought they had a democratic right to shape their own system of public transport. In addition, the policy of deregulation (see Chapter 3) removed monopoly status from local passenger transport authorities, forcing them to reject social pricing criteria and compete with private companies according to the 'get rich' ethic.

The Local Government and Housing Act of 1989 gave central government powers to increase the number of services for which charges could be made. Moreover, the subsidising of council house rents was to stop from 1990–1 when the Housing Revenue Account was to be 'ring-fenced'.

There are profoundly political implications when public services make charges, including the following:

(1) *Less democracy*. Increased allocation of resources through the market (commodification) means that the sphere in which decisions are made by democracy is contracted.

(2) *Less equality*. Differing abilities to pay result in different levels of service: Eton and Harrow for the rich, Grimesworth comprehensive for the rest.

(3) *Less service*. Services will not be offered which do not generate profits. Old people's homes must close.

(4) *Hidden tax*. Where profits are made, users are in effect paying extra tax.

(5) *More social tension*. The above effects create social unrest as the have-nots turn envious eyes upon the haves.

Essentially, charging tends to undermine the ideal of social democracy. Where the justification for receiving a service is the ability to pay, citizenship rights disappear.

Taxing times

The importance of local taxation goes well beyond the funding of local services. It is of deep constitutional significance because it gives autonomy from the centre; without this local democracy can be nothing but hollow pretence. Until the Thatcher era this independence was regarded as sacrosanct, a veritable constitutional convention. Indeed, it may also be seen as a plank of liberalism:

the right of communities to economic self-determination is analogous to that of individuals to shop around in the great *laissez-faire* supermarket. However, the 1980s were to reveal double standards as new terms such as 'rate-capping', 'community charge' and 'poll tax' entered the lexicon.

The rates

Until 1990 the rates system, devised in 1601, was the basis for local taxation. It was a property tax based on notional annual rental value (termed rateable value – RV). An authority would levy a rate of x pence in the pound (rate poundage – RP), derived by dividing the amount needed from the rates by the total rateable value of all the property in the area. Property owners would then pay accordingly: if RP was 50 pence in the pound, a property of RV £700 would yield £350. There were two categories of rateable property, domestic and non-domestic (business premises). By the twentieth century the system appeared to have overrun its constitutional sell-by date, accused of being:

(1)   Regressive (taking a larger proportion of the income of the poor than of the rich).

(2)   A disincentive to property improvement.

(3)   Lacking buoyancy (unable to rise automatically with inflation).

(4)   Insufficient in yield.

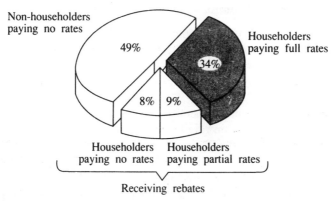

Figure 11.2   Proportion of electorate paying full or partial rates, 1984–5. Source: HM Government, 1986, p. 6.

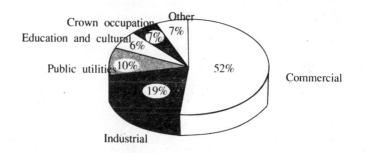

Figure 11.3 Non-domestic rate revenue by sector: England, 1984–5.
Source: HM Government, 1986, p. 11.

Moreover, it was highly unpopular. Unlike income tax, pain-lessly extracting money under the anaesthetic of the PAYE sys-tem, the rates were highly visible, reminiscent of the methods of Dick Turpin. With its basis in property, and rebates for the poor, the system seemed fiendishly designed to target the middle classes. Figure 11.2 reveals that over 50 per cent of the population escaped. Loud complaints also came from commercial and industrial inter-ests, which contributed around 50 per cent of the total while being denied a corporate vote; a case of taxation without representation (see Figure 11.3).

Rates and central control – into the neutral waters

Until the mid-1980s the autonomy conferred by the rates was ac-knowledged with good grace as a feature of pluralist democracy. In 1980 Tom King, Conservative Minister for Local Government, declared in response to criticism of grant cuts: 'If we'd started to determine . . . rate levies . . . then I'd accept that that would be a major threat to local democracy' (Douglas and Lord, 1986: 31).

The only restraint on rate levels was believed to lie in the local ballot box. Hence, the Thatcher government, in trying to reduce local expenditure, reasoned that if central grants were squeezed, there could be little compensatory rate rise. However, this proved a miscalculation, councils discovering they could lower the bucket further down the well without sustaining electoral fatalities. The result of the resistance was an astonishing assault. King's words were to mock him as the government sailed into the politically demilitarised zone.

Rate-capping

The first wind of an assault came in 1981 when the government toyed with the idea of compelling authorities to hold referendums before levying supplementary rates to compensate for grant loss. The belief was that no one in their right mind would actually vote *for* greater taxation. This intuition was confirmed when the city of Coventry held its own advisory referendum. The event was rather less spectacular than an earlier attempt to reduce local taxation in the same city: 25 per cent of the population turned out to vote, which was more than the solitary Peeping Tom who, in the eleventh century, lustfully eyed the naked Lady Godiva as she rode through the streets. However, the referendum suggestion raised such indignation from government back-benchers and Conservative authorities that it was jettisoned. Despite this, the Local Government Finance Act 1982 removed local authority powers to levy supplementary rates altogether.

The 1983 general election put new wind into Conservative sails. A system of 'selective rate limitation' was introduced, soon dubbed 'rate-capping'. It targeted particular, allegedly profligate, authorities. Maximum annual expenditure levels were specified and excess rate demands were rendered *ultra vires*. In the first year eighteen authorities were penalised, sixteen of them Labour controlled.

Charging the community – the poll tax

Like so many central offensives, rate-capping failed. Moreover, it fell well short of the full-scale reform demanded in the leafy shires. Hence, buoyed up by yet another general election victory in 1987, the Conservatives felt sufficiently bold to initiate a reform not contemplated beyond the arcane laboratories of right-wing think-tanks (in this case the Adam Smith Institute). This replacement for the rates was not called a tax at all: it was a 'community charge', quickly dubbed the 'poll tax' because the idea was to place a flat-rate levy on everyone of voting age. The ancient constitutional cry, 'No taxation without representation', was reversed to read: 'No representation without taxation'. It was said to be 'fair' in that everyone would pay the same for services in the way that they did for cauliflower or bread, and it would promote greater local accountability since more voters would be paying for the consequences of their choices. For the Conservative Party it offered the additional allure of making Labour councils unpopular.

The case against the charge was overwhelming. Most obviously it was profoundly regressive. The equal charge for cauliflower analogy was completely irrelevant because the very definition of a tax is that it is *not a charge for services*. Thus, for example, childless people pay for education and healthy people pay towards the NHS. Indeed, for all its defects, the rates system was actually more progressive in both gross (before rebates) and net terms.

Moreover, the poll tax was to cost far more to collect (some 2.5 times as much (*Daily Telegraph*, 16 November 1988)) since it was to be paid by 38 million rather than 14 million. In addition, set-up costs were estimated at around £270 million (Travers, 1989: 21–3). Although one of the main criticisms of the rating system was its antiquity, this replacment was over two centuries older, last imposed in 1381 when it occasioned the famous Peasants' Revolt led by Wat Tyler.

In 1990 it was the middle-class peasants who were revolting. If in much of its earlier legislation the government had appeared to shoot itself in the foot, this time it was a kneecapping. The loss of popularity was astounding, the Conservatives regularly trailing Labour by some 20 per cent in opinion polls. In February 1990, eighteen Conservative councillors in West Oxfordshire actually resigned from the party and, in the local elections the following May, their leader David Walker defeated the party's official candidate by 516 votes to 146. Indeed, these elections delivered a stinging rebuke; the pattern of voting, if replicated in a general election, would have returned a Labour government with a commanding majority of sixty-six (*The Guardian*, 5 May 1990).

Just recapping

The government claimed that the problems were caused by 'overspending authorities' and resorted to another ploy. Instead of rate-capping there was to be community-charge-capping, and twenty-one Labour authorities suffered. So much for the increased local accountabilty promised. Chris Patten, the Environment Secretary brought in for the purpose of damage limitation, was obliged to confess in the Commons to 'problems, anomalies and difficulties'. The flat-rate principle was buckling under pressure and developing some progressive contours. In June 1990 Patten announced a gigantic £3.5 billion package for an *ad hoc* patchwork of safety nets in an attempt to retrieve lost popularity.

The national non-domestic rate (NNDR)

Non-domestic rates were retained, though in a quite different guise. A highly centralised NNDR system was established with rateable values reassessed in 1990 and a single national rate poundage set by central government (34.8p in the pound for England). The yield was to be collected centrally and reallocated to local authorities on the basis of population.

There were profound implications in the change, with both losers and gainers. The latter tended to be Conservative outer London boroughs, the south-east, the south-west and the West Midlands, while the north, the north-west and inner London lost out. On the other hand, London and the south experienced dramatic rises both in rateable value and rate poundage, while the reverse occurred in the north. There was also a general shift of the burden from manufacturers to retailers, with hundreds of thousands of small shopkeepers living over their premises hit particularly hard by having to pay both poll tax and NNDR (*Sunday Times*, 8 April 1990). Moreover, in the early years 'safety nets', in which gainers subsidised losers, were to operate to ease the transition, and the costs of these again hit the south-east.

The beginning of the end?

The unpopularity of the poll tax proved to be a major embarrassment to the Conservative Party and was to contribute to the momentous events of November 1990 in which Margaret Thatcher was challenged for the leadership by Michael Heseltine. Unable to win on the first ballot she withdrew in order to permit certain of her Cabinet colleagues to stand. The result was that John Major, Chancellor of the Exchequer, emerged victorious after a second ballot. During the campaign Heseltine had made much of the poll tax issue, promising dramatic revision if not outright abolition. Significantly the new Prime Minister made Heseltine a member of his first Cabinet as Secretary of State for the Environment, which included responsibility for the community charge. Clearly the days of the poll tax in its present state were numbered, although many thought that the new minister had been handed a poisoned chalice. However, he instigated a wide-ranging inquiry and in March 1991 announced some 'interim conclusions' to the House of Commons. The proposals were coupled with Chancellor Norman Lamont's Budget of a few days before which had placed an extra 2.5 per cent on VAT in order to raise money to ease poll tax charges by an average of £140 per head. To some extent this was little more than an attempt to rob Peter in order to pay Paul, but it was only a short-term measure. The longer-term solution was to replace the poll tax with a new system of local tax based upon property (that is, the rates principle) but retaining a poll tax element through an adjustment for the number living in the property.

The alternatives

Various alternatives to the rates and poll tax have been proposed, including fuel tax, vehicle tax, sales tax and even an earmarked proportion of national income tax. All have been rejected for technical or political reasons. In 1976 the Layfield Report recommended a local income tax (to supplement rather than replace rates) but this was unattractive to central government because it would increase local autonomy. It was additionally distasteful to the right because (being progressive) it would have placed a greater burden on the middle class – not at all what Conservative voters understood as the objective of reform. It was particularly repugnant to the Thatcher government, which was dedicated to reducing direct taxation.

At the same time the Labour Party agonised over its own alternative. Initially there was talk of a kind of rates system based on the capital value of property, derided by Conservatives as a 'roof tax'. However, by mid-1990 the proposal being canvassed was little more than a return to the weary old rates system, but with some fresh paint (extensive rebates and more sophisticated valuation), to be called 'fair rates'. In this dismal quest one could wonder that neither party had come up with something more modern, such as the seventeenth-century 'window tax'.

Pennies from heaven – central grants

With its limited taxation base, local government cannot be entirely self-financing and has relied upon grants from central government. These are justified on the grounds that many local responsibilities are centrally imposed. There is also a social justice factor, the grant serving an *equalisation* function: taking from the rich parts of the country and giving to the poor (see Figure 11.4), a principle

Figure 11.4 Equalisation between English regions, 1984–5, through local grants. Source: HM Government, 1986.

generally disliked by the right. However, from the point of view of the centre there is a further and rather different purpose of the largesse: gaining control on the 'who pays the piper' rule. The total central grant is termed the *Aggregate Exchequer Grant* (AEG) and comprises specific and general grants.

Specific grants

These are made for particular services (housing, education, police and so on), usually given as a percentage of the cost incurred. Specific grants can be criticised on the following grounds:

(1)   They favour wealthy authorities, which can spend money to attract money.

(2)   They increase the power of central government by enabling it to target or ignore services.

(3)   They can lead to unnecessary expenditure merely to attract the grant. For example, in the 1950s and 1960s authorities erected high-rise flats when they had quite enough space for low-density development.

General (or block) grants

A general grant is a supplement to an authority's tax income, hence its title, Revenue (previously Rate) Support Grant (RSG). It offers the following advantages:

(1)   It is relatively easy and cheap to administer.

(2)   It permits autonomy from the centre and is therefore more conducive to local democracy.

(3)   It is socially equitable in that it facilitates equalisation.

Conversely, block grants have the following disadvantages:

(1)   They can be hostage to maverick authorities which use the money in idiosyncratic ways.

(2)   They can have an anti-egalitarian effect. For example, in education, some authorities spend more per head than others.

The evolving system

Central government began to make grants towards services in the nineteenth century to support the efforts of voluntary societies and *ad hoc* bodies. As the municipal institutions began to take over these were inherited as specific grants, soon to be rationalised into a single block. Indeed, the consolidation of specific grants into block grants has been a repeating tendency, happening on a large scale in 1888, 1929, 1958 and 1974. During the twentieth century the relative size of the central grant grew steadily to become, by the 1960s, the lion's share of local income. However, the collapse of the long boom in the 1970s saw a pulling on the reins, with a system of *cash limits*. During the 1980s government moved towards a greater reliance on the more centralist specific grants.

Determining the RSG – mixing the cake and slicing it up

The calculation of the RSG has a highly complex and technical appearance. Formally the task falls to the Local Government Finance Policy Directorate located deep within the Department of the Environment. It works rather like the painters of the Forth Bridge: when the civil servants reach the end of the annual cycle they immediately begin the whole operation again. There are two basic tasks: determining the overall size of the cake and deciding how to apportion it between authorities.

Mixing the cake
The global size of the block grant is determined by the Public Expenditure Survey Committee (PESC) process, which fixes the expenditure levels of all government programmes. Local government can make its views known through a special advisory body, the Consultative Council on Local Government Finance (CCLGF) (see p. 222). However, the final decision is ultimately a political one reflecting the goals of the party in power.

Slicing it up
This second operation is no matter of simple division. Like a just parent with different-sized children, central government is supposed to ensure that the slice on each authority's plate is fair. The tendency has been to base the size of the grant upon

two factors: the *needs* within the area (for example, the number of old people, road mileage and so on) and the *resources* (for example, number of industries, amount of highly rated housing) available. In 1966 a *domestic* element was added to subsidise domestic ratepayers. However, in 1979 the wise parent was replaced by the nineteenth-century workhouse master. It was felt by the Thatcher government that the formula was biased in favour of Labour-controlled city authorities and the grant became an overtly political weapon.

The block grant in the 1980s

The Local Government Planning and Land Act 1980 replaced the needs and resources elements of the RSG with a new *block grant*, calculated in a complex, not to say arcane, manner (Douglas and Lord, 1986: 27). Yet in principle it was the essence of simplicity, merely replacing decisions made by negotiation and calculation with political diktat. The government wished to secure two things: a general reduction in the overall level of expenditure and a means of clipping the wings of the Labour-controlled prodigals.

Each authority's grant was calculated on the basis of a Whitehall assessment of what it should spend, the Grant Related Expenditure Assessment (GREA), and an assessment of what it should raise in rates, the Grant Related Poundage (GRP). If an authority exceeded the prediction its grant would be cut. However, this did not secure the desired reductions. After the May 1981 local elections the number of Labour-controlled authorities rose, and the total defiant overspend for the year was almost £1 billion.

The result was a tightening of the screw. A system of centrally determined expenditure 'targets' was imposed, backed up with grant 'holdback'. These were made increasingly severe so that by 1985–6 it was by no means only the Labour-controlled authorities in which the pips were squeaking. Yet still the centre was thwarted. Wily authorities responded to their gamekeeper role by resorting to the poaching tactics of 'creative accounting'. Some even went on to reach a stage of receiving no grant at all, leaving them like the philosopher Diogenes who, living in a barrel, could scorn Alexander the Great, with nothing to fear from the emperors of Whitehall.

From rate support to revenue support

In 1990, as part of the poll tax package, came further modification. The GREA was replaced by a Standard Spending Assessment (SSA) of what each authority should spend in order to achieve a common standard of service. This contained an equalisation element but was calculated on a simpler formula than before (based on needs in the following categories: education, social services, highways, police, fire, other, and capital finance). Whitehall would also set a notional poll tax (£380 in 1991) which authorities were supposed to accept. Thus a prediction of an authority's tax income could be based on its poll tax yield (notional figure multiplied by eligible population) plus its share of the NNDR. The amount each authority would receive in RSG would then be calculated by subtracting total tax income from the SSA. In contrast to the old, the new RSG was immutable once set at the beginning of each financial year; any marginal expenditure rises were to be passed on disproportionately to poll tax (thus a 1 per cent expenditure rise could mean a 4 per cent poll tax rise, an effect termed 'gearing'), thereby increasing the pain on local electors.

Borrowed time – financing capital development

If we cannot afford a holiday in Florida we do not go, but if we want a car or a house, we borrow because we see it as an investment. Similarly, local authorities borrow for *capital* expenditure but not for current expenditure. If they did the latter, they would soon end up in Queer Street, like the council of Liverpool when it fought central government in 1986 by refusing to collect rates and borrowing from the fabled gnomes of Zürich.

Borrowing is repaid from current income over time. This has the additional advantage of sharing the burden with future users. Loans are raised from the same sources as the private sector (banks, finance houses, foreign countries), as well as a government-sponsored Public Works Loans Board.

The hand of the centre

Central government has always taken an interest in local borrowing. Before 1981, authorities were obliged to gain approval via a

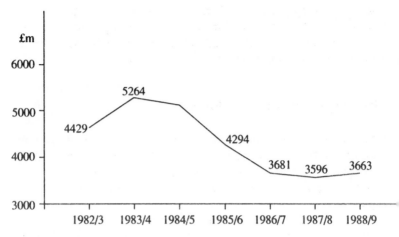

Figure 11.5   Local government expenditure – 1986–7 prices.
Source: data from CIPFA, 1988, table 4.2.

loan sanction process, though they were free to purchase capital assets from other income sources. The original purpose was centrally imposed efficiency, but in the post-war era the process became an instrument of economic demand management.

Although the Thatcher government renounced Keynesianism, its interest in local borrowing was greater than ever. A reduction in the Public Sector Borrowing Requirement (PSBR) was a key element in early monetarist strategy. In the Local Government Planning and Land Act 1980 the loan sanction procedure was replaced with a general central power to set ceilings on total capital expenditure, making authorities more than ever 'appendages of the central departments of state' (Duncan and Goodwin, 1988: 110). Figure 11.5 reveals how real reduction in capital spending was one of the Thatcher government's greatest successes. Subsequently the government allowed authorities to top up these annual capital expenditure allocations with capital receipts. However, these receipts became exceedingly large and provided authorities with another opportunity to practise the art of 'creative accounting', giving the central government further pause for thought.

With the introduction of the poll tax the process was changed again. The government gave itself the power to make *credit approvals* to authorities, covering all agreements to acquire capital goods. The intention was to force them to use capital receipts (money earned by the sale of capital, such as council houses) for paying off debts rather than further capital development. The bulk of the approvals were reserved for authorities with low capital receipts, mainly inner cities.

Looking at the books – the audit

Like all commercial undertakings, local authorities must submit their accounts for annual audit. Before 1983 this was undertaken by impartial district auditors. The purpose was to ensure good accounting practice, to root out corruption and detect *ultra vires* expenditure.

In 1983 the system was toughened up with the creation of a new Audit Commission, a centralised quango. Although the reform had been envisaged in the 1976 Layfield Report, the emphasis in 1983 was more Thatcherite, with a focus going beyond mere legality to consider value for money in commercial terms. The commissioners went into an authority more in the nature of management consultants, placing emphasis on cuts and criticising matters such as overtime bonuses, the payment of housing benefit (in 1988 Sheffield was accused of over-payment of £35,000 per week) and even recommending redundancies. The new commission was soon seen as a highly political instrument (with its director making controversial media statements), a development to be criticised by the accounting profession itself.

Conclusion – calling the tune

For many it seemed that local government had, during the 1980s, been subjected to a death of a thousand cuts. Yet the fact that the central financial assault was so prolonged and multifaceted testifies not only to its vehemence, but to a general incompetence. There was an air of desperation in the way that one thing was tried after another. Even the opening gambit, the great Land and Planning Act of 1980, was found to be illegal and retrospective legislation (the Local Government Finance Bill 1987) was needed to remove egg from the official face. The continuing farrago of 'repetitive legislation' forced the government to jettison its early pseudo-

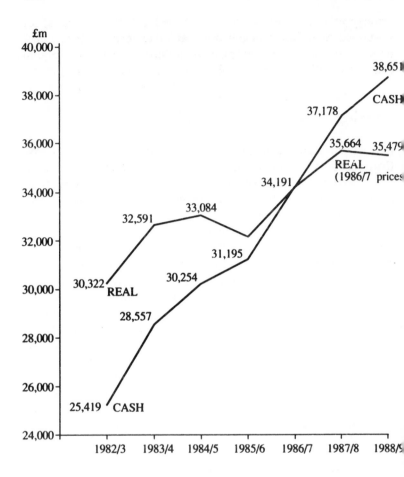

Figure 11.6 Local government current expenditure. Source: data from CIPFA 1988, table 4.2.

scientific jargon to reveal its political distaste for authorities controlled by its political opponents. Despite the rhetoric of saving and of curbing wasteful authorities, the extent to which real cuts were achieved remains debatable (Rhodes, 1988: 239–52).

Although capital spending certainly fell, Figure 11.6 reveals that current expenditure in both cash and real terms rose steadily in the period 1982–3 to 1988–9. However, within the totals there were variations between services. While education and social services were squeezed, expenditure on the police rose (there was also a shift from central to local government of responsibility for housing benefit in the early 1980s). In addition, inner-city Labour-controlled authorities with high levels of need suffered dispropor-tionately. Hence, the general effect has not been so much to reduce local expenditure as to increase the burden on the poor and most vulnerable.

However, with or without cuts, the effects of the financial re-forms clearly moved in the direction of greater central control. Criticism of this was by no means confined to political opponents. The Comptroller and Auditor General and Parliament's Public Accounts Committee saw in the developments greater inefficiency, less accountablity and less democracy. Even the Director of the Audit Commission observed grimly that, if the pattern continued, 'local government will be replaced by local administration – to the ultimate disbenefit of us all' (*The Guardian*, 26 April 1986).

12

Local Government Under Pressure

Local politics neither begins nor ends in the town hall; it can take to the streets in dramatic ways. We may be asked to sign petitions in the shopping precinct or witness rowdy demonstrations, council meetings can be disrupted by chanting protesters, parents may lie before oncoming rush-hour traffic to demand a zebra crossing for their children. Such events are very much part of politics. The number of people fighting elections will always be small but the number who will be drawn into some sort of local political activity is potentially limitless.

Not that it is always democratic. In secret meetings in the anonymous offices of the town hall, local notables may sip tea with the chief executive and treasurer discussing decisions which may cost local taxpayers millions of pounds, render people homeless, or even jeopardise the community's health with polluting forms of industry. This chapter opens a political Pandora's Box. After defining and classifying pressure groups, the chapter identifies the channels of communication and asks why some groups have better access than others. Finally we confront the big question of power within the community: at the end of the day, who gets what, and why?

What is a local pressure group?

The classic definition sees a pressure group as a body of individuals bound together by a common concern and desiring to influence public policy without actually gaining office. A local pressure group is one wishing to influence the policy of the council (or of some other public body active in the area). This definition distinguishes groups from political parties, which are primarily concerned with gaining office, but the distinction is by no means clear cut and can even be misleading. Many groups spend much time and energy in fighting elections and are very pleased if able to win seats. Indeed, at the local level the distinction is particularly blurred.

Another distinction is that between a 'pressure group' and an 'interest group'. Put simply the latter is an association of people sharing a common interest. It is only when they begin to act politically that it becomes a pressure group. Thus, interest groups outnumber pressure groups; indeed, Newton (1976: 38) identified over 4,000 organisations in the city of Birmingham alone, each a potential pressure group.

As in the case of parties, it is misleading to think of local interest groups entirely in parochial terms. While sewing circles, hanggliding clubs and preservation groups may be essentially local, many of the major groups active in local politics are really branches of national organisations. The big voluntary societies such as MENCAP, Age Concern or the NSPCC are nationally organised, as are the associations of the chief officers, local authority professions and unions such as NALGO and NUPE. In addition, the main economic interests, unions and employers associations, form themselves into 'peak organisations': the TUC and CBI. Even the beleaguered ratepayers organise themselves as the National Union of Ratepayers Associations. This centralisation is an important factor in understanding both the strategy and level of success of local political pressure.

Studying local groups

For many years orthodox textbooks paid scant attention to local interest groups. This reflected both a tendency to conceive local government as an apolitical branch of public administration and a traditional preoccupation with legalistic interpretations. Yet the omission was gravely misleading since, from the beginning, the balance of community power has been more important to an understanding of municipal events than legal rules. The tradition began to change with greater emphasis on behaviourism within the social sciences, although this area remains somewhat cloudy.

Classifying groups

Whose interest?

It is usual to classify interest groups as sectional or promotional. The former look out for themselves while the latter are concerned with the promotion of some ideal.

Sectional groups
These are sometimes termed economic groups since the common interest is often economic. Membership is usually restricted to those directly involved. There are many examples of sectional groups in local politics (tenants' groups, shopkeepers' associations and so on). The nature of the locality will help determine the kinds found; in rural areas the National Farmers' Union is highly visible, but in the industrial towns, factory owners and trade unions have dominated. Large firms can often act as pressure groups in their own right but smaller ones may band together as chambers of commerce or local branches of the CBI. A particularly important category comprises the various sections of the authority's own massive work-force: the associations of the professions and the public sector trade unions. In addition, there are hundreds of organisations and societies which can at some time expect to find their fate lying in the hands of a council (say a rugby club threatened with the loss of its ground, parents threatened with the closure of the local school and so on).

Promotional groups
These pursue goals other than the direct interests of members; they are sometimes called cause groups. The League Against Cruel Sports opposes activities such as foxhunting, the National Council for Civil Liberties is concerned with civic freedom and so on. Sometimes the fight is on behalf of those too weak to speak for themselves; thus Shelter is concerned with housing for the poor, the National Society for the Prevention of Cruelty to Children with

child abuse, and the Howard League presses for penal reform. Sometimes it is a matter of self-help as with, for instance, Alcoholics Anonymous. Its responsibility for collective consumption services makes local government a prime target for promotional groups and the 1980s saw a dramatic rise in the number of voluntary organisations attempting to plug the gaps in a crumbling welfare state.

Holding together

Another basis for classification concerns the reason that groups form and the way they maintain cohesion. American political scientist Gabriel Almond (Almond and Powell, 1966: 70–80) suggested the following four categories:

(1) *Institutional groups*. These do not exist primarily to influence government (churches, business associations, trade unions, sports clubs, voluntary associations and so on). Mancur Olson (1968: 143) sees this type as by far the most successful because they have a ready-made power base in the form of a large membership, considerable expertise and secure funds. Business associations are particularly effective, as are many voluntary organisations. There are also some very powerful local institutional groups within the public sector, including the local authorities' own bureaucracies.

(2) *Associational groups*. These form specifically for the purpose of influencing government. Thus, for example, CND would in all probability cease to exist if governments abandoned nuclear weapons. Groups of this kind are very evident in local politics, often associated with new road schemes, hospital closures, educational changes, housing and so on. Lacking any other basis for membership, they have more difficulty in holding together.

(3) *Non-associational groups*. These are people sharing a common interest but not formally organised. They may be regarded as potential, or latent, groups ready to mobilise should a threat emerge. Examples abound in local politics, such as ethnic groups, social classes (or sub-classes), estate residents, parents and so on. It is argued that they are influential because decision makers take cognisance of their interests to prevent them hardening into organised groups and becoming awkward.

(4) *Anomic groups*. These are sections of the population with little feeling of involvement, bargaining power or sense of organisation. Generally they comprise the most severely underprivileged, who during the 1980s began to form a new underclass. Anomic groups tend to resort to violent, extreme, though ultimately ineffective, modes of action. They can include squatters, drug dependents and alcoholics living on the fringes of society in the decaying inner cities. Their problems are often closely associated with homelessness, bringing them into confrontation with the local authorities. However, although unable to help themselves, their cases may be put by voluntary associations.

Individuals and groups

Pressure groups are not soulless collectivities; they comprise individuals, some of whom are energetic political activists. A study of the 'British poverty lobby' revealed that of thirty-nine groups concerned with income maintenance (Age Concern, Gingerbread and so on) around half were run by 'political entrepreneurs' (Whiteley and Winyard, 1984). The highly visible Shelter was formed by a small group stirred by the celebrated television drama-documentary *Cathy Come Home*, highlighting the harrowing plight of Britain's young homeless. Group leaders can become local notables, as well known as councillors. Trade union and business leaders similarly use their organisations as power bases for personal political activity. All are part of a local 'stage army' manning a host of committees, boards and working parties orchestrating community life (Hill, 1970).

Pathways to power

Local groups require channels of access to decision makers. Broadly there are six: the public at large, the council itself, the 'local executive', political parties, the bureaucracy and the non-elective sector. In addition, there is a quite different avenue via central government.

The public

If a group can create a favourable climate of opinion life is much easier. A council will be far more willing to adopt a popular proposal than one likely to incur vote-losing hostility. Some start with a great advantage in that their missions are widely approved. Groups espousing children's causes can invariably count on widespread sympathy but those seeking help for drug abusers or the wives of convicted criminals, for example, cannot expect their collection boxes to gain great weight as they stand in the high street.

There are various ways of alerting public opinion. Marches and demonstrations can win publicity but if violence breaks out, perhaps involving grim confrontations with the police, the publicity can be adverse. Indeed, such tactics are a last resort after other avenues have been denied, or have failed. The local media can provide publicity either by reporting a group's activities or by publishing letters and articles from members. However, the local press is generally controlled by the political right, so that many typical local groups cannot expect a favourable image projection. The 'loony left', a skilful creation of the tabloids during the 1980s, was a major factor in British politics.

It is possible to influence public opinion in a more subtle manner, by feeding a subliminal message of what is proper, reasonable and desirable. This is easier for the political right as it is largely accomplished through the press, including the increasing use of free sheets force-fed through unprotected letter-boxes. These are financed by advertising and generally implant a right-wing view of life, stressing the virtues of local businesses, which are usually portrayed as guardians of the local community rather than as footloose, profit-hungry cosmopolitans ready to pull up local roots once commercial prospects look cloudy.

The council

The local council can be approached as an entity or through individual back-benchers. A common device is the petition signed by a large number of local residents and presented at a council meeting. Being so formal an approach, it is difficult for the council to sweep the issue under the municipal carpet and the presence of the press can mean a chance for publicity. In meetings councillors themselves can function as spokespersons for particular causes. They may also sit *ex officio* on the boards of various associations where they can become familiar with their aims and aspirations. Alternatively groups may get members coopted onto a relevant council committee; they may even get a representative elected directly onto the council.

The 'local executive'

It is even more useful if a group is able to gain the support of one of the council's leading lights: a member of the Policy and Resources Committee, a committee chairperson, or even the council leader. Of course, privileged access of this kind is not available to all: it is linked with the next channel.

The parties

The distinction between pressure groups and parties breaks down when it is realised that the Labour and Conservative parties have deep historic links with certain interests, the former with the unions and the latter with business. In each case the relationship is a financial one, and when the interest groups pay the piper they will be expecting no small say in the tune. Moreover, the interest group members will often be central party figures, controlling the selection of candidates as local oligarchs.

The mandarins

The municipal officials, with their inestimable power to shape policy, spend much of their time closeted with representatives of various local interests. This may range from a confrontation with a group of irate parents to membership of a high-powered consultative body drawing together members of the local business elite to consider major developments – a new supermarket, sports stadium or multi-storey car park, for example. In addition, there are less formal bureaucractic avenues; officers are paid-up members of the middle class, speaking the same language as the local notables who dominate community life and meet at golf club, church and masonic lodge.

The non-elective sector

A quite different avenue for local groups to pursue their ends comes in the enlarging non-elective sector (see Chapter 4), where there are centres of power no less important than the municipal

'If we can stall long enough they'll become part of our heritage.'

institutions. District health authorities and urban development corporations making major decisions affecting the quality of local life are themselves prey to the attentions of groups, though here there is less democratic imperative to follow open patterns of consultation.

Central government

The existence of this avenue highlights the danger of conceiving local government as a miniature state rather than as part of a wider political system. If local groups are unsuccessful they can have a further bite at the cherry if they are able to turn to Westminster to persuade central government to override the local authority. Of course, not all groups can take this route; those that are part of national organisations are best placed. Very often a local dispute escalates to national proportions. Thus, if teachers feel aggrieved by their local authority they can call on the NUT to bring its full might to bear on the Department of Education and Science, the minister, and even the Cabinet.

It is generally weakening to local democracy if groups are able to do this. Business interests are particularly well placed to call for assistance. Cockburn's Lambeth study found that 'deals that matter most to them, over taxation and employment policy, grants and control, are deals done at Westminster and Whitehall' (Cockburn, 1977a: 45). The effect is particularly hard on associations of ordinary working-class people. What is the use of petitioning a local council to prevent, for instance, an environmentally damaging supermarket development, if the thwarted multinational giant, perhaps pouring money liberally into the coffers of the Conservative Party, can secure ministerial intervention?

Insiders and outsiders

It is clear that not all local groups enjoy the same quality of access. This fact leads to a crucial distinction between what are termed *insider* and *outsider* groups.

Insider groups

These are able to command the ear of power with relative ease. They are invited to sit on consultative bodies and their leaders are usually able to telephone the town hall for an informal chat when some information or favour is desired. Groups of this kind usually possess the following important political resources:

(1) *Knowledge*. The authority can depend heavily upon groups for information. Thus businessmen know most about the economy, architects are the experts on building, voluntary organisations best understand the problems of the homeless and so on.

(2) *Veto power*. There are policy areas where implementation would be impossible without group cooperation. Voluntary associations play a major part in service delivery, and local employment levels are dependent on businessmen. The authority's own

work-force has enormous veto power, fear of which contributed to Conservative contracting-out policy which weakened the in-house unions.

(3) *Communication.* The local authority frequently needs to address sections of the community. By speaking to a few chosen group leaders it can disseminate information and target particular audiences.

(4) *Legitimation.* If councillors can show that they have gained the assent of group leaders potential protesters will find much of the wind removed from their sails. This is particularly the case in planning, where the environmental lobby's approval is a *sine qua non* of progress (Lowe and Goyder, 1983: 95).

Thus we find in many localities a closed community where the party activists, burghers, freemasons, rotarians and various local notables meet regularly on this or that committee, advisory board or consultative council. At the informal level favours will be exchanged and a nod, a wink, or a special handshake will ensure that business takes place both on the surface and beneath. Although not so secretive as the private sector, this is a rather shadowy world where from time to time corruption, such as the notorious Poulson affair, is scandalously uncovered. Although such activities rarely find their way into standard textbooks, the 'Rotten Boroughs' column of *Private Eye* gleefully keeps readers informed.

Of course the kinds of group granted insider status will vary, particularly with the political complexion of the council. In the Conservative shires the agricultural interest is dominant as landowners hunt profits and fish favours in the county halls (Newby *et al.*, 1978: 235), while in left-wing authorities such as Sheffield (Hampton, 1970) the trade unions and trades councils are close to the decision makers.

Outsider groups

These inhabit a colder world. Their causes are often unpopular, concerned with the weak, vulnerable and despised in society (single-parent families, women's movements, ethnic minorities, slum communities, claimants' unions and so on). From the first industrialisation produced inequality, and many major studies of poverty have been urban based, in areas such as London and

Chicago. Even in housing, an area of particularly acute concern to the poor, it was found that ordinary citizens' groups were excluded in favour of establishment interests (Dunleavy, 1981). One result of this exclusion is a tendency to take to the streets. The politics of the outsiders is not that of the club or the warm carpeted office; it happens in the derelict house, the rumbling street, to the sound of breaking glass, chanting, and sometimes the beating of shields by riot-masked special police groups. The protesters ask forlornly, 'Whose town is this?' But they will usually lose, sometimes to the crack of the firearm, the truncheon and the sight of blood. Although their strategies can expect little success, they have few alternatives.

Who governs? Power and local politics

How do interest groups fit into the local political process? Various perspectives are taken on the all-important questions of power in the state. Can these throw light into the dark corners of the town halls?

Local pluralism

Pluralism is a theory of the democratic state which sees power fragmented between various public and private institutions. Such a model is accepted by orthodox political scientists in the liberal tradition. It is characterised by features such as the following:

(1)   All are free to form or join any association they wish: the fundamental right to freedom of assembly.

(2)   Public policy is the outcome of discussion and compromise. The government is more referee between competing interests than policy maker.

(3)   No single interest will gain disproportionate influence because all balance each other.

(4)   The system is fairer than elections (one person, one vote) because those with the strongest feelings can work harder to get more from the system.

(5)   Those not in groups will be considered because they will be regarded as latent groups, ready to mobilise if threatened.

(6) Policies will be moderate, legitimate and conducive to stability. No one is entirely a loser.

Robert Dahl (1961), doyen of US pluralists, conducted a celebrated study of local government in New Haven which presented a relieved liberal establishment with a benign picture approximating to this model. But how realistic is it? It belongs to a liberal orthodoxy which favours minimal government, a political version of the *laissez-faire* economy which argues that if everyone looks after him/herself the end result for society is the best possible allocation of resources. However, this idea is bogus; for some it is a state of anarchy where the strong hold sway, with as little state impediment as possible. Similarly, pluralism can be seen as a form of political anarchy in which certain interests (the insiders) are far better placed than others.

Local corporatism

This alternative view of pressure group activity takes account of their uneven access. The government is not seen as a passive referee; it sets up elaborate patterns of consultation (incorporation), some interests being warmly embraced while others are excluded.

Local government possesses some highly corporatist features. There are formal provisions for incorporation including a network of local consultative committees and advisory bodies meeting regularly to unite the locally great and good. There is even provision for incorporation into the very heart of the policy-making process by cooption onto the authority's all-important committees (up to one-third of the membership). It is generally the business interests which enjoy the closest relationships, particularly with officers. The introduction of corporate planning after 1974 tended to increase opportunities for this cosy marriage (Cockburn, 1977a: 35).

In addition, many voluntary organisations work hand in glove with official agencies delivering services. These provide information, sit on joint consultative councils, conduct joint research and receive large grants. The Seebohm Report (1968) on local authority personal social services enthusiastically urged such incorporation, recommending that social services departments be focal points in a partnership relationship.

This is a world of exclusion as well as inclusion, the favoured groups not having to compete with rivals as in the pluralist model.

There is little need to take to the streets, squat, demonstrate, or beat one's head against a brick wall of bureaucratic intransigence. Here difficult decisions can be discussed over a round of golf or on a trip to Spain. The movement towards contracting-out offers increased incentives for business interests to seek close relationships with decision takers.

Interest group activity around the non-elected sector is even more secretive. Urban development corporations may consult with whatever groups they choose, and their businessmen leaders will have their strongest affinities with capitalist interests. This is a world unknown to elective government, a world of multinational enterprise lubricated with backhanders, slush-funds and sweeteners.

Local elitism

Elitist theory argues that the great mass of people in any community naturally falls prey to domination by the few (see pp. 246–7). In one famous study Floyd Hunter (1953) showed local social and political life in the US to be dominated by small wealthy cohorts. C. Wright Mills (1959: 126n.) argued that pluralism was more 'ideological hope' than true description. Many British case studies (such as Dearlove, 1973; Cockburn, 1977a; Saunders, 1980) discern high levels of local elitism.

Elitism is not only to be measured in terms of the advantages of wealth. Chapter 9 revealed it to be woven into the fabric of local administration (Wilson, 1988). For Pahl (1975: 207), the local elite become the managers of urban life. 'The controllers, be they planners or social workers, architects or education officers, estate agents or property developers, representing the market or the plan, private enterprise or the state, all impose their goals and values on the lower participants in the system'. The bureaucrats are at their most comfortable with those from similar backgrounds. They can sincerely 'believe that they are behaving quite properly and . . . not see that they are consulting a minority opinion' (Hill, 1974: 87). In this insulated capsule of professional power, elitism produces a form of local government best termed gin-and-tonic corporatism.

The local capitalist state

Local government in its nineteenth-century pomp was the very essence of elitism. Those dominating both society and the municipal institutions were the local business magnates, and to this day they gaze down upon younger generations from the splendour of their aldermanic portraits lining the stately town hall corridors.

Domination arising from economic structure leads to a Marxist explanation. Here the key to power in society is believed to lie in ownership of the vital materials (factories, machines and so on) needed by a community for survival. Under capitalism these are not owned by the community but by a small number of individuals. As a result they become enormously powerful, effectively controlling the government because without their cooperation the economy will crash.

Today the economy operates on a national and international scale. Is it still possible for business interests to dominate local politics? Dearlove (1973) found business leaders on first-name terms with officers in the London Borough of Kensington and Chelsea, while Saunders (1980) revealed the councillors of the London Borough of Croyden to be working hand in glove with capitalist interests in planning the commercial development of the town centre. Cynthia Cockburn's study of Lambeth (1977a) shows that, even when an authority is a Labour stronghold, its most important policies favour the business elite. Moreover, the Thatcher era saw a reassertion of the rights of the small entrepreneur, often demonstrated in a strengthening of the hands of local chambers of commerce. The commercial interests run on the inside track because they are able to cultivate the view that what is best for them is also best for the community. Although business development means more profits, more profits mean more jobs, a better city and so on.

This perspective not only tells us about council decision making, it speaks on the nature of urban life, which is a social formation designed in sympathy with production (Castells, 1983). Earlier chapters have noted how the cities grew up as great dormitories to house the giant labour force required by factory mass production methods. However, this imposes costs. The urban way of life has long been synonymous with tension, pain, danger and loneliness (Wirth, 1938). Urban transport systems take workers, like sardines, to and from the city centres; roads jam with high-density (high-polluting) traffic; schools place utilitarian skills before wider education; mass housing is made as cheaply as possible and those with no place in the productive process will have difficulty in being housed at all. In a post-Fordist era the big factories give way to the out-of-town, small, hi-tech industries and the deserted inner cities decay, housing only those unable to stake out new territories in the leafy countryside (see pp. 257–8).

Those suffering will struggle for improvements in living standards and will petition local authorities for basic rights (to housing, health, amenities and so on) and social services (Offe, 1985). Urban riots reached a crescendo in Britain during the first term of the Thatcher government as unemployment peaked, and re-emerged in the third term (Benyon, 1984; Benyon and Solomos 1987). However, because social services must be paid for by taxes on profitability there will be strict limits on the concessions made. Hence it is inevitable both that urban protest movements will form and that they will be resisted by the local state institutions. This is a recipe for tension.

Tipping the balance

Central government can influence mightily the balance of local interests. This can be particularly well illustrated in the long series of attempts to deal with the problems of the inner cities. The 'rediscovery of poverty' by Peter Townsend in the 1960s (see Chapter 4) (Townsend, 1975) was a signal for a variety of local outsider groups to join the chorus, pointing out that they had been talking prose on this subject for some time. Various initiatives followed which sought to mobilise local groups behind council efforts, partly under the inspiration of the large-scale Anti-Poverty Programme mounted in the US in the early 1960s (Higgins *et al.*, 1983).

This was followed by *Community Development Projects* which made reports highly critical of the power of businesses to destroy local economies. The 1970 Conservative government commissioned professional consultants to conduct *Inner Area Studies* in three of the most problematic areas – Lambeth, Liverpool and Birmingham – which confirmed the diagnoses (Department of the Environment, 1977: 297). However much a local authority might want to cooperate with groups representing the underprivileged, they would have a Sisyphean task in the face of the imperatives of capitalism.

However, the New Right was generally opposed to pressure groups. Olson (1982) argued that their natural tendency was to increase public expenditure, while Beer (1982: 31) lamented that Britain had reached a point of 'pluralist stagnation' in which over-loaded governments were unable to govern. This analysis applied most appositely to those groups concerned with expensive collective consumption services, and the willingness of authorities to listen to them was seen not as an attempt to solve the problem, but as one of its principal causes.

Privatising the community

The result was a series of initiatives designed to shift the locus of local political power even more firmly in the direction of the local business interests (Massey, 1982: 443). Enterprise zones were designated where businesses would receive a variety of profit-enhancing incentives. After the menacing riots at Toxteth the government established the Merseyside Task Force, a body of White-hall mandarins and local business interests under the Secretary of State for the Environment to rebuild the local economy. This became the model for the urban development corporations set up in other large urban areas. Their urban recycling programmes were mainly for the benefit of the young and aspiring, with little meaning for members of outsider groups inhabiting the colder regions of the capitalist economy.

The policy of increasing the power of local business interests went even further after the 1987 Conservative general election victory. A policy of *Action for Cities* reflected an atavistic desire to re-create the nineteenth-century municipal model when local businessmen ruled the roost: 'The inner cities need to rediscover the sense of civic pride that once united residents and businesses' (Cabinet Office, 1988). At the very time that grants to councils were being slashed, a City Grants Scheme in 1988 gave funds directly to local businesses; over £100 million was distributed in 1987–88.

The strategy aroused sustained opposition from the excluded groups. It was part of the motive behind the rise of the New Urban Left, though the failure of the movement was to stand as a vivid illustration of the might of capital. The approach posed burning moral questions. In 1985 the Right Reverend Robert Runcie, Archbishop of Canterbury, set up an inquiry into the inner cities, and its report, *Faith in the City,* was a crushing indictment of the government.

Conclusion – who wins?

Although there are many interest groups in the local political process it is seriously misleading to conclude that policy is the outcome of benignly pluralistic process. Some interests are much
more powerful than others, and generally these are the representatives of capital. Pressure from organisations representing the
underprivileged can gain concessions, but when they threaten
private-sector profitability (as they did in the 1980s) the centre will
step in to ensure the well-being of the capitalist interests.

Although the idea of local pluralism is partly mythical, it is vital
to establishment interests. It helps legitimate the distribution of
power by suggesting that, even though some may do rather better
than others, all start the race from the same tape and run along a
level track; here the winners are worthy of their prizes and the
losers have only themselves to blame. Hence, the Thatcher ploy to
eliminate consultation from the process of government (central
and local) was a high-risk strategy. Social life in Britain's cities
becomes increasingly tense as the number of outsiders increases.

13

Local Government at Westminster and Whitehall

It has been apparent throughout the chapters of this book that local government exists in a highly centralised state. Hence it is not surprising that the central institutions are particularly concerned with municipal matters. Policy towards local government emerges from a complex process and its source is often difficult to pin down. This chapter examines the Westminster–Whitehall complex, looking particularly at institutions concerned with municipal affairs. It then takes a wider perspective on the other interests involved in the process – the local government policy community or sub-government. The conclusion assesses the relevance of the corporatist view today.

Policy for local government

The simple model of representative government asks us to believe that ordinary people make policy by voting for politicians on the basis of manifesto promises. This is naïve; no government can present all its policies, few people read manifestos, advertising hype and a largely right-wing media corrupt political choice, no one can anticipate what day-to-day decisions must be made by government during its term, and so on. To counter the manifest deficiencies in the system we have the theory of pluralism, which argues that the real way people influence policy is not by voting but through a continuing process of lobbying.

However, pluralism does not work in the way apologists claim, since some pressure groups are excluded altogether while others enjoy disproportionate influence, and we are left with a rather selective form of pluralism which is better termed corporatism.

This secretive network is fragmented into smaller sub-systems concerned with particular areas of policy and known variously as sub-governments, policy communities and policy networks, formed around certain departments of state where particular interests reign supreme. Sometimes the groups use collective intermediaries such as, for instance, the Confederation of British Industry (CBI) (Grant and Marsh, 1977). These are 'peak organisations' which amalgamate a large number of congruent interests in a single voice. They are key features in the idea of corporatism; the aggregation of interests reduces competition and makes groups more compliant and 'reasonable' towards government.

These considerations suggest the framework of this chapter. Can a local government sub-government be identified? Do local authorities form peak organisations? How can local government influence the policy made by central government? The chapter begins with the Westminster–Whitehall machinery and then extends the focus to the other actors in the process.

Local government at Westminster

Parliament has long been interested in local matters. The founder members of the House of Commons were knights representing their shires before the royal authority. Indeed, the right of towns to return an MP was one of the advantages of incorporated borough status.

The golden age

In the nineteenth century Parliament's role in local government became vital. The great Reform Act of 1832, which gave the vote to the urban bourgeoisie, produced profound changes in the composition of the House of Commons, giving power to the new industrial interests, intent on constitutional reform through legislation.

The period 1832–67 is often described as the 'golden age' of parliamentary government. It was also a golden age for lawyers, who grew fat as a great tidal wave of public and private legislation swept through Parliament, building the modern system of local government.

Public legislation included some major enactments which established the modern municipality (see pp. 28–31). Public Acts could be *permissive*, in that authorities were empowered, but not compelled, to apply the measures or *mandatory*, meaning that they were obliged to follow them.

The increase in private legislation was even greater. This was a result of the movement for the creation of *ad hoc* bodies (whereby citizens of an area gained the authority to operate a service) and of the desire of certain go-ahead municipalities to acquire additional responsibilities. Local MPs were expected to play a key role in fighting for Bills from their constituencies.

So great was the deluge that Parliament was obliged to develop special procedures to speed things up. In both the Lords (much used for private legislation) and the Commons, small expert committees were created and, from 1846, the practice began of sending private Bills to Whitehall for examination. Parliament sometimes extended the provisions of a good private Act to cover all areas by passing a public Act. Alternatively it would pass adoptive Acts, containing provisions which local authorities could pick up 'off the shelf' and incorporate in their own legislation with a considerable saving in lawyers' fees. Thus, for example, the Town Improvements Clauses Act 1847 set out, in 216 sections, provisions in areas such as paving, street lighting, street cleaning and so on.

Golden sunset

However, the golden age was soon to become a golden sunset. Further franchise extension and the rise of disciplined mass party machines was to erode MPs' independence. The idea of Parliament as a place to represent local interests become a fiction; the parties became more concerned to represent their backers from the trade unions and the oak-panelled board-rooms.

Nevertheless, MPs retain the basic right to speak on behalf of their constituencies and will be advised by councils when local issues, such as new bypasses or power stations, are being debated.

In addition, Parliament can debate, question and criticise the government, an ability greatly enhanced since the entry into the Commons in 1989 of the unblinking eye of television. Parliament may also use scrutiny committees to ferret into departmental processes. The Select Committee on the Environment and those concerned with education, police and social services are particularly interested in matters municipal. Yet pressure on the timetable (guillotined debates, the rota for parliamentary questions and so on) means that little time can be devoted to local government. Moreover, the Environment Committee has proved one of the more lethargic of its kind, with few reports and poor attandance by members (Englefield, 1984: xix).

Perhaps most importantly, MPs can exert influence through back-bench revolt. This can only happen if members of the party in power become involved, but the tendency increased in both Houses from the 1970s (Norton, 1985; Baldwin, 1985). The Acts to reform local government in London in 1962 and in England and Wales in 1972 were both subject to modification as a result of pressure in the Commons and in the Lords. Some MPs and lords are extremely experienced in local government (they can even be members of councils).

The Paving Bill to prevent elections in the GLC and metropolitan counties prior to their abolition was dramatically defeated in the Lords, the Local Government Planning and Land Act of 1979 was withdrawn for amendment and the Bill to introduce local referendums before levying supplementary rates was withdrawn altogether. In March 1988 a revolt led to concessions in the poll tax legislation in the form of a £130 million rebate package and, in the following month, the government was obliged to head off a threatened rebellion over housing benefit with concessions worth £100 million.

Beyond the formal processes on the floor of the House, MPs can exert influence through the parliamentary parties which regularly bring leaders into contact with back-benchers. There are also cross-bench territorial groupings and beneath the surface are the ongoing informal relationships which characterise Westminster life. Ministers may be accosted in the tea-rooms, bars and corridors, and a government must constantly consider 'what the lads will stand'. Such liaisons are a prime responsibility of the party whips.

The national parties

Specialised machinery exists within the parties to shape policy towards local government.

The Conservatives

When Labour stormed Westminster in the dramatic post-war landslide, the Conservative Party began to contemplate its policy navel in considerable earnest. A subcommittee on local government was formed which become the National Advisory Committee for Local Government (NACLG). Today this comprises party group leaders from various local authorities, Conservative members of the local authority associations (see pp. 221–2), backbench MPs, a peer and various advisers. When in opposition front-benchers also attend (Gyford and James, 1983: 31). Within the NACLG is a smaller Policy Liaison Group and various specialist committees. In addition to advising on policy, NACLG acts as a sounding-board on grass-roots feeling and mobilises support for the leader. Central Office also has a Local Government Organisation Department, although this is concerned more with administration than policy.

The annual conference usually includes at least one debate on local government and, in addition, there is a special one-day local government conference and a policy weekend – jamborees to reward and inspire. They allow the faithful toilers at the parish pump to draw near and admire their princes and princesses. However, during the Thatcher years harmony was less evident, with some delegates denouncing their leader's policies.

More specific policy advice can come from the Research Department, considerably beefed-up under Mrs Thatcher. However, it has not been particularly interested in local government (Ramsden, 1980). During the Thatcher era the real inspiration came from various satellite think-tanks, particularly the Centre for Policy Studies set up by Sir Keith Joseph. The New Right nostrums brewed here were to have profound implications for local government. Indeed, the Adam Smith Institute not only proffered much advice on the introduction of free-market techniques into the municipal sphere, it reinforced its wisdom with sustained political lobbying (Forsyth, 1980).

Labour

The Labour constitution makes the party conference the supreme policy-making body although in practice the NEC (see p. 107) is the centre of authority. However, its composition does not make provision for direct local government representation. Councillors may serve on it, as shown by the election to the NEC in 1983 of David Blunkett, leader of Sheffield City Council, but not as of right. Among the NEC policy committees is a Regional and Local Government Subcommittee (RLGS), and the party also appoints a Local Government Officer with a research staff. Since 1956 there has been a three-day national conference for local councillors which is attended by party leaders. Unlike the main conference, resolutions do not automatically become policy.

The Labour ward and constituency organisations have a greater say in policy than their Conservative counterparts, but the consensus years saw little interest in local government, with few conference resolutions and debates (Craig, 1981). However, the post-1979 Thatcher assault concentrated the collective mind and the value of local democracy began to feature on the agenda. Even so, the New Urban Left was never popular with moderates and local government was not specifically considered when six policy review groups were set up after the 1987 general election defeat.

Local government at Whitehall

For centuries the central state had been content to leave parish and borough matters largely alone. However, the rising nineteenth-century bourgeoisie had a different view. Whitehall machinery emerged with a specifically municipal orientation.

Towards a Ministry for Local Government

The poor law reform of 1834 was highly symbolic. It placed a non-elected, high-handed, central Poor Law Commission, not responsible to Parliament, over locally elected authorities. The model was unpopular and in 1847 the Commission was replaced by a Poor Law Board, a veritable ministry for the poor under a responsible minister. The model was cloned for the administration of sanitation with the creation, in 1848, of a Central Board of Health to supervise local health authorities. Again the Central Board was unpopular and in 1858 its functions passed to various other government departments.

Developments were partly a response to exogenous forces. In the second half of the nineteenth century British industrial superiority was being challenged by the United States and Germany. Economic decline caused a crisis of confidence in the liberal state, making the case for stronger central government more insistent. At the same time, this was becoming more feasible as the machinery of state was modernised following the Northcote–Trevelyan report of 1853.

In 1871, a Royal Commission on sanitary conditions recommended the creation of a single central ministry to galvanise local authorities into action. The result was the Local Government Board (LGB), which assumed responsibility for the Poor Law, public health and various municipal interests of the Home Office. The status of the LGB was raised in 1879 when it took over the audit of the local accounts from authorities themselves, enabling it to extend its tentacles beyond the Poor Law and public health into other areas of local government.

Yet complete control remained elusive. The LGB lacked any clear policy, the existence of the rates meant that it had no control over poor relief levels and it was plagued by internal disharmony. Moreover, it was obliged to share its municipal responsibilities with other departments, including the following:

Privy Council. Various medical functions including the control of poisons, medical registration and supervision of midwives. A committee of the Council supervised the central grant to the school boards established by the 1870 Education Act.

Home Office. Industrial disease, inspection of mines and quarries, asylums, reformatories, inebriates, workmen's compensation and industrial schools.

Board of Education. Set up in 1902 when local authorities took over from the school boards.

The Board of Agriculture. Oversight of the sale of food and drugs and diseases in animals.

The Board of Trade. Shipping and water supply.

The National Health Insurance Commission. Established under the 1911 National Insurance Act.

In 1919 a Ministry of Health replaced the National Insurance Commission and LGB, and took over various functions connected with local administration and health which had been held by other departments. Thus a single ministry was responsible for a wide range of functions including health, the Poor Law, national insurance pensions, local government finance, local government boundaries, housing and town planning.

Health functions were subsequently removed with the creation of the NHS and in 1951 the Ministry of Housing and Local Government (MHLG) was established. In 1974, as part of the fashion for giant Whitehall departments, the mighty Department of the Environment (DoE) emerged (subsuming the MHLG and various other responsibilities). Although more a loose conglomerate than an integrated whole (Painter, 1980: 142), it was a powerful empire and the Secretary of State became a major government figure.

However, the multi-functional portfolios of local authorities mean that various other departments (the DES, DSS, DH and the Home Office) continue to take considerable interest in their activities. Perhaps the greatest interest is taken by Her Majesty's Treasury, with its hands forever on the nation's purse-strings.

The Treasury

Any consideration of Whitehall policy making must accord a special place to Her Majesty's Treasury. Heclo and Wildavsky (1974) characterise Whitehall as an intimate village community where the Treasury conducts endless bilateral negotiations with the spending departments: haggling over costs, questioning new policies and weighing the demands of one programme against another. All policy will ultimately bear the Treasury imprimatur. Under Mrs Thatcher the character of the Treasury changed, with the Keynesians of the post-war era usurped by the monetarists. The general ethos of public expenditure cuts was to increase Treasury power within Whitehall; departments concerned with local services (education, housing and so on), as well as the DoE itself, were particularly weakened. Ministers resisting cuts were obliged to appear before a high-powered Cabinet committee known forbiddingly as the 'Star Chamber'.

The Cabinet

At the heart of the policy making process stands the Cabinet, chaired by the Prime Minister. During the 1980s the centralising tendencies in British government reached an apogee when Margaret Thatcher effectively ended any debate that she was merely *primus inter pares* (first among equals). Essentially the Cabinet consists of ministers heading the departments; there are no 'policy ministers'. This means that, although it is supposed to work collectively, the Cabinet is a fiercely competitive forum, with each minister expected to fight the departmental corner. Within the Cabinet there is a hierarchy, with some positions (such as Chancellor and Foreign Secretary) carrying more weight than others. Those concerned with local government are, with the exception of the Home Secretary (responsible for the police), not the most prestigious. They cannot expect to win many arguments if powerful colleagues are ranged against them.

Yet today the Cabinet is almost a dignified part of the constitution, most work being done through its committees, chaired by ministers, junior ministers, civil servants and the Prime Minister. The radical policies of the 1980s saw a Local Government Affairs Committee chaired by Margaret Thatcher herself, as well as *ad hoc* committees to consider the abolition of the GLC and metropolitan counties, rates reform, the poll tax and so on. The system is paralleled by a network of official committees where civil servants discuss the same issues in advance, in order to prepare the way for ministers: one of the many formidable sources of mandarin power.

Notwithstanding the pomp and ceremony of the formal Westminster–Whitehall process, the policy making landscape has not yet been fully charted. The official machinery is surrounded by an informal cluster of interests and pressures constituting a local government policy community. The relationships are symbiotic; the groups want government help but they provide valuable information, assist in the implementation of policies and, in the final analysis, can prove awkward if not appeased.

Walking the corridors of power – the policy community

Final parameters can never be drawn around this community. Some groups are core members, while others come and go

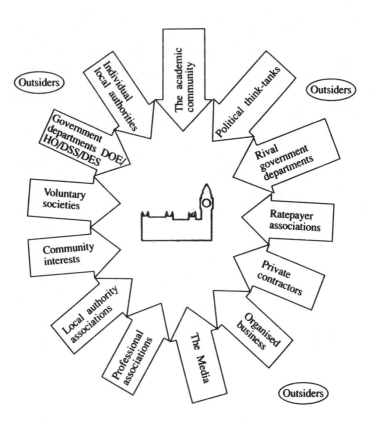

Figure 13.1 The local government policy community.

according to the shape of the agenda (see Figure 13.1). There are also the excluded interests, although they may sometimes gatecrash the party as uninvited guests. The following sections examine local authority associations, voluntary societies and professional bodies involved in local administration. In addition, the anti-local-government lobby and the outsider interests condemned to stand forlornly on the sidelines are also considered.

Talking collectively – the local authority associations

Local authorities may be seen as interest groups representing their areas. Their demands include economic growth, more territory, larger grants, responsibility for important functions and so on. However, many of these desires are shared in common (inner-city development grants for urban authorities, green-belt protection in the shires and so on) and associations have evolved machinery to develop collective views and present them to central government. These are peak organisations, visible signs of the climate of corporatism in which policy for local government is made.

Not surprisingly, the associations are products of the nineteenth century (Keith-Lucas and Richards, 1978: 181). The reorganisation of 1974 led to their recasting into the Association of Metropolitan Authorities (AMA) (to represent the top- and lower-tier authorities in Greater London and the metropolitan areas), the Association of County Councils (ACC) and the Association of District Councils (ADC). Within the AMA the London boroughs form the Association of London Authorities (ALA), and within the ACC and ADC the Welsh authorities have additional meetings, as do the twelve largest urbanised districts. However, in Scotland there is a single Convention of Scottish Local Authorities (COSLA).

The associations are highly organised, each headed by a council. Members are usually from the majority parties on their home councils so that the associations themselves are under party control. Although the ACC and ADC are generally more Conservative, while the AMA is Labour, the party of opposition at Westminster tends to dominate the associations. The long-standing Conservative hegemony on the ACC was lost in 1986 with the collapse of the Conservative vote in the local elections. COSLA has remained steadfastly Labour.

Much policy making takes place through subcommittees of the councils and the chairpersons can become well-known public figures. The associations also maintain bureaucracies to organise, administer and advise. Although these are relatively small (Isaac-Henry, 1984: 134), they can call upon full-time local government officers for help and can be highly influential.

The corporatist network binding local authorities, their associations and Whitehall has many strands, both formal and informal. The former involves numerous consultative councils, working parties and interdepartmental committees orbiting in the Whitehall galaxy. Some of these can be the great high-profile Royal Commissions producing major reports, while others labour in relative obscurity in the bowels of Whitehall. Of particular importance has been the Consultative Council on Local Government Finance (CCLGF), which brings together representatives of local authority associations, civil servants from various departments and ministers, including the Secretary of State for the Environment, who plays a leading role. Much of the work of the CCLGF is done through committees and working groups, producing papers setting out different policy options and their consequences (Chandler, 1988: 119).

There are also high-level *ad hoc* meetings between ministers and leading councillors, while informal contacts arise in countless ways. Politicians on both sides communicate within and between parties, while ministers foster relationships with opposition councillors in order to discover their views (Chandler, 1988: 82). Channels also link bureaucrats, ranging from a friendly telephone conversation to a round of golf or a drink in an exclusive London club. Central government corporatism generally takes place in the male, white, establishment world of pin-striped suits and upper-crust accents. The local government policy community does not have the aroma of prestige and power of the business communities but it can be closed and secretive to outsiders.

One alleged weakness of the associations is their plurality. Some advocate their replacement by a single body to articulate a unified local government view (Redcliffe-Maud, 1969, vol. I: 32, 107). However, such a recommendation reveals political naïveté. The differences between the urban areas and the shires are too great for a common front. The more likely outcome of a merger would be to weaken the organisations by submerging political debate.

Voluntary societies

There are hundreds of voluntary societies with close interests in social policy. These bear little resemblance to the Victorian philanthropic organisations which are their forebears. They are led by dynamic political operators with sophisticated skills (Salisbury, 1969). Des Wilson, the first director of Shelter, became a national political figure, while Frank Field was leader of the Child Poverty Action Group before going on to become an outspoken parliamentarian. These groups take part in formal and informal consultations with the DoE and other Whitehall departments, sit on consultative councils, meet mandarins and ministers and appear as media pundits. The 1980s saw their presence increased as the official welfare state looked increasingly anorexic.

Professional associations

Chapter 9 showed local government to be heavily professionalised and professional associations have a very visible presence in the policy community. One way they enter is as advisers to the local authority associations (Rhodes, 1986: ch. 3), and some leading municipal lawyers, treasurers and chief executives achieve political prominence in this way. The professions are also approached directly by central government, invited to sit on advisory bodies in their own right. In addition, informal relationships can develop between central and local officials. They meet at regional and national conferences and through the pages of their journals; 'parish magazines' of a professional community furthering a sense of common interest.

As leading pressure groups the professional associations are able to cast off their constitutional obligations to impartiality and contribute to wider political debate as policy experts. It is in their interest to depoliticise the agenda so that their voice, rather than that of the politicians, becomes the clarion of authority and orthodoxy. Yet, as with all pressure groups, self-interest comes before public interest. Thus were the architects able to visit upon the nation the horrific high-rise (high-suicide-rate) housing 'solutions' of the 1960s (Dunleavy, 1980: 107).

The anti-local-government lobby

Classical pluralist theory holds that, in a kind of Newtonian law of political motion, for every interest there is an equal and opposite one which will act as a counterbalance. Yet it is not common to speak of an anti-local-government lobby. Is such an idea fanciful? By no means.

Petit bourgeois interests

In the first place there are the ubiquitous ratepayer associations which oppose local expenditure in principle. They have a natural place in the heart of the Conservative Party. Moreover, in a capitalist state the fact that local government provides many of its services outside the market makes it intrinsically threatening. Firms which could make profits by offering a wide range of services, from school meals to refuse collection, are denied the opportunity. When capitalist interests speak in the decision making process they will call for less local provision and more contracting-out.

The capitalist state

Collective consumption services provided by local government threaten profitability in a fundamental way. Although they can be seen as socialising the costs of production, and hence in the interests of capital, they cost money which is raised through taxation. Once the economy falters, as in the mid-1970s, then a fiscal crisis of the state occurs in which industry is unwilling to provide the necessary funds (O'Connor, 1973; Gough, 1978). Indeed, anti-local-government sentiments reached an apogee in the thinking of the New Right expressed in various think-tank reports (Chapter 15). In the 1980s the state itself was part of the anti-local-government lobby, as was shown in the development of complex local state machinery outside council control (Chapter 4) and the movement towards privatisation (Chapter 3).

Central bureaucracy

A further source of opposition can come from the mandarins of Whitehall. Not only do they view their local administrative cousins with disdain; they see councillors, with their local mandates and policies, as irritating grit in the state machinery. This attitude was inlaid in the structure of public adminstration in the nineteenth century by the utilitarians, who created not only the modern local government system but also a profoundly elitist civil service. The heirs of Chadwick preserve their sense of superiority by deliberately remaining aloof, rarely visiting the authorities and cultivating blissful ignorance of the details of local administration (Chandler, 1988: 54).

Competing policy communities

There is considerable competition within the public sector, much of it institutionalised in the public expenditure system (see Chapter 11). In the struggle, each department can be assisted by those pressure groups associated with it (the links between the National Farmers' Union and Ministry of Agriculture, Fisheries and Food are well known) so that the policy communities can be said to be fighting each other. Guns or schools? parks or trunk roads? are classic dilemmas, and local government services will often lose out in the annual scramble for resources.

Moreover, there is competition within the municipal sub-government. Rhodes (1988) notes the existence of smaller policy communities or 'networks' within the larger community. Thus there are territorial policy communities, concerned with government strategy towards certain parts of the country, and various service-based communities concerned with, for instance, education or housing. In addition there are communities formed by distinctive professional groups and producer communities concerned with particular industries. Finally there are communities which form around a particular issue, such as inner-city regeneration. There is competition for resources between and within these networks. Indeed, there is no end to competition; it is also found between local authority associations and between the local authorities themselves (Rhodes, 1986).

The media

The press and broadcasting media traditionally showed little interest in municipal matters. This changed during the 1980s as the Thatcher assault and retaliation by the New Urban Left made local government front-page news. Generally the press and (to a lesser extent) the broadcasting media favour the right in politics (Curran and Seaton, 1981). This leads to an anti-local-government stance. Apart from the very direct attacks in the 1980s, when 'loony left' stories became *de rigueur*, the general anti-welfare statism and the 'scrounger' obsession tend to undermine local government, since much of its *raison d'être* lies in providing for collective consumption.

As noted in Chapter 8, there is a general tendency to poke fun at councillors, social workers and even teachers. It has been argued that the loony left strategy was seized upon by Conservative Central Office as a means 'not merely to gain local votes but as a national propaganda tool' (Lansley *et al.*, 1989: 175). However, it would be wrong to say that the media is entirely against social democracy; some radio and television programmes make strong social points (rousing the wrath of Conservative politicians during the 1980s). At the same time *The Guardian* newspaper is generally social democratic in its line (though itself subject to jibes from the right).

The outsiders

Not all local government interests enjoy the warm corporatist embrace; some shiver in the cold. To a considerable extent this is the case with trade unions representing the great mass of local authority employees in the lower reaches of the hierarchy. Unions such as NALGO and NUPE have enjoyed statutory representation on the Whitley Councils determining public sector pay and conditions of service, but are by no means as close to the corridors of power as the professional associations. Neither NUPE nor the GMWU gave evidence to the important Redcliffe-Maud Royal Commission (Chandler, 1978: 91). Even a professional union such as the NUT can find itself treated with disdain. Similarly, there are many voluntary associations promoting unpopular causes such as women's rights, racial issues, aid for prisoners' wives and so on. This category became larger in the 1980s as government policy turned a hard face towards those most in need of social services.

One response to the official cold shoulder is recourse to strikes and noisy publicity campaigns designed to rouse popular sympathy, but this is a two-edged sword, likely to rouse public hostility, as happened in the 'winter of discontent' of 1978–9 and the teachers' strikes of the 1980s. Moreover, even if the propaganda battle is won, as was the case in the campaign to save the GLC, an obdurate central government can still push through its policy (Duncan and Goodwin, 1988: 188–215).

Conclusion – twilight of corporatism

It is apparent that the process of making policy for local government is complex and labyrinthine. Beyond a vague agreement on the desirability of local self-determination for communities, there is no single local government interest as such. Rather, there is multilayered competition between and within policy communities.

However, by the 1970s, the corporatist heyday of British government appeared to be past (Lehmbruch and Schmitter, 1982). Edward Heath's relationship with the unions had reached an all-time low and the right bewailed 'ungovernability crises' and 'pluralist stagnation'. The humiliating collapse of Callaghan's 'Social Contract' with the unions led to the accession of the Thatcher government and it became clear that the days of beer and sandwiches at Number Ten were over.

The lack of appetite for consultation was to make itself felt in the local government policy community (Rhodes, 1986). The government even wrapped up the Burnham negotiating machinery created to deal with teachers' pay. The CCLGF became, not a forum for discussion, but a captive audience before which ministers would issue diktats. Major policies such as the GLC abolition and the poll tax were introduced with no attempt at discussion with interested parties. The broad central–local dimension of the policy community came to the fore as a result of an overriding desire of the centre to reduce local government activity across a broad front. It is to this relationship that the following chapter turns.

14

Intergovernmental Politics

It is clear from the discussion in this book that the scent of central power permeates every corner of the municipal system. In this chapter the specific focus is on what orthodox texts call the study of central–local relations. However, this term implies that the matter belongs to the dry and politically antiseptic world of organisational theory rather than the messy, and sometimes torrid, world of politics. The result is to technocratise one of the most important sites of political struggle off the political science agenda. This is why the events of the 1980s came as such a profound shock, leading to alarmist charges from left as well as right that the constitution was in crisis. It will be seen that the area is better termed 'intergovernmental relations'; this chapter looks at confrontations which are essentially and indelibly political.

This chapter starts by recapitulating the myriad ways in which the hand of the centre insinuates itself into municipal life, noting the constitutional definition of the relationship (in so far as there is one) and its historical development. After this it examines the rising political temperature of intergovermental relations since 1979. The final section assesses models developed to illuminate the relationship.

The hand of the centre

Throughout this book it has been seen that the political culture in which local government subsists is essentially centralist in character, conditioned by the nationally orientated media and a national economy. The centre decides which services will be provided by local government, and these can be removed at the stroke of a Whitehall pen. The local administrative landscape contains an oppressive central presence in the form of various non-elected field agencies and quangos. Even the boundary map has been subject to redrawing by Whitehall. Local bureaucracies are heavily influenced by their cousins at the capital, many entirely happy to take orders from Whitehall HQ. Overriding all is the question of finance; if the local piper will not play, Whitehall will not pay. Indeed it will go further and slip light-fingered hands into the piper's pocket with 'clawback', 'holdback', and rate- and poll tax-capping.

There is also political centralisation. The so-called local parties are essentially branches of giant national mass organisations, as are the major pressure groups. When people vote in ostensibly local elections they deliver a verdict on the national government. Councillors may be thought to be peculiarly localist in orientation, yet there is a continual brain-drain in which leading players on provincial stages are drawn irresistibly to the glitter of the Westminster big-time.

The sovereign centre – local government under elective despotism

Anti-localism was woven into the very fabric of the nineteenth-century constitution through the doctrine of the sovereignty of Parliament. Today this means the sovereignty of the leaders of the majority party: the Cabinet and the Prime Minister. This is a despotic power denied monarchs and presidents under written constitutions; local government finds itself subject to an astonishing concentration of power. There are four principal fronts upon which the centre can advance: legislative, administrative, judicial and financial.

(1) *Legislation.* Bound by the doctrine of *ultra vires* local government has no authority other than that conferred by statute. However, Parliament is entirely under the thumb of the majority party, which can make any law it chooses. One of the first shots fired under Mrs Thatcher was the Local Government Planning and Land Act 1980, which was intended to rock local government to its

foundations. Other dramatic Acts abolished the GLC and metropolitan counties and introduced the community charge, although there were countless others (over fifty between 1979 and 1989 – Benyon, 1989: 177). There are no municipal parts which the centre cannot reach; there was even darkly foreboding legislation forcing authorities to adopt oppressive attitudes towards homosexuals.

(2) *Administration*. A continuing torrent of instructions, circulars and advice cascades from Whitehall, the degree of domination varying from one department to another (Griffith, 1966: 515) but always present. Moreover, in certain services (for example police and education), there are the roaming *apparatchiks* – Her Majesty's Inspectors – with their ever-open eyes and ears. The Thatcher government revealed, through its common core curriculum for schools, the extent to which a determined government can go. In addition, ministers have reserve powers to take over services if an authority displeases. Lothian Regional Council, for example, was forced to make expenditure cuts by the Secretary of State, who threatened that a non-elected commissioner would usurp their role.

(3) *Judicial*. The relationship can be dragged before the judges. *Ultra vires* behaviour can be judged by the courts and central government can apply for various High Court writs compelling authorities to act or preventing them from doing so. Throughout the history of local government there have been various *causes célèbres*. One of the most important concerned what is now termed 'Poplarism', when five Labour members gained effective control of the parish of Poplar in East London. To the outrage of the establishment, they revolted against the inhuman conditions of the workhouses and poor law system. In the course of a long and complex political battle the councillors (men and women) were committed to prison in 1921, to which they were escorted by a popular procession waving banners. One of them, George Lansbury, addressed the crowd from his cell window (Keith-Lucas and Richards, 1978: 65–71). Use of the courts is by no means dead (Grant, 1986), as was seen in 1981 when Lord Denning ruled in the House of Lords against the GLC's 'Fares Fair' policy. Norwich Council, accused of foot-dragging in the sale of council houses in line with the 1980 Housing Act, was warned by the courts to 'get a move on'.

(4) *Finance*. As dependence on central grants increased this became the most potent weapon. In the 1980s the systems of grants,

borrowing, charging and even the hitherto sacrosanct right of a local authority to tax, were drastically remodelled in favour of central domination (see Chapter 11).

However, this framework of constitutional authority tells only part of the story. It belongs to the old-style analysis of central–local relations and is more appropriate to the study of civil service field agencies. Local government is not entirely unable to resist the centre. In a constitution replete with fictions, the reality of power can only be assessed in terms of what actually happens. In the real world of politics the relationship is infinitely complex.

A brief history of intergovernmental relations

Chapter 2 noted a long centralist tradition in local government, reflecting the desire of the monarch to rule by means of local agents based in the shires. There was also a localist tradition, beginning with the parishes and maintained in the large market towns which applied for Royal Charters, making them free from central jurisdiction. These traditions had an important bearing on the development of the relationship between the two levels of government.

Casting the mould

The industrial revolution, which spawned the modern local government system, was to exert a profoundly centralising impetus. The great Philosophical Radical movement was on the side of the industrial bourgeoisie against the *ancien régime* of landed aristocracy. It is not difficult to see why the emerging capitalist order, anxious to remove the ancient barriers which blocked its way to power, found Bentham's ideas so attractive. The model he prescribed involved no fewer than three tiers, each subordinate to the one above, all meeting at a grand nexus in Parliament (conveniently replete with radical Whigs after the Reform Act of 1832). Although local 'headmen' and 'sub-legislatures' would be elected they were to be subject to one of Bentham's most cherished administrative principles: a vigilant regime of central inspection. The reforms of the Philosophical Radicals in poor law and public health administration were relentlessly centralising.

Yet the voice of localism was not entirely silent before the onslaught. It was heard from the great cities where, unlike the shires, the bourgeoisie had already taken control. The Municipal Corporations Act of 1835 allowed them much autonomy, which they were able to safeguard against the highly centralising Act of 1888 by remaining outside the two-tier system as all-purpose county boroughs. Clearly, the bourgeoisie only insisted on the values of centralism where it suited them.

There were also localist voices arguing from a traditional conservative standpoint. The most notable advocate of localism, seen in parish and borough, was J. Toulmin Smith. He saw in these a noble tradition of community, democracy, local autonomy and citizenship:

> The fundamental idea of Centralism is *distrust*. It puts no Faith in man; believes not in hope, not in the everlastingness of truth . . . Its synonyms are, irresponsible control; meddling interference; and arbitrary taxation. (Smith 1851)

In 1882 a German scholar, Rudolph von Gneist, published *The History of the English Constitution (Das Englische Verwaltungsrecht)* in which he portrayed parish government as an ideal (von Gneist, 1891). J. S. Mill, though a Philosophical Radical sharing the bourgeois dread of full democracy, had also argued in favour of localism, seeing it as a means of educating the masses into the bourgeois view of representative democracy, in which the working classes would vote for competing members of the superior classes rather than be so impertinent as to seek office themselves.

Municipal socialism

By the end of the nineteenth century there was a new political force in the form of the Labour Party, which saw in localism a basis for socialism. This drew its intellectual sustenance from the Fabian Society, combining such eminent figures as George Bernard Shaw, Sidney and Beatrice Webb and Annie Besant.

The Fabians recognised that elites would not relinquish power easily, but saw local government as an ideal vehicle for the gradual, non-revolutionary road to social and economic reform which was the hallmark of their philosophy. This was to be 'municipal socialism', free from the autocratic hand of the centre and based on communal goodwill and common interest. In the 1930s the Fabians went further

in their faith in localism arguing, along with the socialist thinker
G. D. H. Cole, that territorial representation was not enough; men
should also be represented in local government in terms of their
location in the production process. This was functional representation
allowing guilds and unions to be represented on councils.

Consensus politics – consensus central–local relations

The attitude of the British left has been of great significance in the
development of central–local relations. There has been a constant
quest by the Labour movement for 'respectability' in the eyes of
the capitalist establishment and this has entailed a preference for
parliamentary rather than municipal action. Thus, for example,
Herbert Morrison, even when Mayor of Hackney, strongly opposed the Poplarism movement (Donoghue and Jones, 1973: 47).
Although it was the industrial city which called the British left into
existence, and although the city has always constituted a fundamental threat to the right and a natural constituency for the left,
the British Labour Party deliberately muted the idea of municipal
socialism, fearing its radical image.

Labour interest in municipal socialism completely evaporated
once the heady idea of power at Westminster ceased to be a pipe
dream. The social democratic state after the Second World War
was highly centralist in character. This was seen as necessary to
ensure efficiency and equity in the provision of social services.
Moreover, the increased role local government was asked to perform demanded more financial support from the centre, a further
instrument of control. The centripetal tendency was also enhanced
with the acceptance of central management of the economy under
the name of Keynesianism. In this period of economic boom few
mourned the loss of local autonomy; cross-party consensus was
matched by central–local consensus. Local government accepted
its role as junior in a harmonious partnership. The emphasis was
on the technological fix of life's problems (see pp. 144–5).

Beyond consensus – ending the masquerade

However, in the mid-1970s this consensus was to cave in as the
lean years replaced those of plenty. It became evident throughout

the capitalist world economy that the long boom, based upon free markets and the Bretton Woods Agreement of fixed exchange rates tied to the US dollar, was drawing to a close. Technological obsolescence, inflation, unemployment and stagnation all came together to be exacerbated by the oil crises (see p. 174). In 1974 the government forced the reduction of local government spending through the imposition of cash limits.

Events led inexorably to the ascent of New Right Thatcherism with its aggressive repudiation of the consensus ideal. The temperature of central–local relations was to reach white heat; no longer was the old terminology appropriate; the consensus-based central–local relationship was to be replaced by a process of 'intergovermental politics'. Ironically, the era of welfare state consensus had, through its incipient centralisation, produced the very tools needed by the New Right, and they did not hesitate to set about the job. The result was the long saga of attacks detailed in the chapters of this book.

Central–local becomes intergovernmental – central New Right versus New Urban Left

The centralist attack was not uncontested. In Britain's large urban areas the New Urban Left emerged as a local resistance movement. Essentially this arose under the localist dynamic from left-wing councils. They came to battle with both shield and sword; the former was to defend the welfare state and local democracy while the latter was to promote a new vision of the role of local government.

The shield

Government policy was recognised by Labour councils, particularly in urban areas with a strong ideological commitment to collectivist provision of social services, as an assault on the concept of the welfare state. The councils saw their role as maintaining a commitment to services, some of which were felt to be needed more than ever because of the traumas of rising unemployment. The tactics entailed various means of resisting grant cuts and much propaganda. However, the threat was seen to go beyond services to imperil local government itself. The erosion of local autonomy which, like smoking, had not seemed a serious threat to the young lungs of the post-war welfare state, had been insidiously sapping its strength to the point of crisis. The movement was fighting for local democracy itself, which is why many other interests, including Conservative councils, became involved (see below).

The sword

Some socialists accepted elements of the New Right diagnosis, expressing disillusionment with the centralist socialism of post-war Labour governments. This had spawned large alienating public bureaucracies, a paternalistic welfare state dominated by technocrats and a national health service distanced from local government. It was felt that social democracy needed the medicine of local democracy.

Many left-wing authorities began to act on their local economies, taking a number of new policy initiatives in areas such as industrial incentives and job creation (Chandler and Lawless, 1985). When Ken Livingstone became leader of the GLC in 1982, he widened the vision of what an authority with limited powers could do. From public transport subsidies and cycle lanes, policies moved into areas of personal morality, including positive orientations towards women, racial minorities and homosexuals (he alarmed Labour traditionalists in various ways, not least by declaring 'everyone is bisexual'). At the time David Blunkett argued:

> There has been a shift from seeing local councils as local administration, to seeing them again as *government* . . . Local government can be a tool for achieving socialist change. This has been submerged in parliamentary, centralist views of progess. (Blunkett, 1984: 244)

For some, local politics offered a means for attacking capitalism itself, a site for class struggle. Such movements could be seen as a natural consequence of advanced capitalism (Castells, 1977).

The contingencies for action

Mere dissatisfaction with central policies could not in itself produce a resistance movement. The following factors made it possible for the New Urban Left to become a distinct political force:

(1) *Growth of Labour power in local government.* The normal electoral swing towards the party of opposition increased the

number of urban councils under Labour. This had three consequences: it gave local parties the opportunity to take control, produced the moral authority of a local mandate and provided a transfusion of new blood.

(2) *The new breed*. This development was at the heart of the movement. As Labour won control of councils in the early 1980s, the left began to displace the right within party associations (see p. 132). Figures such as David Blunkett, Ken Livingstone, Bernie Grant, Derek Hatton, Ted Knight and Martha Osamor became well-known *bêtes noires*, to both right and soft left.

(3) *A new strategic position*. The loss of political power as a result of both genuine popular enthusiasm for Thatcherism and the perversity of the electoral system began to appear a long-term, if not terminal, problem for the British left. This could be seen to elevate the importance of the local stage as a base for socialism and challenge to the right.

(4) *Tension within the Labour Party*. The movement was further fuelled by the internal tension within the Labour Party. The endemic moderate–extremist division paralleled the centralist–localist conflict. Younger members, some sympathetic to Labour's 'Militant Tendency', saw urban socialism as a means of advancing more extreme policies within the party by weakening the traditional hierarchies.

The amazing multicoloured coalition

The possibility of fighting capitalism from the town halls gained support from those not traditionally attracted to Labour. Associations of the far left, churches, community organisations, women's movements, radical sections of the public-sector unions, black rights groups, environmentalists and CND became involved, in many cases renewing alliances forged during the Community Development Projects of the 1960s. Even the Anglican Church ceased to look like the Conservative Party at prayer with its *Faith in the City* report, while the Bishop of Durham labelled government policies 'wicked'. The movement began to look like the kind of alliance which scholars such as Eric Hobsbawm had long advocated as a panacea for the British left. Indeed, the threat to democracy pushed the coalition beyond the left. Conservative MPs and councils, the three local authority associations and even the House of Lords became involved in a general desire to reaffirm the value of local government.

In addition, the Thatcherite assault threatened a large number of politically innocent bystanders, including the great army of around three million local authority employees: teachers, planners, social workers, as well as the legions of lesser bureaucrats and functionaries. These, as core members of the social consumption sector, could expect to be the first in line when redundancies threatened. There was increased militancy among what is a highly unionised work-force, which joined councillors to resist abolition of the GLC and the metropolitan counties and to oppose rate-capping.

Councils encouraged developments with overtly political appointments at the top, changed management structures (sometimes bypassing the chief officers), mobilisation of radical elements within the local government unions and measures to raise the political awareness of employees (Blunkett, 1984: 248). Promises of 'no redundancies' were an important factor in identifying employees' interests with those of councils. It was thanks to bureaucratic cooperation that authorities were able to use the 'creative accounting' weapon.

End of the dream

The centre attacked on many fronts through grant ceilings, restrictions on rates, use of the auditor, disqualification and crippling surcharge (of the councillors of Lambeth and Liverpool), the threat of bringing in commissioners (for example, in Lothian and Norwich), curtailment of functions, the complete abolition of certain authorities, recourse to the courts up to the House of Lords and an incessant battery of legislation. In addition, a clamorous propaganda battle raged in the media.

Despite gallant rhetoric and certain short-term triumphs, the left generally fared badly. One strategy was to wage a war of attrition in the hope of a change in the majority party at Westminster. Yet, with harsh irony, the battle itself weakened Labour, as the right-wing media fanned 'loony left' and 'reds in the town hall' scares. The left's vision of innovative collectivist state provision did not win popular support (Lansley, 1989: 195). Hence, when the

Conservatives cruised home in the 1987 general election it was time to admit defeat, to accept the bitter pill of 'new realism'.

The result concentrated the minds of the Labour leadership, which took a tough line with left-wing constituency organisations, in some cases banishing them altogether. By early 1988 many of the councils once in the van of hard left developments were accepting political reality. Hardliners, such as Ted Knight of Lambeth, were marginalised and reduced to a rump as the 'soft left' began to take over key positions and ruefully effect expenditure cuts. As Thatcher's popularity waned with the poll tax fiasco, and more and more councils fell to Labour, the party steadfastly refused to attack on the urban front, all attention being directed at Westminster.

In this the British left may be contrasted with that of a number of other West European countries where the city has been seen as a key site for political activity with the potential to pursue policies of redistribution and planning and to advance the concept of civic responsibility (Mort, 1989: 262). Of course, the position of the national Labour Party was to contribute greatly to the legitimation of the Thatcher assault.

The Conservatives, buoyant after the electoral fillip, took an uncompromising line in dispensing victor's justice. Appeals by rate-capped councils for reassessment were met with demands for detailed central determination of spending patterns and foreign lenders, who had increasingly been coming to the aid of stricken authorities, were frightened off with a firm declaration that the British government would not stand by any local government debt (Wolmer, 1987).

During the engagement the government set up the Widdicombe Committee to examine the unwelcome politicisation of local government which, while making some nods in the direction of local democracy, stressed that local government exists only on the basis of the goodwill of the centre, so that 'its continued existence . . . depends on the contribution it can make to good government' (Widdicombe, 1986a, ch. 3, para. 49). And what exactly is 'good government'? This is something to be decided by the centre!

Post-mortem – the Ex-Urban Left?

The New Urban Left cannot be considered to have been a philosophical or practical counterpoise to the New Right. In the first place it lacked homogeneity. The coalition was liable to disintegrate once its basic anti-centralist aims were achieved. Goals of the moderates (higher collectivist spending on basic social services) are not necessarily compatible with demands for the eradication of racism and sexism within bureaucracies. The Hatton-led militant forces of Liverpool had very little in common with the permissive values of the GLC. Again, the goals of the town hall unions essentially reflect members' interests in terms of job security, wages and conditions of work. They are not necessarily identified with the localist cause. Moreover, the movement lacked the clear intellectual articulation of the New Right, with its think-tanks and gurus, and many of its basic ideas lacked the advantage of novelty, being largely a reaffirmation of the welfare status quo. Matters were not helped by the youth and inexperience of many of the new councillors, with a fistful of ideas but little notion of how to implement them (Lansley, 1989: 194).

In the final analysis the movement was more a protest than a strategy for lasting political power. David Blunkett, as leader of Sheffield City Council, said: 'We may lose, but we will lose honourably and lose in the traditions of the Labour movement that fought and struggled and didn't keep its head down' (Blunkett, 1984: 247). For this reason, the main body of the Labour Party remained resolutely centralist in its strategy and ambitions. The transfusion of new blood contained the virus of extremism and was subject to violent rejection by the antibodies of the old guard, even resorting to witch hunts and expulsions. It is salutary to note that Blunkett, Livingstone and Grant had already begun to accept the doctrines of *realpolitik* and pursue centralist political careers, all entering Parliament in 1987.

Modelling the relationship – central–local to intergovernmental

Various models have been advanced to explain the puzzling relationship between local and central government. They should not be seen as mutually exclusive; each can help illuminate particular circumstances and historical periods. Nor can it be said that one is right and the others wrong; indeed, the real mistake would be to entertain the idea that any one of them could hold the key entirely of itself.

All orthodox models share the view that local autonomy can be explained by reference to the constitution, central government institutions and the actions of individuals (ministers and mandarins) occupying the key offices. They differ only in the degree of autonomy they ascribe to local government. It is through these that the orthodox approach to the study of central–local relations is developed. This section discusses three such models, which may be termed agency, partnership and stewardship, and is followed by an examination of the power–dependence model, which is essentially different.

Agency

The idea that local government should be an agency of the centre, with little will of its own, is essentially a centralist, Benthamite position. It may be argued that Parliament creates local authorities to do a job for the central state; they are little different from civil service field agencies. From the 1930s, W.A. Robson (an academic and local councillor) began a loud lament for what he saw as the death of local government (Robson, 1966), arguing that local initiative had been sapped by the centre's agency thinking.

Partnership

Post-war opinion seemed to suggest that Robson had been scaremongering; although local actors *felt* a sense of oppression (with the loss of functions and some highly centralist legislation such as the 1944 Education Act), the agency model was systematically discredited as an explanation of the central–local relationship. Boaden (1971), for example, argued that differentials in levels of *per capita* spending on particular services (education, housing) in different authorities demonstrated their autonomy. This was confirmed for spending on social services (Davies, 1972). It was argued that central and local government existed together in a largely harmonious partnership, a well-adjusted marriage, with give and take on both sides. The potentially draconian constitutional powers of the centre, so feared by Robson, were but fictions; the costs of using them would be odium such as would be bestowed by the neighbours of a man who beat his wife, and central government would pay the price at the ballot box.

Stewardship

However, the spending variations between authorities were only marginal and could be said to have lain within parameters entirely acceptable to central government. Some husbands do not permit their wives out of their sight, while others allow them to go to evening classes, badminton clubs and even watch male all-in wrestling. The leeway afforded by the tolerant spouse does not necessarily betoken any absence of dominance; indeed it may be a sign of confidence that the partner would not dare overstep the line of propriety.

This leads to the idea of stewardship, where a servant manages an estate in the absence of the landlord. The stewardship model undermines the claim of those who believe that 'British authorities still retain considerable discretion over the way in which they run their services' (Goldsmith, 1986a: xiv). The leeway of authorities to make decisions is merely that desired by the centre in order to make its own life easier; the steward is on the spot and has greater understanding of local problems than the landlord. The steward may at times even persuade the master to adopt or modify a policy, but deference is expected at all times, otherwise the steward can be replaced (Chandler, 1988: 185–6). Councillors acting *ultra vires* can be barred from office like the burghers of Clay Cross, Lambeth and Liverpool, functions can be transferred to special commissioners appointed by a minister and authorities can even be abolished altogether.

Power–dependence

This model begins to move us towards behavioural reality. It goes beyond constitutional rules to stress that local authorities, like other organisations, are actors engaged in politics, and as such they have a number of potent resources: expertise, organisation, information and a crucial role in policy implementation (central government being largely *non-executant*) (Rhodes, 1981). In addition, the very concept of local government confers two resources denied other bodies: a democratic base with a local mandate and access to a separate means of taxation. The relationship is thus seen as a series of skirmishes between two governments, and there is no reason to believe that it will always run along predictable constitutional rails. Central–local relations becomes intergovernmental relations. Although it was criticised (see for example Hampton, 1981: 64; Dunsire, 1982: 21), the model opened up new analytical vistas. It was to offer the most cogent explanation of the events of the 1980s.

Conclusion – bloody and only dubiously victorious

For many, the developments of the 1980s confirmed the agency model as the best description of local government's relationship with the centre. It seemed as if central government was a matador in some surrealistic bullring, with the ability to file the bull's horns, change the rules, and call upon the picadors to gouge out the bull's eyes and rip its entrails from its belly. The blood-lusting audience has given (in 1983 and 1987) two resounding 'Oles!'.

Yet this is a simplistic judgement. The rise of the New Urban Left, the need for repeated legislation on the part of the centre in order to plug the loopholes found by irrepressible local authorities (Rhodes, 1988), and the fact that local government expenditure did not fall in real terms (see pp. 191–2) amply demonstrate local government's formidable potential to resist. A final testimony to this ability comes in the extent to which the Thatcher government sought to erase it from the map altogether, either by outright abolition or by removing functions and appointing non-elected alternatives. In the 1980s the central government (and the centralists within the Labour Party) emerged bloody, and only dubiously victorious.

Neither central–local nor intergovernmental models give all the answers to our questions. They remain confined within an analytical framework which sees the actors as boxers in a ring, insulated by thick ropes from the rest of the world. As narrow-range models, they largely ignore the totality of the state. The intergovernmental battle is enacted in a vast political amphitheatre and its nature and outcomes are to a considerable extent determined by great endogenous (and even exogenous) political forces. Accordingly we must complement our analysis with a consideration of broad-range, or holistic, models which encompass the wider influences. This leads to the final chapter.

15

Local Democracy and the State

As argued throughout this book, local government is but a sub-system of a greater political system. In addition, it is situated in a capitalist economy operating locally, nationally and even internationally. This dependence was graphically illustrated in the oil crises of the 1970s, which reverberated throughout the capitalist world to reach every town and city.

This concluding chapter examines local government in the totality of the state. However, there is no single theoretical perspective on the democratic state. Liberal, socialist, pluralist, corporatist, elitist, Marxist and neo-liberal models are considered, and the chapter concludes by looking from the uncertain present into an uncharted future.

Local government in the liberal democratic state

The liberal democratic state was created during the industrial revolution when the new bourgeoisie took over and reformed just about every institution from the monarchy to the military. At the heart of this movement was the extension of the franchise which, in the view of the constitutional expert Albert Venn Dicey, made the House of Commons the supreme body in the constitution. This supremacy was derived on the moral grounds of popular sovereignty rather than on any legal precepts.

The constitution was fashioned to the liking of the bourgeoisie and the term 'liberal' was essential to its meaning. Freedom was the supreme value, but it was a limited freedom. Individuals were to be free to pursue their business interests in the *laissez-faire* economy without impediment. In other respects there was little freedom from the state, which took a firm line on the protection of profit and property. It was a state which offered what Lenin described as 'the best possible shell' for a capitalist economy.

In this state local government played a crucial role, furnishing the infrastructure needed for industry and housing the giant workforces. Broadly speaking the bourgeoisie promoted localism where they were in control (the new industrial towns) and centralism where they were not (the old towns and rural areas).

Local government in the social democratic state

The liberal idea of the minimal state was mythical. The state even intervened in economic life with legislation (such as factories acts) to protect individuals from the ravages of capitalism (and hence to protect capitalism from itself). Even so, the inter-war years saw a dismal performance by the economy and a great depression which seemed to confirm Marx's grim prophecy of capitalism's inevitable collapse. However, all was saved in the post-war era when, within an outward shell of liberal democracy, Britain became a social democracy. No longer was the state to stand in the wings. It was to enter the hallowed precincts of the free market in accordance with the novel doctrines of economist John Maynard Keynes, and was to furnish a comprehensive welfare state.

In this new state local government was to play an even more important role as the main provider of social services. Yet the position was one of handmaid to the centre; the egalitarian principles of social democracy and citizenship limited scope for local initiative. In addition, the commitment to centralised management of the economy prohibited local initiative on the economic front. Local government became more like local administration.

Local government in the pluralist state

Pluralist theory has been the great saviour of the liberal democratic constitution. Where it was palpably evident that the representative institutions did not deliver popular democracy in the way claimed by nineteenth-century apologists, it become possible to argue that the free association of people into pressure groups created a state in which real power was fragmented and a process of continuing bargaining gave everyone an equal chance to influence policy. Politics was a great game of football, with the state no more than a neutral referee (Bentley, 1967: 208). The result was an optimum allocation of political values based on fair compromise.

In such a scenario it is possible to see local authorities individually and collectively as interests in society with a fair chance of influencing policy. There is certainly some truth in this; local authorities do act as pressure groups for their areas, and the local authority associations represent collective views. In this local authorities can be seen to offer a constitutional protection against overweening government, diffusing power in what is otherwise a highly centralist state (see Jones and Stewart, 1985).

Yet the inequalities persisting in British society render the pluralist apologia rather implausible. The game which local authorities play is hardly a fair one and the referee is by no means neutral. Indeed, unlike many others, the British constitution is specifically anti-pluralist, being unwritten and with no bill of rights to guarantee minority interests; unitary, with no separation of powers and, most significant for local government, with no element of federalism.

Local government in the corporatist state

The corporatist model accepts the pluralist proposition that society consists of competing interests but argues that government is not a neutral arbiter, neither is access equal. Some interests are 'incorporated' into the process of government, joining a closed 'policy community' centring around the corridors of power at Whitehall, while others are excluded (see pp. 219–20).

The early decades of the century saw a corporatist bias in the British state (Middlemass, 1979: 372), which developed further after the Second World War when the CBI and the TUC emerged as peak organisations. It was seen in Chapter 13 that local government fitted into this system with a policy community forming around the Department of the Environment. However, by the 1980s corporatism seemed a thing of the past (Lehmbruch and Schmitter, 1982). The Thatcher government, avowing that 'government should govern', had closed the doors to the state consultation chambers.

Local government in the elitist state

This approach to power in society was pioneered by the classical elite theorists of the early twentieth century. It repudiates not only liberal democracy but pluralism as well. Broadly speaking it posits the existence of a cohesive, collusive, self-seeking minority of the population who are able to dominate the mass. Elites are able to conceal the full reality of their power by keeping issues off the political agenda altogether (making them 'non-decisions') so that ordinary people do not even know that a controversial point of issue affecting their interests hangs in the balance (Bachrach and Baratz, 1970). Representative government can do little to prevent this happening, though it provides a myth of participation which the elite will be happy to foster in order to conceal its dominance. Studies in this tradition tend to focus on the personal backgrounds, education and family linkages of those in the top positions in various walks of life: the army, the civil service, the board-rooms of industry, the City and so on. The elite even has its own educational service, the public school–Oxbridge system, existing outside the mainstream education provided for the masses. The evidence is compelling indeed; Britain is a society with a very clearly discernible 'upper class' (Scott, 1985).

The implications of the elitist state for local government lie in its centralist tendencies, collusion being a defining characteristic of an elite. This is not a soil in which the tree of local democracy and autonomy can flourish. From the time of Bentham there has been an incessant drumbeat of central superiority.

There is also the elitist veneration of the professional: 'Only elites who can apply the necessary time and steady attention to public matters' can end the 'profitless and barbarising forms of conflict [election, pluralism, class war, etc.] . . . in developed societies' (Field and Higley, 1980: 17). Professionalism pervades the culture of local administration. It was seen in Chapter 10 that local officials, who can so easily dominate elected representatives, belong to supremely elitist associations (the Law Society and so on) led by fully paid-up members of the middle class. In addition there is the dependence of the officers on their Whitehall cousins who, nurtured in the public school–Oxbridge womb, retain close familial links with the other bastions of the establishment. The officials also prove their skill in the art of making 'non-decisions' when they technocratise matters off the political agenda.

Local government in the capitalist state

The classical Marxist position holds that the institutions of government pale to unimportance against the overriding power of the interests of capital. Marx's famous aphorism depicts the state as nothing more than a 'committee for managing the common affairs of the bourgeoisie'. However, the extent of this control is a matter of considerable debate. French Marxist philosopher Louis Althusser (1969) sees the actions of individuals, committees and institutions as entirely determined by the forces inherent in the mode of production (the *structure*). Their actions are merely those of players on a stage, obliged to follow prescribed roles, their triumphs and disasters laid down by the script. Voluntaristic behaviour, reflecting individual motivations, cannot count in a truly 'scientific' explanation of power. In considering local government, Harvey (1985) notes how the very geography of urban life is constantly restructured by the movements of national and multinational firms to and from this or that locality (see Massey, 1984).

Not all Marxists share this view; indeed, Marx himself argued that, although subject to powerful external forces, 'men make their own history' (1977: 300). The capitalists may be powerful but the state retains a significant degree of autonomy and can be made to operate in the interests of the working class. Local government can be a particularly important source of such autonomy.

Urban local government has been crucial to capitalism. Chapter 2 showed that it was largely created by the nineteenth-century bourgeoisie to serve their economic interests. However, subsequent developments of advanced capitalism led the bourgeoisie to withdraw from the local scene to concentrate on the national and international institutions of state. Yet the nineteenth-century model of local government remained as a site for working-class political action. Why was this? At least part of the answer lies in legitimation, the process whereby people are led to accept the principles under which they are governed. Local government, with its provision for the election of ordinary people to political office, is necessarily a potent instrument of legitimation. If people feel able to exert some degree of real influence at local level they will be more likely to accept decisons made in the central arena.

Moreover, autonomous local government can genuinely serve the interests of the capitalist class in the following ways:

(1)   The division of social services between local elected agencies can limit levels of provision; in middle-class areas local taxpayers can bring anti-socialist pressures to bear even when a Labour government rules at Westminster.

(2)   Autonomous local authorities are vulnerable to pressure from footloose industries, which can play one off against another in seeking local tax concessions, planning permission, and a benevolently blind eye to antisocial side-effects such as pollution.

(3)   The system inhibits the emergence of a united local government front. Thus in the New Urban Left movement authorities were unable successfully to coordinate their resistance and one by one they caved in (Lansley *et al.*, 1989: ch. 10).

(4)   The idea of local politics as a site for working-class action is belied in practice. As seen in Chapter 8, the majority of councillors are from the owner-occupier class with *petit bourgeois* values.

(5)   Chapter 9 showed that the local government professions are peopled by members (or committed servants) of the middle classes. They are thereby afforded a powerful basis for dominance in society.

(6)   The central state can use an autonomous local government system for buck-passing unpopular policies. Thus the Conservative government loudly trumpeted the message of loony left, high-spending authorities as the explanation for high poll tax levies in 1990.

While serving the capitalist state, autonomous local government at the same time poses a threat. The local arena represents a chink in the armour; advances may be made which might seriously undermine long-term profitability (Castells, 1987: 1). This has always been a sensitive area in local politics; in the nineteenth century there were the 'economisers', in the twentieth the ratepayers' parties. It was also the basic issue in the Poplarism of the early twentieth century (see p. 230) and emerged again during the 1980s with central government's multi-pronged attack on local government finance.

Chapter 3 noted the distinct roles of central and local government, the former being mainly concerned with policy for investment in the economy and the latter with social consumption (see pp. 39–40). Saunders (1984: 24) associates these with two distinct modes of decision making broadly characteristic of the two levels of government: central government is seen as a closed corporate system, dominated by capitalist interests, while local government is relatively open, permitting the involvement of non-capitalist interests.

This dual state thesis is not entirely borne out by reality; it is intended as an 'ideal type' rather than a true description. As such it is very useful because it sheds further light on the key question in the previous chapter: the relationship between central and local government. In the total context of the capitalist state this can be seen to generate intergovernmental tension at the following four levels:

1. *Functional* (investment versus consumption policy).

2. *Political* (corporatism versus open participation).

3. *Ideological* (market allocation of resources versus collectivist provision to meet need).

4. *Organisational* (central politicians and bureaucrats versus their local counterparts).

Thus, while local government can be seen as an importantly autonomous element of the capitalist state, the odds will always favour central domination because the interests of capitalism must come first. In other words, capitalism needs democratic local government, but also needs to keep it in check.

Local government in the neo-liberal state

It has been apparent throughout the pages of this book that from 1979 local government was coloured by the rise in British politics of the New Right. This comprised a rather strange rag-bag of ideas, many disinterred from the nineteenth century by right-wing think-tanks and others little more than the *petit bourgeois* prejudice which had always lamented the post-war welfare state and permissive ethos of the 1960s. Yet the ideas commanded attention because, when the Thatcher government took office, they were to leave the snug bars of the pubs and the masonic halls of the home counties (as well as the more esoteric corners of senior common rooms) to become the driving force of radical challenge to the social democratic consensus.

The collapse of the long boom revealed that only economic abundance had enabled capitalist interests to tolerate the social democratic advances. Prominent Conservative Lord Hailsham used the opportunity of an invitation to deliver the BBC Dimbleby Lecture in 1976 to voice the right-wing unease that Britain had become dangerously democratic. He warned darkly that government was an 'elective dictatorship', the logical consequence of a mass electorate regularly returning Labour governments.

The free market anti-social-democracy doctrines, preserved throughout the post-war era by the economist F. A. Hayek (see, for example, 1982, vol. III), were retrieved from obscurity. The eccentric arch-monetarist Milton Friedman (1962) of the Chicago School, whose dominant thesis was that capitalism is the mother of freedom, became a respected guru of the new orthodoxy of individualism. In addition, a curious body of thought termed public choice theory sought to apply the individualistic logico-deductive reasoning of classical economics to politics and public administration with bizarrely anti-communitarian results.

The public choice theorists were savage critics of state bureaucracy and social democracy. Public administration was seen, not as protecting citizens' rights, justice or equality, but as a labyrinthine world of spendthrift public officialdom. Bureaucrats were depicted as incorrigibly self-interested budget maximisers, perennially preoccupied in the old game of empire-building (Niskanen, 1971: 38). Local government may be expected to suffer particularly acutely from this tendency because of its high level of professionalisation.

Pluralism and corporatism also came under attack because pressure groups were intent upon inflating public expenditure with selfish demands (Olson, 1982). The result was an 'oversupply' of public goods. The problem was seen as particularly acute in local government because of the large categories of working-class beneficiaries who, with their pressure groups and voting potential, were able to outgun the defenceless ratepayers (Pirie, 1981: 11).

Though there was little evidence of any clearly thought-out strategy (Mather, 1989: 212), Thatcherite neo-liberalism carried devastating implications for local government. Distributing services according to need rather than wallet size, it stood in direct contradiction to the market order. Moreover, its independent ability to tax was a deep threat to the overriding mission to reduce public expenditure. Finally, being under the control of Labour councillors it was a tantalisingly red rag to the new post-Falklands spirit of John Bullish Thatcherism. It represented that part of the state which the government was committed to 'roll back'. Margaret Thatcher had declared her intention to bury socialism and to do so it would be necessary to bury local government.

It is apparent from the chapters of this book that the impact of these ideas was profound indeed. There was a generally debilitating atmosphere of financial cuts and an anti-statist ethos emanating from Downing Street which shattered morale. Those who had worked in the post-war era on the construction of the great cathedral-like edifice of the social democratic state were faced with the despairing sight of the oncoming bulldozers preparing the way for a new supermarket state.

The future – backwards or forwards?

The neo-liberal programme was in large measure an atavistic longing for the Victorian order when businessmen reigned in the town halls. Yet, with or without the political desire, there are insistent pressures for change from the evolving mode of production. The old capitalist model, based upon mass production supported by mass consumption (Fordism) has since the 1970s been giving way to more flexible, small-scale patterns arising from new technologies (post-Fordism). Where do the towns and cities fit into this economy? British local government is in a state of extreme flux; the only certainty today is the uncertainty of tomorrow. The fraught 1980s provided some clues to the shape of the local authority of the future, ranging from the 'field authority' to the 'communitarian authority'.

The field authority

Although it was under the social democratic consensus that much post-war centralism had occurred, and notwithstanding the New Right veneration for freedom, the 1980s saw authorities increasingly under the Whitehall thumb. The reason for this was political expediency rather than ideology. Moreover, the demise of the corporatist era left little opportunity for local government to talk back to the centre through the policy community. Post-Widdicombe restrictions on councillors threatened to enhance the importance of officers, who would more willingly see themselves as servants of Whitehall.

The tightening of the central grip tool place despite prolonged local resistance from Conservative-controlled councils as well as the New Urban Left. Indeed, the resistance may in itself have contributed to the vehemence of the central assault. For example, if rate-capping had been allowed to work the community charge might not have materialised. By the end of the 1980s many thought local government was looking more like an agency of the central state than it had been in the days when Robson wrote seminally of his fears of centralism.

Of course, an agency model for local government fitted snugly within the general approach to government developed during the Thatcher era, where the expressed preference was for 'doers' rather than thinkers, and where discussion and dissent, even within the Cabinet, was frowned upon. The extensive hiving-off of parts of the civil service to form semi-autonomous agencies as recommended in the Ibbs Report of 1988 testified further to the agency thinking. Indeed, the civil service itself was pushed towards an agency style with promotions in the mandarin class closely monitored by the Prime Minister herself, asking the relentless question: 'Is he one of us?' (Kingdom, 1991: 374–5).

The competitive authority

Competition is a key idea in neo-liberalism. The idea of increased charging for services, poll tax and competitive tendering, as well as deregulation and the ending of subsidies, made local government but one more hustler in the economic marketplace. The main basis for measuring the quality of a service must be how cheaply it is done. This strategy calls for high use of technology and a shedding

of the labour force. It is difficult to know where competitive behaviour should stop, or indeed whether it should stop at all, as
central government sees scope for profit-making in all manner of
services. Citizens, expecting services by right, become 'customers',
getting what they can afford. Coupled with this is an increased
stress upon marketing, which means spending public money, not
on providing services, but on mind-bending and window-dressing.

Authorities can even be made to compete with each other for
residents. Charles Tiebout (1956) argued that people would 'shop
around' for the cheapest place to live, voting not with their hands
but with their feet. Authorities would be forced to cut expenditure
in order to attract these nomadic tax-avoiders, and the problem of
over-supply would be solved. In such a model the humane goal of
equalisation (see pp. 184–6) is wiped out at a stroke and democracy is completely engulfed by the market. Those without the
resources to be spatially mobile remain static, mute and impotent,
their once-prized vote a chip in a bankrupt casino.

The enabling authority

The term 'enabling authority' has become much in vogue in the
early 1990s. Instead of providing services the local authority merely arranges for the job to be done by others: voluntary societies
(sparing the taxpayer by confining their fund-raising to the altruistic), quangos (with members circumventing the ballot box by
means of central patronage) and private profit-maximising firms.
Contracting out and local management for schools were steps in
this direction. Some have seen in the concept of the enabling authority an optimistic non-Thatcherite future, with councils taking
firm control over social and economic conditions through a regulatory role (Clarke and Stewart, 1988).

However, a capitalist economy, where the free market holds the
answer to all problems, has little appetite for regulation. Local authorities trying to enforce contract compliance in the 1980s were
attacked by central government. Indeed plans to regulate the privatised state industries always advocated the 'light touch'.
Ominously, the competitive tendering provisions introduced various
rules to ensure that the private sector was not disadvantaged (such
as too many contracts put out to tender at once, or strict rules on
workers' conditions, salary levels and so on). Restrictions were

placed on the questions an authority might ask a private firm in evaluating its bid, some in the areas of policy towards the employment of handicapped workers and those from ethnic minorities. In addition, there was provision for private firms to take action against an authority if unhappy with the outcome of their tenders.

The managerial authority

Earlier chapters (see Chapter 10) have revealed how the movement towards managerialism in local government has been a constant post-war trend. Under the guise of a quest for efficiency it has shown a basic propensity to place power in the hands of officials at the expense of the elected councillors. The call was no less insistent under the Thatcher regime, though here managerialism and efficiency were often code words for centralism and cuts.

However, the ideas of the competitive and the enabling authority carry further implications for the power of the urban managers. Tasks such as setting charges for services at a profitable level and awarding contracts on the basis of tenders can be seen largely in technical terms. It can easily be argued by the managers that such decisions, which are common to the private sector, are not ones which ordinary people elected as councillors can ever be competent to make. Lawyers and accountants rule.

The late-lamented authority

A council in an enabling authority might be expected to meet only a few times a year to award contracts. However, an even more extreme scenario is one in which local government disappears altogether. This could hardly be described as fanciful in view of the abolition of the GLC and the metropolitan counties and serious talk of eliminating the historic county system. A threatening creation was the urban development corporation (and a plethora of locally based quangos) as an alternative to an elected council. Here central government patronage could ensure that the right people (businessmen) controlled the destiny of communities. Of course, abolition does not have to be done with the bludgeoning weapons of ideological rhetoric and legislation. Authorities can be allowed to wither on the vine like the old parishes. If one by one the functions go, little is left but ceremony and display.

The communitarian authority

The attack was not without grave risks. In the first place, as the power–dependence model suggests, there could be no certainty that the centre could achieve all its goals and there were some humiliating failures during the 1980s. There is also the risk that, having pursued its policy of high centralisation, Westminster will find that it has over-reached itself (Stewart, 1989: 253). Perhaps the greatest danger lies in losing the legitimacy derived from the idea that people can vote for local representatives to control their services. This consideration might be the one to prevent the destruction of local government. Although Margaret Thatcher displayed little concern with legitimation she pursued a high-risk strategy which frightened many Conservatives. The change in the party leader in November 1990 signalled a more conciliatory line.

Of course, the future is partly dependent on which party reigns at Westminster. What alternative scenario could the left offer? The portents were not particularly good. It has been seen that the post-war socialism of Labour did not recognise the potential for the left in city politics and saw little virtue in local authorities pursuing separate policies which undermined interpersonal equality. Moreover, the New Urban Left, which sought to revive the principle of municipal socialism, received little encouragement from leaders. Even so, the party generally expressed a more sympathetic view of local democracy during the 1980s.

Blunkett and Jackson argue that some degree of local autonomy should be constitutionally entrenched, with a defined area of jurisdiction for local authorities and a genuinely independent right to tax its citizens. They also argued that authorities should have the right to pursue economic policies in the manner they had attempted before they were swamped by business-led quangos (Blunkett and Jackson, 1987: 189). This would obviously introduce a new era of intergovernmental relations. However, under a system of this kind the left would have to face up to two problems. In the first place, compromise would be required over the goal of equality and secondly, a government would have to accept the probability of far-right councils, such as those of Wandsworth, Westminster and Bradford in the 1980s, going their own way.

Some argue that Labour councils can pursue a communitarian (or collectivist) approach by breaking the old Labour statist and bureaucratic image, with decentralisation and other means of participation (in voluntary groups, neighbourhood councils, workers' cooperatives) and as consumers. Local councillors will no longer be able to rely on a mandate as a blueprint for action, they will aim to develop policies in continuing consultation with local people (Lansley *et al.*, 1989: 204). The enhanced legitimacy derived from community involvement would strengthen local government's right to play a strategic role in social and economic development.

Perhaps the traumas of the New Right attack will actually revive local government by forcing a reappraisal, and rejuvenation, of its communitarian ethic. This possibility is enhanced by the fact that the quality of newly privatised services proved poor, and in-house workers won contracts more easily than expected. Moreover, tenants and parents showed little enthusiasm for opting-out. Significantly, the Widdicombe research found much popular support for municipal institutions.

The wired-up authority

Although the idea of cable radio and television and other forms of electronic communication are largely confined to private-sector developments they present unique possibilities for the left to promote the communitarian goals of local government. Communal life is about people and groups talking together, which is the essence of the new communications technology. In the United States a 'wired city' movement grew out of Lyndon Johnson's social programmes aiming to build 'participatory, community-based cities' (Mulgan, 1989: 267). It becomes possible to link homes and town hall on a two-way transmission basis for video services, community information, health education, teleshopping for the old and handicapped, and even instant opinion polls and referendums on political issues. The effect can be to break down the social fragmentation associated with the traditional city. Networks of this kind can bind dispersed minorities: ethnic groups, women, the old and the handicapped.

Bank card technology, although developed to fuel consumerism and extend credit, can introduce further possibility for asserting citizenship. The idea of the 'town card' can offer services such as cheap shopping, transport, libraries and cultural facilities. The cards can be used to confer opportunities on a selective basis or even universally. Sheffield's 'Passport to Leisure' system enabled all citizens to enjoy a wide range of facilities from municipal golf to indoor football. The break-up of utilities through privatisation (telephones, electricity, water) offers further long-term possibilities for municipalisation and community control and collective provision. Cards can also facilitate giving to local charities and the holding of opinion polls (dipstick democracy).

The soft-focus authority

The loss of functions by local authorities leaves them with fewer means of shaping their communities. One alternative way forward is to seek new areas of action. It is possible to find a role, not in dealing with planning applications and building the hard infrastructure of roads and retail Disneylands, but in creating a soft infrastructure in the form of a pleasing communal *milieu* in which to meet, talk, think and drink. This was part of the strategy of the metropolitan counties and the GLC which, of course, had very few functions from the outset. It became increasingly relevant during the Thatcher era which was marked by official disdain for the idea of community, social culture or the arts, and displayed more than a whiff of aggressive philistinism.

This approach is particularly justified in post-Fordist society where the city loses the centripetal force of factory-based production. Ways in which the *milieu* can be enhanced are numerous and can include arts funding, theatres and concert halls. Streets can be lined with trees, cycle lanes can be designated, community policing can be encouraged, derelict factories can be disguised with murals and so on.

There is a pay-off for the *milieu*-conscious authority in the form of an economic multiplier effect. Jobs in the arts directly generate jobs elsewhere. Visitors create multiple demands for services. More importantly, if the place is convivial, people will want to live there and firms will be induced to relocate. Many cities wishing to attract firms will stress the non-city aspects of the environment. This partly explains developments in cities such as Cardiff (media city), Sheffield (World Student Games), Bradford (museums), Liverpool (garden festival), Merseyside (pop music Mecca) and Glasgow (European City of the Year in 1990). Some such as York and Edinburgh (cities of great beauty with pre-industrial origins) have a head start in the politics of *milieu*.

The down side to this approach is that what is created is a wine-bar *milieu* of high art, opera and ballet, convivial to a middle-class clientele but offering less to those most vulnerable to the desolation of post-Fordist culture: the young, the old, ethnic communities and the poor in the run-down estates.

Conclusion – justifying local democracy

The legislation following the Widdicombe Report confirmed that, even if nothing else changed, the role of councillors would be reduced. Those that might remain were expected to be 'businesslike' rather than representative (Adam Smith Institute, 1989). Was local democracy to be jettisoned as excess baggage on the soaring New Right airbus? Can it still be justified in the hi-tech, post-Fordist world where the sense of community is eroded and customer sovereignty is supposed to replace the sovereignty of the people?

The British constitution, based on the supremacy of Parliament, is unequivocally unitary and centralist. Actual political behaviour makes it more so, with the death of Cabinet government and an oppressive concentration of power in the hands of the Prime Minister. Does this mean that central government has an unalloyed right to override local democracy? The answer to this is not as simple as the lawyers might claim. A living constitution is more than a collection of rules; it embodies the spirit of a political culture in which are embedded normative moral expectations.

Britain has a long history of self-determination by communities. In ancient times, when kingly interest in the localities was concerned with raising taxes, recruiting an army and maintaining order, the monarch did not interfere in the collective decisions a community might make. In spite of changing patterns, faith in 'localness' as a democratic virtue has persisted (Hill, 1974: 27). Democracy avows that only the person in the house knows where the draught comes in; only the dwellers in a community know whether they want, and are prepared to pay for, subsidised bus fares, cycle lanes, community policing, free nurseries and so on. Without a degree of real local democracy one of the capitalist state's most important legitimating devices is lost and the penalty for this may be rather greater than imagined by those who see the destruction of the municipal dimension as a prerequisite for private profitability and short-term political ends.

Market-based neo-liberal individualism is ultimately self-destructive. For example, every day arteries to the cities are jammed with belching vehicles, polluting the atmosphere and producing the potentially fatal global warming, yet the solution of the New Right is to hound the GLC though the courts for providing subsidised public transport. Alternatively, we may save money in taxes if we cut back state education, but who will treat us when we are sick if chidren have not been made into doctors? These are illustrations of the famous fable of the 'tragedy of the commons', which declares that when each fights for himself rather than the community everyone is ultimately worse off.

The alternative is collectivism, where the good of all comes before that of the richest, and democratic local government can be one of its clearest expressions. This is not to say that local government should seek to return to the past. Standardised mass-produced collective consumption, itself reminiscent of the typical product of the factory of the Fordist era, may no longer be appropriate under post-Fordist conditions. Local democracy implies not welfare state paternalism, but the right to determine collective consumption patterns. The evidence of other countries demonstrates that community values can be effectively expressed in various different ways (Norton, 1986). What matters is that ordinary people should be able to control their environment. Without this it will be difficult to describe Britain as a democracy.

It is worth remembering that for the ancient Greeks, who invented democracy long before the birth of Christ, the city-state or *polis* (from which we get the word politics) was the natural unit of community life. They believed size to be a vital factor in real democracy and the *polis* was essentially human in scale. Today, as the international economy (and the giant multinational corporations that bestride it) erodes the boundaries of the nation-state and constricts its autonomy, towns and cities become even more vital to social life. They are community units to which people can feel a sense of belonging and, through participation, gain a sense of control over their lives in society. The dismissal and destruction of local democracy which took place in Britain during the 1980s represented a leap into a chilling constitutional void.

Bibliography

Adam Smith Institute (1989) *Wiser Counsels: The reform of local government*, London: Adam Smith Institute.

Alexander, A. (1982) *Local Government in Britain since Reorganisation*, London: Allen and Unwin.

Almond, G. A. and Powell, G. B. (1966) *Comparative Politics*, Boston: Little Brown.

Alt, J. E. and Chrystal, K. A. (1983) *Political Economy*, Brighton: Harvester Wheatsheaf.

Althusser, L. (1969) *For Marx*, Harmondsworth: Penguin.

Anwar, M. (1986) *Race and Politics*, London: Tavistock.

Ascher, K. J. (1987) *The Politics of Privatisation: Contracting out public services*, London: Macmillan.

Association of Councillors (1987) *Support Services for Councillors*, London: Charles Knight.

Bachrach, P. and Baratz, M. S. (1970) *Power and Poverty*, Oxford: Oxford University Press.

Baddeley, S. and James, K. (1987) 'From political neutrality to political wisdom', *Politics*, vol. 7, no. 2, pp. 35–40.

Bains, M. A. (1972) *The New Local Authorities: Management and structure*, London: HMSO.

Baldwin, D. J. (1985) 'Behavioural changes, a new professionalism and a more independent House', in Norton, P. (ed.), *Parliament in the 1980s*, Oxford, Basil Blackwell, pp. 96–113.

Baldwin, R. and Kinsey, R. (1982), *Police Powers and Politics*, London: Quartet.

Batty, K. and George, B. (1985) 'Finance and facilities for MPs', in Norton, P. (ed.), *Parliament in the 1980s*, Oxford: Basil Blackwell, pp. 169–81.

Beer, S. H. (1982) *Britain Against Itself*, London: Faber.

Benn, M. (1985) 'Policing women', in Baxter, J. and Benn, M. (eds), *The Rape Controversy*, London: NCCL.

Bennington, J. (1976) *Local Government Becomes Big Business*, London: Community Development Project Information and Intelligence Unit.

Bentley, A. F. (1967) *The Process of Government*, Cambridge, Mass: Harvard University Press (first published 1908).

Bentley, S. (1972) 'Intergroup relations in local politics: Pakistanis and Bangladeshis', *New Community*, vol. 2, no. 1, pp. 44–8.

Ben-Tovim, G., Gabriel, J., Law, I. and Stredder, K. (1986) *The Local Politics of Race*, London: Macmillan.

Benyon, J. (1984) (ed.) *Scarman and After: Essays Reflecting on Lord Scarman's Report*, Oxford: Pergamon.

Benyon, J. (1989) 'Ten years of Thatcherism', *Social Studies Review*, vol. 4, no. 5, pp. 170–8.

Benyon, J. and Solomos, J. (1987) *The Roots of Social Unrest*, Oxford: Pergamon.

Birch, A. H. (1959) *Small Town Politics*, Oxford: Oxford University Press.

Birkenshaw, P. (1985) *Grievances, Remedies and the State*, London: Sweet and Maxwell.

Blaug, M. (1963) 'The myth of the old poor law and the making of the new', *Journal of Economic History*, vol. 23, pp. 151–84.

Blunkett, D. (1984) 'Local socialism: the way ahead', in Boddy, M. and Fudge, C. (eds.), *Local Socialism?*, London: Macmillan, pp.242–84.

Blunkett, D. and Jackson, K. (1987) *Democracy in Crisis*, London: Hogarth.

Boaden, N. (1971) *Urban Policy Making*, Cambridge: Cambridge University Press.

Boateng, P. (1985) 'Crisis in accountability', in Baxter, J. and Koffman, L. (eds) *Police, The Constitution and the Community*, Abingdon: Professional Books Ltd, pp. 237–45.

Boddy, M. (1984) 'Local councils and the financial squeeze', in Boddy, M. and Fudge, C. (eds), *Local Socialism?*, London: Macmillan, pp. 215–41.

Brier, A. P. (1970) 'The decision process in local government: a case study of fluoridation in Hull', *Public Administration*, no. 49, pp.153–68.

Brindley, T. and Stoker, G. (1987) 'The privatisation of housing renewal: dilemmas and contradictions in British urban policy', in van Vliet, W. (ed.), *Housing Markets and Policies under Fiscal Authority*, New York: Greenwood.

Bulpit, J. G. (1967) *Party Politics in English Local Government*, London: Longman.

Byrne, T. (1981) *Local Government in Britain*, Harmondsworth: Penguin.

Cabinet Office (1988) *Action for Cities*, London: HMSO.

Castells, M. (1976) 'Theory and ideology in urban sociology', in Pickvance, C.G. (ed.), *Urban Sociology: Critical essays*, London: Tavistock.

Castells, M. (1977) 'The class struggle and urban contradictions', in Cowley, J., Kaye, A., Mayo, M. and Thompson, M. (eds), *Community or Class Struggle?*, London: Stage 1.

Castells, M. (1983) *The City and the Grass Roots: A cross cultural theory of urban social movements*, London: Edward Arnold.

Castells, M. (1987) *City, Class and Power*, London: Macmillan.

Chandler, J. A. (1988) *Public Policy-making for Local Government*, London: Croom Helm.

Chandler, J. A. and Lawless, P. J. (1985) *Local Authorities and the Creation of Employment*, Aldershot: Gower.

Checkland, S. G. and E. O. A. (eds) (1973) *The Poor Law Report of 1834*, Harmondsworth: Penguin.

Chittenden, M. (1988) 'Freemasonry "rife" among top police', *Sunday Times*, 10 April.

Church of England (1985) *Faith in the City: report of the Archbishop of Canterbury's Commission on Urban Priority Areas*, London: Christian Action.

CIPFA (1988) *Local Government Trends*, London: Chartered Institute of Public Finance and Accountancy.

Clapham, D. and English, J. (1987) *Public Housing: Current trends and future developments*, London: Croom Helm.

Clarke, M. and Stewart, J. (1988) *The Enabling Council*, London: Local Government Training Board.

Cockburn, C. (1977a) *The Local State*, London: Pluto Press.

Cockburn, C. (1977b) 'Why women get involved in community action', in Mayo, M. (ed.), *Women in the Community*, London: Routledge and Kegan Paul.

Cole, G. D. H. (1948) *A History of the Labour Party from 1914*, London: Routledge.

Coombes, M. G., Dixon, J. S. Goddard, J. B., Openshaw, S. and Taylor, P. J. (1983) 'Functional regions for the population census of Great Britain', in Herbert, D.T. and Johnston, R. J. (eds) *Geography and the Urban Environment*, vol. 5, Chichester: Wiley.

Craig, F. S. W. (1981) *Conservative and Labour Party Conference Decisions 1945–1981*, London: Parliamentary Research Services.

Crewe, I. (1986) 'On the death and resurrection of class voting: some comments on *How Britain Votes*', *Political Studies*, vol. XXXIV, pp. 620–38.

Crewe, I. (1987) In *The Guardian*, 15 June.

Crick, B. (1964) *In Defence of Politics*, Harmondsworth: Penguin (2nd edn 1982).

Crosland, C. A. R. (1956) *The Future of Socialism*, London: Jonathan Cape.

Crossman, R. H. S. (1975) *Diaries of a Cabinet Minister*, vol. 1, London: Jonathan Cape.

Curran, J. and Seaton, J. (1981) *Power Without Responsibility: The press and broadcasting in Britain*, London: Fontana.

Dahl, R. (1961) *Who Governs?*, New Haven: Yale University Press.

Darke, J. and Darke, R. (1979) *Who Needs Housing?* London: Macmillan.

Davies, B. (1972) *Variations in Children's Services among British Urban Authorities: A causal analysis*, London: Bell.

Davies, T. (1981) 'Implementing employment policies in one London borough', in Craig, G., Mayo, M. and Sharman, N. (eds), *Jobs and Community Action*, London, Routledge & Kegan Paul.

Dearlove, J. (1973) *The Politics of Policy in Local Government*, Cambridge: Cambridge University Press.

Dearlove, J. (1979) *The Reorganisation of Local Government*, Cambridge: Cambridge University Press.

Dennis, N. (1972) *Public Participation and Planner's Blight*, London: Faber and Faber.

Department of the Environment (1977) *Policy for the Inner Cities*, Cmnd 6845, London: HMSO.

Department of the Environment (1983) *Streamlining the Cities*, Cmnd 9063, London: HMSO.

Department of the Environment (1988) *The Conduct of Local Authority Business: The government response to the report of the Widdicombe Inquiry*, Cmnd 433, London: HMSO.

DES (1987) *Grant Maintained Schools: A consultative document*, London: Department of Education and Science.

Donoghue, B. and Jones, G. W. (1973) *Herbert Morrison: Portrait of a politician*, London: Weidenfeld and Nicolson.

Douglas, I. and Lord, S. (1986) *Local Government Finance: A practical guide*, London: Local Government Information Unit.

Downs, A. (1957) *An Economic Theory of Democracy*, New York: Harper and Row.

Duncan, S. and Goodwin, M. (1988) *The Local State and Unequal Development*, Oxford: Polity Press.

Dunleavy, P. (1980) *Urban Political Analysis*, London: Macmillan.

Dunleavy, P. (1981) *The Politics of Mass Housing in Britain: Corporate power and professional influence in the welfare state*, Oxford: Clarendon Press.

Dunleavy, P. and Husbands, C. T. (1985) *British Democracy at the Crossroads: Voting and party competition in the 1980s*, London: Allen and Unwin.

Dunleavy, P. and Rhodes, R. A. W. (1986) 'Government beyond Whitehall', in Drucker, H., Dunleavy, P. Gamble, A. and Peele, G. (eds), *Developments in British Politics 2*, Basingstoke: Macmillan, pp. 107–43.

Dunleavy, P. and Rhodes, R. A. W. (1987) 'The Conservatives and sub-central government', *Social Studies Review*, vol. 2, no. 5, pp. 19–26.

Dunsire, A. (1982) 'Challenges to public administration in the 1980s', *Public Administration Bulletin*, vol. 39, pp. 8–21.

Easton, D. (1953) *The Political System*, New York: Knopf.

Eckstein, H. (1958) *The English Health Service*, Cambridge, Mass.: Harvard University Press.

Englefield, D. (ed.)(1984) *Commons Select Committees: Catalysts for progess?* Harlow: Longman.

Field, G. L. and Higley, J. (1980) *Elitism*, London: Routledge & Kegan Paul.

Finer, S. E. (1952) *The Life and Times of Edwin Chadwick*, London: Methuen.

Flinn, M. W. (1963) *An Economic and Social History of Britain Since 1700*, London: Macmillan.

Flynn, R. (1982) 'Managing consensus: the infrastructure of policy making in planning', in Harloe, M. (ed.) *New Perspectives in Urban Change*, London: Heinemann.

Forrest, R. (1987) 'Privatisation, marginality and council housing', in Clapham, D. and English, J. (eds), *Public Housing: Current trends and future developments*, London: Croom Helm.

Forsyth, M. (1980) *Re-servicing Britain*, London: Adam Smith Institute.

Fraser, D. (1973) *The Evolution of the British Welfare State*, London: Macmillan.

Fried, A. and Elman, R. (1971) (eds) *Charles Booth's London*, Harmondsworth: Penguin.

Friedman, M. (1962) *Capitalism and Freedom*, Chicago: Chicago University Press.

Gamble, A. (1979) 'The Conservative Party', in Drucker, H. (ed.), *Multi-Party Britain*, London: Macmillan.

Gerth, H. H. and Wright Mills, C. (1957) *From Max Weber*, London: Routledge & Kegan Paul.

Gladden, E. N. (1967) *Civil Services of the United Kingdom 1855-1970*, London: Frank Cass.

Goldsmith, M. (ed.) (1986a) *New Research in Central-Local Relations*, Aldershot: Gower.

Goldsmith, M. (1986b) 'Managing the periphery in a period of fiscal stress', in Goldsmith, M. (ed.), *New Research in Central-Local Relations*, Aldershot: Gower.

Goss, S. (1984) 'Women's initiatives in local government', in Boddy, M. and Fudge, C. (eds), *Local Socialism?*, London: Macmillan, pp. 109-32.

Gough, I. (1978) *The Political Economy of the Welfare State*, London: Macmillan.

Grant, M. (1986) 'The role of the courts in central-local relations', in Goldsmith, M. (ed.), *New Research in Central-Local Relations*, Aldershot: Gower, pp. 191-206.

Grant, W. (1971) ' "Local Parties" in British local politics: a framework for empirical analysis', *Political Studies*, vol. xix no. 2, pp. 201-12.

Grant, W. and Marsh, D. (1977) *The CBI*, London: Hodder and Stoughton.

Greenwood, R. *et al.* (1980) *Patterns of Management in Local Government*, Oxford: Martin Robertson.

Griffith, J. A. G. (1966) *Central Departments and Local Authorities*, London: Allen and Unwin.

Griffiths, R. (1988) *Community Care: Agenda for action*, London: HMSO.

Grigsby, J. (1985) ' "Jobs for the boys" move delayed', *Daily Telegraph*, 1 November.

Gyford, J. (1976) *Local Politics in Britain*, London: Croom Helm.

Gyford, J. and James, M. (1983) *National Parties and Local Politics*, London: Allen and Unwin.

Gyford, J., Leach, S. and Game, C. (1989) *The Changing Politics of Local Government*, London: Unwin Hyman.

HM Government (1986) *Paying for Local Government*, London: HMSO.

HM Government (1987) *Housing: The government's proposals*, London: HMSO.

Hambleton, R. (1978) *Policy Planning and Local Government*, London: Hutchinson.

Hampton, W. (1970) *Democracy and Community: A study of politics in Sheffield*, London: Oxford University Press.

Hampton, W. (1981) 'Who calls the tune?', *Public Administration Bulletin*, no. 36, pp. 63–6.

Harvey, D. (1973) *Social Justice and the City*, Oxford Basil Blackwell.

Harvey, D. (1985) *Consciousness and the Urban Experience: Studies in the history and theory of capitalist urbanization*, Oxford: Basil Blackwell.

Hayek, F. A. (1944) *The Road to Serfdom*, London: Routledge & Kegan Paul.

Hayek, F. A. (1982) *Law, Legislation and Liberty*, London: Routledge and Kegan Paul.

Heclo, H. and Wildavsky, A. (1974) *The Private Government of Public Money*, London: Macmillan.

Hedley, R. (1990) 'Members' role under scrutiny', *Local Government Chronicle*, 22 June.

Henney, A. (1984) *Inside Local Government: A case for radical reform*, London: Sinclair Browne.

Herbert, Sir E. (chairman) (1960) *Report of the Royal Commission on Local Government in London 1957–60*, Cmnd 1164, London: HMSO.

Higgins, J., Deakin, N., Edwards, J. and Wicks, M. (1983) *Government and Urban Poverty*, Oxford: Basil Blackwell.

Hill, D.M. (1970) *Participating in Local Affairs*, Harmondsworth: Penguin.

Hill, D. (1974) *Democratic Theory and Local Government*, London: Allen and Unwin.

Himmelweit, T., Humphreys, P. and Jaeger, M. (1985), *How Voters Decide*, Milton Keynes: Open University Press.

Hirst, F. W. (1931) *Gladstone as Financier and Economist*, London: Ernest Benn.

Hoffman, J. D. (1964) *The Conservative Party in Opposition 1945–51*, London: MacGibbon and Kee.

Hoyle, S. (1987) 'Deregulation: the view from the bus stop', *Transport*, June, pp. 115–16.

Hunter, F. (1953) *Community Power Structure*, Chapel Hill: University of North Carolina Press.

Ingle, S. (1987) *The British Party System*, Oxford: Basil Blackwell.

Isaac-Henry, K. (1972) 'Policy processes in local government: a case study', *South Western Review of Public Administration*, vol. 11, pp. 29–37.

Isaac-Henry, K. (1984) 'Taking stock of the local authority associations', *Public Administration*, vol. 62, no. 2, pp. 129–46.

Johnson, T. I. (1972) *Professions and Power*, London: Macmillan.

Jones, G. W. (1969) *Borough Politics: a study of Wolverhampton Borough Council 1888–1964*, London: Macmillan.

Jones, G. W. (1988) 'Against local government', *Local Government Studies*, vol. 14, no. 5, pp. 1–11.

Jones, G. W. and Stewart, J. (1985) *The Case for Local Government*, London: Allen and Unwin (2nd edn).

Keith-Lucas, B. and Richards, P. G. (1978) *A History of Local Government in the Twentieth Century*, London: Allen and Unwin.

Kettle, M. (1980) 'The politics of policing and the policing of politics', in Hain, P. (ed.), *Policing the Police*, London: Calder, pp. 9–64.

Kingdom, J. E. (1986a) 'Public administration: defining the discipline - part 1', *Teaching Public Administration*, vol. VI, no. 1, pp. 1–13.

Kingdom, J. E. (1986b) 'Public administration: defining the discipline - part 2', *Teaching Public Administration*, vol. VI, no. 2, pp. 1–21.

Kingdom, J. E. (1987) 'Public administration: is it a useful discipline?' *Teaching Public Administration*, vol. VII, no. 2, pp. 1–9.

Kingdom, J. E. (1990) Public administration or public implementation – a discipline in crisis', *Public Policy and Administration*, vol. 5, no. 2, pp 5–29.

Kingdom, J. E. (1991) *Government and Politics in Britain*, Oxford: Polity Press.

Kingdon, J. W. (1967) 'Politicians' beliefs about voters', *American Political Science Review*, vol. 61, pp. 137–45.

Klein, R. (1989) *The Politics of the National Health Service*, London: Longman.

Laffin, M. and Young, K. (1985) 'The changing roles and responsibilities of local government chief officers', *Public Administration*, vol. 63, pp 41–59.

Lansley, S., Goss, S. and Wolmar, C. (1989) *Councils in Conflict: The rise and fall of the municipal left*, Basingstoke: Macmillan.

Lasswell, H. D. (1936) *Politics: Who gets what, when, how?* New York McGraw Hill.

Lasswell, H. D. and Kaplan, A. (1950) *Power and Society*, New Haven Yale University Press.

Leach, S. (1989) 'Strengthening local democracy?', in Stewart, J. and Stoker, G. (eds), *The Future of Local Government*, Basingstoke Macmillan.

Lee, J. M. (1963) *Social Leaders and Public Persons*, Oxford: Clarendon Press.

Lehmbruch, G. and Schmitter, P. (eds) (1982) *Patterns of Corporatist Policy Making*, London: Sage.

Lewis, N., Seneviratne, M. and Cracknell, S. (1986) *Complaints Procedures in Local Government*, Sheffield: Centre for Criminological and Socio-Legal Studies, University of Sheffield.

Lipset, S. M. (1959) *Political Man*, London: Heinemann.

Lowe, P. and Goyder, J. (1983) *Environmental Groups in Politics*, London: Allen and Unwin.

Magnus, P. (1954) *Gladstone*, London: John Murray.

Malpass, P. N. (1975) 'Professionalism and the role of architects in local authority housing', *Royal Institute of British Architects Journal*, vol. 82, pp. 6–29.

March, J. (1990) 'What happens when the smoke clears?', *Municipal Journal*, 12 May, pp. 10–12.

Mark, Sir R. (1978) *In the Office of Constable*, London: Collins.

Marx, K. (1977) *Selected Writings*, McLellan, D. (ed.), Oxford: Oxford University Press.

Massey, D. (1982) 'Enterprise zones: a political issue', *International Journal of Urban and Regional Research*, vol. 6, pp. 429–34.

Massey, D. (1984) *Spatial Divisions of Labour: Social structures and the geography of production*, London: Methuen.

Massey, D. (1985) 'Geography and class', in Coates, D., Johnston, G. and Bush, R. (eds), *A Socialist Anatomy of Britain*, Cambridge: Polity Press, pp. 79–96.

Mather, G. (1989) 'Thatcherism and local government: an evaluation', in Stewart, J. and Stoker, G. (eds), *The Future of Local Government*, Basingstoke: Macmillan.

Maud, J. (chairman) (1967a) *The Management of Local Government*, vol. 1, London: HMSO.

Maud J. (chairman) (1967b) *The Management of Local Government*, vol. 2, London: HMSO.

McKenzie, R. T. (1963) *British Political Parties*, London: Heinemann (2nd edn).

Michels, R. (1962) *Political Parties*, New York: Collier.

Middlemas, K. (1979) *Politics in Industrial Society*, London: André Deutsch.

Miliband, R. (1984) *Capitalist Democracy in Britain*, Oxford: Oxford University Press.

Mill, J. S. (1958) *Considerations on Representative Government*, Indianapolis: Bobbs-Merrill (first published 1861).

Mills, C. Wright (1956) *The Power Elite*, New York: Oxford University Press.

Moore, C., Richardson, J. and Moon, J. (1985) 'New partnerships in local economic development', *Local Government Studies*, September/October, pp. 19–33.

Mort, F. (1989) 'The politics of consumption', in Hall, S. and Jacques, M. (eds), *New Times*, London: Lawrence and Wishart, pp. 160–72.

Mulgan, G. (1989) 'The changing shape of the city', in Hall, S. and Jacques, M. (eds), *New Times*, London, Lawrence and Wishart, pp. 262–78.

Murray, R. (1989) 'Fordism and post-Fordism', in Hall, S. and Jacques, M. (eds), *New Times*, London: Lawrence and Wishart, pp. 38–53.

Newby, H., Bell, C., Rose, D. and Saunders, P. (1978) *Property, Paternalism and Power: Class and control in rural England*, London: Hutchinson.

Newton, K. (1976) *Second City Politics*, Oxford: Clarendon Press.

Newton, K. (1982) 'Is small really so beautiful? Is big really so ugly? Size, effectiveness and democracy in local government', *Political Studies*, vol. 30, no. 2, pp. 190–206.

Niskanen, W. A. (1971) *Bureaucracy and Representative Government*, Chicago: Aldine-Atherton.

Niskanen, W. A. (1973) *Bureaucracy: Servant or Master?* London: Institute of Economic Affairs.

Norton, A. (1986) *Local Government in Other Western Democracies*, Birmingham: Institute of Local Government Studies.

Norton, P. (1985) 'Behavioural changes: backbench independence in the 1980s', in Norton, P. (ed.), *Parliament in the 1980s*, Oxford: Basil Blackwell, pp. 22–47.

Nozick, R. (1974) *Anarchy, State and Utopia*, New York: Basic Books.

O'Connor, J. (1973) *The Fiscal Crisis of the State*, New York: St Martin's Press.

Offe, C. (1985) 'New social movements: challenging the boundaries of institutional politics', *Social Research*, vol. 52, no. 4, pp. 817–60.

Oliver, F. R. and Stanyer, J. (1969) 'Some aspect of the behaviour of county boroughs', *Public Administration*, vol. 47, pp. 169–84.

Oliver, I. (1987) *Police, Government and Accountability*, Basingstoke: Macmillan.

Olson, M. (1968) *The Logic of Collective Action*, New York: Shocken Books.

Olson, M. (1982) *The Rise and Decline of Nations*, New Haven: Yale University Press.

Ostrogorski, M. (1902) *Democracy and the Organisation of Political Parties*, London: Macmillan.

Ottewill, R. M. and Wall, A. L. (1990) *Community Health Services*, Sunderland: Business Education Publishers.

Ouseley, H. (1984) 'Local authority race initiatives', in Boddy, M. and Fudge, C. (eds), *Local Socialism*, London: Macmillan, pp. 133–56.

Pahl, R. (1975) *Whose City?* Harmondsworth: Penguin.

Pahl, R. E., Flynn, R. and Buck, N. H. (1983) *Structures and Processes of Urban Life*, London: Longman.

Painter, M. J. (1980) 'Policy co-ordination in the Department of the Environment, 1970–1976', *Public Administration*, vol. 58, no. 2, pp. 135–54.

Park, R.E. (1952) *Urban Communities: The city and human ecology*, New York: Free Press.

Perry, R., Dean, K. and Brown, B., (1986) *Counterurbanization*, Norwich: Geo Books.

Pirie, M. (1981) 'Economy and local government', in Betler, E. and Pirie, M. (eds), *Economy and Local Government*, London: Adam Smith Institute.

Ponting, C. (1986) *Whitehall: Tragedy and farce*, London: Hamish Hamilton.

RTPI (1986) *Strategic Planning for Regional Potential*, London: Royal Town Planning Institute.

Ramsden, J. (1980) *The Making of Conservative Party Policy: The Conservative Research Department since 1929*, London: Longman.

Ramsden, J. and Jay, R. (1973) 'Lincoln: background to Taverne's triumph', in Cook, C. and Ramsden, J. (eds), *By-elections in British Politics*, London: Macmillan.

Redcliffe-Maud, Lord (chairman) (1969) *Report of the Royal Commission on Local Government in England 1966–69*, vol. 1, Cmnd 4040, London: HMSO.

Redlich, J. and Hirst, F. W. (1958) *Local Government in England, Vol II*, Keith-Lucas, B. (ed.), London: Macmillan (first published 1903).

Reiner, R. (1985) *The Politics of the Police*, Brighton: Harvester Wheatsheaf.

Rhodes, R. A. W. (1981) *Control and Power in Central–Local Government Relations*, Farnborough: Gower.

Rhodes, R. (1986) *The National World of Local Government*, London: Allen and Unwin.

Rhodes, R. (1988) *Beyond Westminster and Whitehall: The sub-central government of Britain*, London: Allen and Unwin.

Ridley, N. (1988) *The Local Right*, London: Centre for Policy Studies.

Robinson, D. (chairman) (1977) *Remuneration of Councillors*, Cmnd 7010, London: HMSO.

Robson, W. A. (1966) *Local Government in Crisis*, London: Allen and Unwin.

Rollo, J. (1980) 'The Special Patrol Group', in Hain, P. (ed.), *Policing the Police*, London: John Calder, pp. 153–208.

Rose, R. (1980) *Politics in England: An interpretation for the 1980s*, London: Faber.

Rothbard, M. (1978) *For a New Liberty: The libertarian manifesto*, New York: Collier.

Rowntree, B. (1980) *Poverty: A study of town life*, New York: Garland (facsimile of 1910 edition; first published 1901).

Salisbury, R. H. (1969) 'An exchange theory of interest groups', *Midwest Journal of Political Science*, vol. 13, pp. 1–32.

Sancton, A. (1976) 'British socialist theory and the division of power by area', *Political Studies*, vol. 24, no. 2, pp. 158–70.

Saunders, P. (1980) *Urban Politics: A sociological interpretation*, Harmondsworth: Penguin.

Scarman, Lord (1981) *The Brixton Disorders, 10–12 April 1981: Report of an Inquiry*, Cmnd 8427, London: HMSO.

Scott, J. (1985) 'The British upper class', in Coates, D., Johnston, G. and Bush, R. (eds), *A Socialist Anatomy of Britain*, Oxford: Polity Press, pp. 29–54.

Seebohm Report (1968) *Report of the Committee on Local Authority and Allied Personal Social Services*, Cmnd 3703, London: HMSO.

Self, P. and Storing, H. (1962) *The State and the Farmer*, London: Allen and Unwin.

Seyd, P. (1990) 'Radical Sheffield: from socialism to entrepeneurialism', *Political Studies*, vol 38, no. 3, pp. 335–44.

Sharp, L. J. (1970) 'Theories and values of local government', *Political Studies*, vol. 18, no. 2, pp. 153–74.

Sherman, A. (1975) 'Fabian rethink local government – forward from elitism', *Local Government Review*, vol. 137.

Smith, D. J. and Gray, J. (1985) *Police and People in London*, Aldershot: Gower.

Smith, J. Toulmin (1851) *Local Self-government and Centralization*, London: n.p.

Spencer, K. M. (1989) 'Local government and the housing reforms', in Stewart, J. and Stoker, G., (eds), *The Future of Local Government*, Basingstoke: Macmillan, pp. 78–100.

Stanyer, J. (1971) 'Why does turnout vary?' *New Society*, 13 May.

Stanyer, J. (1976) *Understanding Local Government*, London: Fontana.

Stewart, J. (1989) 'A future for local government as community government', in Stewart, J. and Stoker, G. (eds), *The Future of Local Government*, Basingstoke: Macmillan, pp. 236–54.

Sundquist, J. L. (1975) *Dispersing Population*, Washington: Brookings Institution.

Tiebout, C. (1956) 'A pure theory of local expenditures', *Journal of Political Economy*, vol. 64, pp. 416–24.

Townsend, P. (1979) *Poverty in the United Kingdom*, Harmondsworth: Penguin.

Travers, T. (1989) 'Community charge and other financial changes', in Stewart, J. and Stoker, G. (eds), *The Future of Local Government*, Basingstoke: Macmillan, pp. 9–29.

Tullock, G. (1967) *The Vote Motive*, London: Institute of Economic Affairs.

Van Den Berg, L. *et al.* (1982) *Urban Europe: A study of growth and decline*, London: Pergamon.

Von Gneist, R. (1891) *The History of the English Government*, London: William Clowes (originally published in 1882 as *Das Englische Verwaltungsrecht*).

Walker, D. (1983) *Municipal Empire*, London: Temple Smith.

Walvin, J. (1984) *Passage to Britain*, Harmondsworth: Penguin.

Webb, S. and B. (1963) *The Parish and the County*, London: Frank Cass (originally published 1906).

Weber, M. (1978) *Economy and Society, Vol. II*, Berkeley: University of California Press.

Wheatley, Lord (1969) *Report of the Royal Commission on Local Government in Scotland, 1966–1969*, Cmnd 4150, London: HMSO.

Whiteley, P. and Winyard, S. (1984) 'The origins of the new poverty lobby', *Political Studies*, vol. 32, no. 1, pp. 32–54

Widdicombe, D. (1977) *Out Fettered Ombudsman*, London: Justice.

Widdicombe D. (chairman) (1986a) *The Conduct of Local Authority Business: Report of the Committee of Inquiry*, Cmnd 9797, London: HMSO.

Widdicombe, D. (chairman) (1986b) *The Conduct of Local Authority Business, Report of the Committee of Inquiry, Research Volume 1: The political organisation of local authorities*, Cmnd 9798, London: HMSO.

Widdicombe, D. (chairman) (1986c) *The Conduct of Local Authority Business, Report of the Committee of Inquiry, Research Volume II: The local government councillor*, Cmnd 9799, London: HMSO.

Widdicombe, D. (chairman) (1986d) *The Conduct of Local Authority Business, Report of the Committee of Inquiry, Research Volume III: The local government elector*, Cmnd 9800, London: HMSO.

Widdicombe, D. (1986e) *The Conduct of Local Authority Business, Report of the Committee of Inquiry, Research Volume IV: Aspects of local democracy*, Cmnd 9801, London: HMSO.

Wilensky, A. (1964) 'The professionalization of everyone', *American Journal of Sociology*, vol. 70, pp. 137–58.

Williams, R. (1961) *Culture and Society 1780–1950*, Harmondsworth: Penguin.

Wilson, D. (1988) 'Inside local authorities', *Social Studies Review*, vol. 3, no. 4, pp. 135–9.

Wirth, L. (1938) 'Urbanism as a way of life', *American Journal of Sociology*, vol. 44, no. 1, pp. 1–24

Wiseman, H. V. (1963) 'The party causus in local government', *New Society*, 31 October.

Wolmer, C. (1987) 'Hard left loses to pragmatism', *The Independent*, 21 October.

Young, K. and Mills, L. (1983) *Managing the Post-Industrial City*, London: Heinemann.

Index